The Changing Constitution of the Present

Essays on the Work of Art in Times of Contemporaneity

Jacob Lund

Sternberg Press

In memory of Hanne Lund

Preface

> *I would go so far as to insist that more than any other time in our brief history on Earth, we are experiencing a clash of temporalities: geological time, the deep time of those processes that fashioned our terrestrial home; historical time; and experiential time. All these times now fold in on one another. We are not used to thinking of time as simultaneous. We think of time as linear: past, present, future. So how do we begin to think about time in a way that takes these concatenations seriously?*
> — Achille Mbembe[1]

> *The internet is not dead. It is undead and it's everywhere. [...] The all-out internet condition is not an interface but an environment. Older media as well as imaged people, imaged structures, and image objects are embedded into networked matter. Networked space is itself a medium, or whatever one might call a medium's promiscuous, posthumous state today.*
> — Hito Steyerl[2]

The Changing Constitution is motivated by the sense that the ways in which we experience time, and how we perceive phenomena like "presence" and "the present," are undergoing substantial changes, occasioned, in particular, by developments in media and communication technologies. The book is driven by the intuition that something has happened and is happening to our relation to time, to our experience of time itself. In other words, we seem to be witnessing a change in the temporal quality of the present, which also means that we need to historicize the meaning of the notion of "the contemporary."

Another motivating factor, is dissatisfaction with the, in many cases, unreflective or imprecise ways in which we conceive of and use the notion "contemporary art," which has replaced modern, and, for a period, postmodern, in describing the art of our time. We, still, need to develop a more critical concept of contemporary art, and to clarify what it might mean. These two motivating factors are closely connected as "contemporary art," in its most immediate sense, is an art of the present; an art that somehow addresses and expresses the present. The question, then, is what this present *is*? And how art expresses or articulates this present? What constitutes our, or perhaps, more objectively, *the* present? What constitutes the *present* present, or the *contemporary* contemporary? When and where did it begin? Who takes part in it? Who is it shared by, who is included in the pronoun "we" that I allow myself to employ — that is, how far does it extend in space and time?

The way in which the contemporary present is constituted differs, I claim, from how the present has been constituted previously. Our present is characterized by contemporaneity in the sense that it is constituted by the bringing together of a multitude of different temporalities at different scales, including deep geological time and different grand narratives and imagined communities developed during modernity. It is formed by an intensified global or planetary interconnectedness of different times and experiences of time, and this interconnection of times at a planetary scale is something historically new. We seem, therefore, to be living in an expanded present, a present in which several temporalities, times and historical narratives take part in what is perceived as present and as presence — and in making presence and the present come into being.

Thus, contemporaneity is at once a periodizing category, in the sense that it describes our era, the time in which we live, and an experiential category, in the sense that it is a particular relationship to time and to history, which may also involve an experience of a loss of history, the loss of a futural moment, which has otherwise defined the basic human experience of the temporal at least since Martin Heidegger.

What interests me most, is how such contemporaneity, and changes in temporality, are registered and articulated in contemporary art, claiming that such registration and articulation is a salient feature in qualifying something as *contemporary* art, and hence important to the development of a more critical concept of contemporary art.

The fundamental point of departure for the essays in this book is therefore to investigate contemporaneity as a defining condition of our historical present. As indicated above, "contemporaneity" refers to the temporal complexity that follows from the coming together — in *the same* space and time, the same here and now — of heterogeneous cultural formations generated along different historical trajectories, across different scales, and in different localities. Or, one might say that contemporaneity occurs through the bringing together of different *Eigenzeiten*, understood with sociologist Helga Nowotny as "the totality of a person's or group's ideas and experiences of time."[3] With the overall aim of questioning how contemporaneity affects our experiences of temporality and the formation of subjectivity in time, my primary material and object of analysis is contemporary art, based on the assumption that art can operate as an advanced laboratory for investigating processes of sense-making and for understanding wider developments within culture and society.

In a nutshell, *The Changing Constitution of the Present* is about how globality and, increasingly, planetarity, affects our experiences of time, and how this is presented in contemporary art and aesthetic practices. More broadly, it is an endeavor to reflect on the cultural implications of the idea of contemporaneity and a globally shared, or at least interconnected, present.

The analyses presented in these essays aim to distinguish themselves from most existing research on "contemporary art" in focusing, firstly, on the issue of temporality and the consequences of contemporaneity for our understanding and experience of time and history; and, secondly, on the significant role of media and information technology in bringing contemporaneity into being and in visualizing it.

The relatively technical conception of contemporaneity with which the book operates is based on the work of philosopher and art theorist Peter Osborne and the work of art historian Terry Smith, who both explicitly relate contemporary art to the issue of contemporaneity. Osborne observes:

> what seems distinctive and important about the changing temporal quality of the historical present over the last few decades is best expressed through the distinctive conceptual grammar of con-temporaneity, a coming together not simply "in" time, but *of* times: we do not just live or exist together "in time" with our contemporaries — as if time itself is indifferent to this existing together — but rather the present is increasingly characterised by a coming together of *different but equally "present"* temporalities or "times," a temporal unity in disjunction, or a *disjunctive unity of present times*.[4]

Whereas Smith understands contemporaneity from a more experiential point of view, as "the constant experience of radical disjunctures of perception, mismatching ways of seeing and valuing the same world, in the actual coincidence of asynchronous temporalities, in the jostling contingency of various cultural and social multiplicities."[5]

Drawing on these highly nuanced conceptualizations of contemporaneity, this book intends to bring greater attention to bear on the ways in which technology conditions temporality and senses of time(s). It goes without saying that technology and so-called digital culture play a highly significant role in the shaping of the world picture and in creating the idea of contemporaneity and planetary co-presence; I am therefore trying to investigate contemporaneity in relation to the media and informational technologies that have helped, and still help, to make it possible.

These technologies, which create an experience of co-presence, are making global-scale circuits of what philosopher Bernard

Stiegler would call transindividuation — or its negative version in the form of disindividuation — possible. Transindividuation designates processes of co-individuation within media or symbolic environments in which the individual "I" and the inter-individual "we" participate and are transformed through one another. It thus conditions all social transformation, and the individual's participation in the social also implies a participation in the much vaster individuation of the media, language, images, etc. through which we communicate — that is, the media that interconnect and make us contemporaneous. Our sense of time and our subjectivity are formed through such processes of transindividuation; and, according to Stiegler, "technics, far from being merely in time, properly constitutes time."[6]

Even though the ambition of this book is to contribute to the development of a critical concept of contemporaneity and of contemporary art, it does not seek to give a systematic analysis of contemporaneity and develop a coherent line of progressive argumentation. In keeping with the matters at hand, its essays — which have been written over the past nine years — should rather be read as analyses and reflections on different interrelated aspects of contemporaneity and contemporary artistic practices.

In dialogue with Stiegler's and philosopher Jacques Rancière's conceptions of the medium as a *milieu*, chapter 1, "Artistic Reappropriation and Reconfiguration of the Medium's Milieu," seeks to address the question of the political aspects of the aesthetic in relation to the notion of medium. Based on the analysis of this theoretical question, the chapter discusses Alfredo Jaar's and Thomas Hirschhorn's artistic projects of reappropriating and reconfiguring conservative symbolic orders and media milieus that have become dissociated.

Chapter 2, "From Embodied to Mediated Memory," asks how we are to transmit and represent the traumatic events collected under the designation the Holocaust *today*? How can the events be represented without being transformed into abstractions, and in a way in which we, who were not alive when they took place, can relate to them? How can that specific past be actualized and re-membered in the present so that we do not forget or simply place the genocide of the European Jews in the archive as completed and past history? Esther Shalev-Gerz's installations *Between Listening and Telling: Last Witnesses, Auschwitz 1945–2005* (2005) and *MenschenDinge/The Human Aspect of Objects* (2006) constitute in each their way specific acts of remembering the Holocaust, while, at the same time, investigating the very workings and nature of remembering. These two works compose the frame for chapter 2, which is an analysis and discussion of some of the main issues involved in current debates on the representation and actualization of the Holocaust.

Chapter 3, "Filmic Montage as an Aesthetics of Contemporaneity," is a reading of Jean-Luc Godard's film essay *Histoire(s) du cinéma* (1988–1998) as an artistic endeavor to resist the synchronizing, standardizing time of global capital, the pervasive uniformity of the global super present, brought about by today's televisual and digital communications, which threaten to trivialize different processes of memory and history, as well as art and culture in general. Taking its point of departure in Stiegler's observation that the final stage of capitalism is the control and synchronization of "available brain time," the chapter argues that Godard's work opposes such control and synchronization through an aesthetics of contemporaneity. The argument is based on the development of a theoretical framework that combines theories of contemporaneity with reflections on the politics of images. Focusing on the ways in which the Holocaust is remembered in *Histoire(s) du cinéma*, the chapter deals with Godard's image-political creation of temporal contemporaneity through a montage of clips of old films and newsreels, photographs, stills, images of paintings, new footage, advertisements, music, sound and voice recordings, textual citation, narration and commentary.

Sharing philosopher and media theorist Boris Groys's concern (and that of a number of other thinkers) that we have lost the future as a political object, chapter 4, "Untimeliness in Contemporary Times," discusses the temporal complexity of our current situation — as well as the extent to which it even makes sense to speak of *our* situation. The aim of the chapter is to provide a critical reading of the notion of *untimeliness*, particularly in philosopher Giorgio Agamben's influential text "What Is the Contemporary?" (2009), as a decisive aspect of being contemporary. Agamben writes of "their time," "their own time," "the epoch," but what is *our* own time and *our* epoch? Who, in the post- or decolonial situation, takes part in the possessive determiner "our"? I argue that it is becoming increasingly difficult to identify a hegemonic "cultural" time in relation to which one can be untimely; that the current contemporaneity makes it practically impossible to be untimely and thus avant-garde in the traditional sense. Claiming that, under contemporary conditions of an intensified global interconnection of different times and social narratives, it is no longer useful to employ Agamben's conception of *untimeliness* when trying to engage with the present in order to reinstall a futural moment, chapter four tries to indicate how a contemporary kind of untimeliness, characterized by operating in relation to several times at once and thus differentiating the presentist present, may be seen to appear in the poetics and artistic practice of Kader Attia.

Chapter 5, "Dematerialization in the Contemporary Present," argues that we need to take the changing historical context of "dematerialization" into consideration when discussing the disappearance and immateriality of the artwork. Today, artistic practices regarding dematerialization have changed from focusing on the development of a critical strategy that obviates commodifiable physical material in favor of ideas and concepts, to critically exploring and disclosing the complexities of the digital society in which we — or at least the large majority of us — live, a society where big data, algorithms and surveillance are put into extensive operation with immense political, social and psychological consequences. The chapter reflects on how the conditions for politically engaged art, for questioning the present, have changed, as our present and its temporal quality is not the same as it was in the 1960s, when conceptual works of art aimed to dissolve their material supports and question the traditional media of art. Our experience of the categories of present and presence has changed, and this changing status and experience of presence also affects our relation to artworks and how they operate. This argument is substantiated through analyses of video installations by Hito Steyerl and by Camille Henrot, which, in different ways, may be said to negotiate the role of media and computational technologies in the interconnection of times and life worlds, and speculate on the impact of the Internet and digitization on the fabric of our everyday lives and our experience of time.

With reference to the "anachronic" exhibition "Soulèvements" (2016–2017) by art historian and philosopher Georges Didi-Huberman, chapter 6, "Anachrony, Contemporaneity, and Historical Imagination," discusses how the notion of contemporaneity relates to the end of a certain history of art, as theorized by Yves Michaud, Arthur C. Danto, Hans Belting, Nicolas Bourriaud, and Didi-Huberman. As part of this discussion, I criticize Agamben's ahistorical notion of the contemporary as an "untimely" *person* or *subject*, capable of entering into a disjunctive or anachronistic relationship with their own time. The overall aim of the chapter is to make an argument for what I call "the contemporary contemporary" as the point of departure for any anachronic relationship with time today; and as the inescapable point of departure for any possible historical imagination.

Chapter 7, "Imagination in the Contemporary Society of the Spectacle," reflects on current changes in the conditions for, and the status of, images: more and more images are networked; cameras and screens are everywhere; image data is geotagged; databases can be navigated in real time; the prevalence of operative images and "machine vision," detached from human control and sense-perception, rapidly increases, etc. These transformations are, of course, closely connected to the digitalization and the digital production of images, which has raised a number of interesting questions about their material support and the infrastructure of their dissemination, about connectivity, circulation, distribution, formats, etc. At first sight, these changes are happening primarily at a technical and infrastructural level, but, naturally — as the chapter seeks to demonstrate — they also problematize the cultural and social significance of images and the role of the human subject. Based on the work of artist Trevor Paglen, among others, the chapter explores how the changes in the status and conditions of images shift how we see — or *do not* see — the world, ourselves, and each other.

Taking Forensic Architecture's project *Triple-Chaser* as its point of departure, chapter 8, "Exhibition as Reflexive Transformation," explores the role of exhibition in contemporary aesthetic and artistic practices. I claim, in dialogue with philosopher and art theorist Juliane Rebentisch, that works of art are capable of producing reflexive transformation of our non-artistic everyday lifeworlds and argue that the act of exhibition, of making visible or perceptible, is a decisive element in such a reflexive transformation of the non-aesthetic and non-artistic social reality that the artwork addresses or in which it embeds itself. As philosopher and novelist Tristan Garcia remarks, the act of exhibition makes something/the work present, but, at the same time, it creates a distance, precisely because the appearance of the work has been arranged and addressed to someone/us; it is exhibited as having been organized and made available to us deliberately. This distance installs a difference, a pensive image, in the language of Rancière, which is what allows for reflexive transformation. When Forensic Architecture makes use of reenactments in their investigations of human rights violations, real space is turned into a model of itself, and a negotiation of what it means can begin. An agency like Forensic Architecture, however, operates in a number of different forums to communicate and exhibit their investigations, of which the forum of art is but one because they see each forum, i.e. place of exhibition, as a distorting lens of its own kind. A decisive aspect of what, nevertheless, makes their — and many other contemporary practices that expand their field of operation beyond the dedicated spaces of art — *aesthetic*, is a certain mode of exhibition or exposition and address, which includes the addressees in the structure of the work and invites them to take part in a process of sense-making.

Earlier versions of the essays in this book have been published in different contexts.

Chapter 1 as "Artistic Reappropriation and Reconfiguration of the Medium's Milieu," *Nordic Journal of Aesthetics*, no. 44–45 (2013) and "Destroying the Image in Order to Save It: Contemporary Image-Politics in the Work of Alfredo Jaar," in *Kreative Zerstörung: Über Macht und Ohnmacht des Destruktiven in den Künsten*, edited by Wolfram Bergande (Vienna: Turia + Kant Verlag, 2017).

Chapter 2 as "Acts of Remembering in the Work of Esther Shalev-Gerz: From Embodied to Mediated Memory," in *Revisiting Holocaust Representation in the Post-Witness Era*, edited by Diana Popescu and Tanja Schult (Houndmills, Basingstoke & New York: Palgrave Macmillan, 2015).

Chapter 3 as "The Coming Together of Times: Jean-Luc Godard's Aesthetics of Contemporaneity and the Remembering of the Holocaust," *Nordic Journal of Aesthetics*, no. 49–50 (2015).

Chapter 4 as "Untimeliness in Contemporary Times," in *Futures of the Contemporary: Contemporaneity, Untimeliness, and Artistic Research*, edited by Paolo de Assis and Michael Schwab (Leuven: Leuven University Press, 2018).

Chapter 5 as "Dematerialization in the Contemporary Present," in *Double Trouble in Exhibiting the Contemporary: Art Fairs and Shows*, edited by Cristina Baldacci, Clarissa Ricci, and Angela Vettese (Milan: Scalpendi Editore, 2020).

Chapter 6 as "Making History Through Anachronic Imagining: Notes on Art History and Temporal Complexity of the Present," in *Retracing the Past: Historical Continuity in Aesthetics from a Global Perspective*, International Yearbook of Aesthetics, vol. 19, edited by Zoltán Somhegyi (Santa Cruz, CA: International Association for Aesthetics, 2017), and *Anachrony, Contemporaneity, and Historical Imagination*, The Contemporary Condition 13 (Berlin: Sternberg Press, 2019).

Chapter 7 as "Imagination in the Contemporary Society of the Spectacle," *The Drouth*, no. 64 (2020).

Chapter 8 as "Exhibition as Reflexive Transformation," *OBOE Journal on Biennials and Other Exhibitions*, vol. 3, no. 1 (2022), https://doi.org/10.25432/2724-086X/3.1.0001.

Notes

1 Achille Mbembe, “How to Develop a Planetary Consciousness,” interview with Nils Gilman and Jonathan Blake, *NOEMA* (January 11, 2022), accessed January 15, 2022, https://www.noemamag.com/how-to-develop-a-planetary-consciousness/.

2 Hito Steyerl, “Is the Internet Dead?,” in *Duty Free Art: Art in the Age of Planetary Civil War* (London: Verso, 2017), 146–147.

3 J.T. Fraser, “An Embarrassment of Proper Times: A Foreword,” in Helga Nowotny, *Time. The Modern and Postmodern Experience*, trans. Neville Plaice (Cambridge: Polity, 1994), 5.

4 Peter Osborne, *Anywhere or Not at All: Philosophy of Contemporary Art* (London: Verso, 2013), 17.

5 Terry Smith, “Contemporary Art and Contemporaneity,” *Critical Inquiry* 32 (Summer 2006): 681–707, 703.

6 Bernard Stiegler, *Technics and Time* 1, trans. Richard Beardsworth and George Collins (Stanford, CA: Stanford University Press, 1998), 27.

The Changing Constitution of the Present

Chapters 1—8

Artistic Reappropriation and Reconfiguration of the Medium’s Milieu

Chapter 1

"The way it is: An Aesthetics of Resistance" was the title given to a retrospective exhibition of works by Alfredo Jaar held in Berlin in the summer of 2012.[1] But what might such an aesthetics of resistance consist of? Is there, indeed, any possibility left for artistic critique of "the way it is" in our post-political society? "The way it is" being a historical situation of post-Fordist cognitive capitalism, in which the production of symbols is a central goal, and in which artistic production has a central function in the process of the valorization of capital.[2] According to Jaar, space for artistic and cultural resistance can still be carved out: "The world of culture is *the only space left* for me to do what I can do, there's nothing else."[3] What Jaar does is a politics of images. He resists the present society of the spectacle by engaging with and reconfiguring the ways in which images and symbols are circulated and exchanged, by reappropriating the medium of the image and by making images occluded by the news media visible.

Before I return — toward the end of this chapter — to three pieces by Jaar and one by Thomas Hirschhorn as examples of the politics of images and artistic reconfigurations and reappropriations of the medium of the image, I take Jaar's "aesthetics of resistance" as my point of departure for a more theoretically inclined investigation of the concept of "medium," with focus on the thinking of philosophers Bernard Stiegler and Jacques Rancière.

I

For a while, there has been a tendency within aesthetics to take a critical stance to employing the notion of the medium. Philosopher Noël Carroll, for instance, is an exponent of this tendency, suggesting in *Engaging the Moving Image* that we "Forget the Medium!," stating:

> Obviously what is meant by the phrase "artistic medium" is very vague, referring sometimes to the physical materials out of which artworks are constructed, sometimes to the implements that are used to do the constructing, and sometimes to formal elements of design that are available to artists in a given practice [e.g. line, color, volume, shape, motion, juxtaposition, and so on, JL]. This ambiguity alone might discourage us from relying on the notion of the medium as a theoretically useful concept. In fact, I think that we might fruitfully dispense with it completely, at least in terms of the ways in which it is standardly deployed by aestheticians. But be that as it may, it should be clear that most artforms cannot be identified on the basis of a single distinctive medium, since most artforms correlate with more than one medium.[4]

The last sentence is, of course, a variation of image and media scholar W.J.T. Mitchell's famous, and nowadays relatively uncontroversial observation that "all media are mixed media."[5] I am not convinced, however, that these observations are sufficient for us to dispense with the notion of medium. Instead, I would like to argue that we need to think the concept of medium in another way. Not least in relation to the mass media of television and digital technology and networks.

Philosopher Wolfgang Welsch, among others, claims that the pictorial demands of visual media codetermine what might count as news, meaning that aesthetic considerations enter, to a much higher degree, into our apprehension of reality. The "real" becomes the "aesthetically presentable." According to Welsch, we witness a "derealization of reality" because of the ways in which our sense of reality — which is largely generated by the media — is affected by the increasingly aesthetic mode of mediation.[6] Reality is presented ever more playfully, and everything is potentially open to manipulation and transformation — "Reality these days, as you know very well, is manipulated to an extreme that makes it virtually impossible for us to actually decipher what is real," Jaar remarks in a conversation with philosopher Simon Critchley.[7] Thus, in many cases, manipulation is not only potential, but also actual: "Consider reports from the first Gulf War, replete with technological simulations and the reality of victims and losses erased. It is often unclear whether we are being shown a playback of reality or an aesthetically effective simulation."[8] Our capacity to distinguish between representations and mere simulations of reality is weakened, and our comprehension of what reality itself consists of begins to change. This general attitude toward media reality has, according to Welsch, been extended to other spheres of everyday life. The overwhelming persistence of media representations does not affect us. On the contrary, it leaves us indifferent. We tend to respond to the ways in which the media works by considering reality as simulation altogether.[9] Artist Iñigo Manglano-Ovalle, for instance, addresses the ways in which reality is derealized and manipulated by the news media in his work *Phantom Truck*, made for documenta 12 in Kassel in 2007. The installation is a full-scale reproduction of a mobile biological weapons lab as described by then secretary of state Colin Powell in his address to the UN Security Council in 2003, prior to the US invasion of Iraq. The sculpture is a hybrid of the renderings used by Powell and photographs of actual trucks taken after the subsequent invasion of Iraq. Powell's manipulated object was used speculatively to justify the invasion, but it turned out not to be capable of the production of biological weapons. The evidence was fabricated. Manglano-Ovalle's installation is cloaked in darkness, illuminated only by natural light, and becomes slowly visible as the light changes or our eyes adjust to its darkness.[10]

II

We may find theoretical help in expanding our understanding of the significance and the function of the medium in the work of Bernard Stiegler and Jacques Rancière, who both in different ways conceive the medium as a *milieu*.

In Stiegler's thinking, the fundamental assumption is that the human being is accidental, is originally in need of technical prostheses, and is therefore fundamentally constituted and conditioned by technics.[11] The human is vulnerable because it is a being that continuously evolves through processes of technical exteriorization that necessarily involve processes of interiorization and the appropriation of technical prostheses and procedures (e.g. speaking, writing, painting, performing, installing, etc.). According to Stiegler, the Aristotelian definition of the human being as a political animal means that I am only human insofar as I belong to a social group.[12]

> This sociality is the framework of a becoming: the group, and the individual in that group, never cease to seek out their path. This search *constitutes* human time. And if the time of the *I* is certainly not the time of the *we*, it takes place within the time of the *we*, which is itself conditioned by the time of the *I*s of which it is composed.[13]

These two dimensions of the temporality of the political animal are tied together by what Stiegler — with a notion he adopts from fellow philosopher Gilbert Simondon — calls "individuation" or "transindividuation." The concept of transindividuation does not refer exclusively to the individuated *I* or to the inter-individuated *we*, but designates the process of co-individuation within a pre-individuated milieu or medium in which the *I* and the *we* are interdependent and in which they are transformed through one another.[14] Transindividuation takes place through an "associated symbolic milieu" where all the members belonging to this milieu participate in it and are functions of it.[15] Transindividuation, then, conditions all social transformation. The work of art takes, or may take, part in a kind of transindividuation, and, according to Stiegler, the question of the reflexive aesthetic judgment is also a question of transindividuation.

Language, of course, is one dimension of the pre-individuated milieu:

> At the very moment I speak to you, I am in the process of individuating myself: individuating myself means seeking to constitute the symbolic coherence of my utterances. But I will only succeed in individuating myself *if I succeed in making you individuate yourselves with me*. If my individuation succeeds, it will have to have succeeded *in you* — but not at all in the same manner, because what I am in the course of telling you I understand and interpret as some thing *that you understand as some OTHER thing*, and this is what is interesting. This is the *condition of the we*, and it is what develops 'potentials,' *powers*, or in Greek, *dunameis*.
>
> However, in individuating the *we together*, you and I separately, and also you and I insofar as we form a group, we participate as well in the individuation of *that which ties us*: language, philosophy, law, etcetera, that which constitutes for us a preindividual fund.[16]

The individual's participation in the social, then, is an element in a much vaster individuation. We also participate in the individuation of *that which ties us*, that is, the media through which we communicate, the symbolic milieu of sign making and exchange: language, images, etc. The individual, the social, and the symbolic milieu of the media are intimately interrelated. This interrelation or interweaving is also stressed in philosopher Paolo Virno's reading of Simondon:

> [T]he *subject* consists of the permanent interweaving of pre-individual elements and individuated characteristics. [...] By participating in a collective, the subject, far from surrendering the most unique individual traits, has the opportunity to individuate, at least in part, the share of pre-individual reality which all individuals carry within themselves. [...] Only within the collective, certainly not within the isolated subject, can perception, language, and productive forces take on the shape of an individuated experience.[17]

The milieu, however, is structurally forgotten because it is what is closest to us — as water is to a fish.[18] The milieu is forgotten because it disappears in front of that which it lets appear, or gives place for.[19] The fact that a milieu always already exists escapes us in the same manner that, as Aristotle observes, "aquatic animals do not notice that one wet body touches another wet body."[20] The fish never sees water because water is what it always sees. Ludwig Wittgenstein's image of the fly in the fly-bottle and the task of philosophy: *Der Fliege den Ausweg aus dem Fliegenglas zeigen*, that is, to show the fly the way out of the fly-bottle, also springs to mind here of course.[21] The glass of the bottle is, for the fly, not a thing, but rather that through which it sees things, that through which things appear.[22] In the same way we as humans see the world through language but do not — at least in everyday life — see language itself.

In Stiegler's thinking, the milieu is something like a general supplement, language is one dimension, technical artifacts consisting of things another. Like Wittgenstein's endeavor to show the fly the way out of the bottle, Stiegler considers the milieu while extracting himself from it in order, through this extraction or abstraction, to bring the milieu into view as the condition of individuation ("the condition of passage from the potential of the intellective soul to its act, to its *for itself*").[23] He tries to contemplate the milieu, understood as "the framework of artifacts forming relations sustaining social relations" — something like a flying fish that intermittently leaves the water, leaves its element — while also making it to perceptible.[24]

III

The ever more omnipresent mass media of television and the Internet poses particularly urgent questions in terms of the medium as milieu — as that which is in between, as that which ties us together and conditions our individuation:

> The human milieu is symbolic, which means that it is a milieu of exchange where exclamations [...] make signs circulate, and that it is a milieu of sign-making where each one participates in symbolic life. Such is the process of trans-individuation by which we co-individuate in symbolic milieus, which are associated milieus. However, the associated milieus have become dissociated. The industrial division of labor has meant that there are producers of symbols and consumers of symbols who do not participate in the elaboration of meaning, causing these symbols to lose their meaning.[25]

Our continuous evolution through the exteriorization and interiorization of prostheses and procedures depends upon an associated symbolic milieu. When this milieu becomes dissociated, the processes of evolution and transindividuation stop and we are made aware of the importance of the association of the milieu — "I believe our daily language is corrupted, dissociated from the truth," Jaar states.[26] A parallel to Stiegler's description of the dissociation of the symbolic milieu may be found in Giorgio Agamben's "Marginal Notes on *Commentaries on the Society of the Spectacle*" of 1990:

> Even more than economic necessities and technological development, what drives the nations of the Earth toward a single common destiny is the alienation of linguistic being, the uprooting of all peoples from their vital dwelling in language. But exactly for this reason, the age in which we live is also that in which for the first time it becomes possible for human beings to experience their own linguistic essence — to experience, that is, not some language content or some true proposition, but language *itself*, as well as the very fact of speaking. Contemporary politics is precisely this devastating *experimentum linguae* that disarticulates and empties, all over the planet, traditions and beliefs, ideologies and religions, identities and communities.[27]

Like Stiegler, Agamben, in an even bleaker manner, points toward how the dissociation of the symbolic milieu and the expropriation of language, of our means of communication, entails the possibility of experiencing language itself, of seeing the media or milieus through which we see the world. This is connected to Agamben's idea of "the being-in-a-medium of human beings" and gesture — not least artistic gestures, for instance the gestures of Samuel Beckett's TV play *Nacht und Träume* — as "the exhibition of a mediality: [...] the process of making a means visible as such."[28] In relation to language, it is the exposure of "the word in its own mediality, in its own being a means, [...] communication of a communicability."[29] Art, in other words, may exhibit the medium or milieu as such, and the way in which we depend upon it and are constituted through it.

As mentioned above, literary books, other kinds of artworks and forms of creative work take — or can take — part in the process of transindividuation. With reference to literary theorist Wolfgang Iser's theory of the aesthetics of reception, Stiegler claims that we can individuate — that is, transform — ourselves by reading a book, or experiencing a work of visual art. A book does not exist as such, it is a process of individuation, which means that a book can be a facilitating power of individuation, but not individuation as such. It is "the long circuit created by the readers, which is the individuation of the book."[30] Stiegler draws upon Iser's understanding of the literary text, according to which it is not simply a representation of a meaning given in advance of the text itself. The text is not actualized until the process of reading; the significance of the text is only created through the reading process. Signification, then, is a result of an interaction between text and reader, not something that is encapsulated in the text per se. The significance of the text is, in other words, produced by the individual reader and therefore appears in an *individual form* — every reader concretizes the artistic artifact in an individual way. This concerns transindividuation in the sense that the creation of circuits is a defining characteristic of transindividuation. Important artists — or philosophers — are, according to Stiegler, singularities who have created new types of circuits that other people can continue (somewhat in the manner of Michel Foucault's concept of "founders of discursivity," such as Marx and Freud, in "What Is an Author?"). The decisive point is not whether the artist has produced a unique work, but whether a new type of circuit has been produced that others can hook themselves up to — that others can appropriate — by building on it. The value of the work depends on its capacity for transindividuation, on how entry to, and continuation of, the circuits is determined.[31]

The conditions for creating circuits of transindividuation are always what Stiegler terms "organological." You have to be able to practice the technics of this organology, you have to have certain technical skills — reading and writing, for instance, or producing music and images — that are common in order to enter the circuits of transindividuation and open spaces for relationships between people. This organological arrangement — understood as the co-individuation of human organs, technical organs, and social organizations — forms the milieu through which we see. As I indicated above, contemporary society, however, is, according to Stiegler's analysis, a society in which organology has become industrial. With reference to Theodor W. Adorno and Max Horkheimer's chapter on "The Culture Industry: Enlightenment as Mass Deception" he locates a change in organology, of transindividuation, that began in the twentieth century when a new organology was developed through the mass media of television, cinema, radio, and further developed in the last few decades through digital technology and networks, which in turn have created a new organization of the circulation of the symbolic:

> Within this new mode of organization, suddenly the production of the symbolic becomes industrial, subject to industrial processes. Here you encounter the production of symbols on the one hand, and the consuming of such symbols on the other — an *aporia* because it is impossible to consume a symbol. The symbol is not an object of consumption; it is an object of exchange, of circulation, or of the creation of circuits of transindividuation. So this situation suddenly produced what I call short-circuiting — of transindividuation.[32]

The destruction of symbolic exchange entails a blockage or short-circuiting of the processes of transindividuation that results in deindividuation, a proletarianization of the consumer. Programs

— a central component of the culture industry — are planned and produced industrially and broadcast through various audiovisual media. According to Stiegler these programs modify our experience of time, as our consciousnesses adapt to their temporalities, which constantly solicit our attention and try to modify our behaviour, especially our patterns of consumption.[33] A telling example of the way of thinking of the program industry is the notorious, herostratic statement by Patrick Le Lay in July 2004 when he was managing director of TF1, the main French TV channel:

> There are many ways to talk about television. But from a "Business" perspective, let's be realistic: basically, TF1's job is to help Coca-Cola sell its product, for example. To make the advertising message well received, the audience's brain must be available. Our shows are here to make the brain available [*disponible*] — to entertain it, to relax it, to prepare it between two messages. What we're selling to Coca-Cola is available human brain time. Nothing is as difficult as securing this availability.[34]

In this situation, the role of contemporary art is to participate in the reconstitution of a symbolic milieu or organology that enables participation in weaving *long* circuits of transindividuation. The role of art is to reconfigure the organology that has been destroyed by the consumerism of the culture industries, and to try to reappropriate and reassociate the media and technical milieus that have become dissociated.

IV

In order better to understand the relationship between art and medium in a political context, and how this reconfiguration may come into being, it seems fruitful to supplement Stiegler's theory of medium with that of Rancière.

Stiegler speaks of "an aesthetic war," *une guerre esthétique*, and claims, in accordance with Rancière, that the political question is an aesthetic question and, vice versa, that the aesthetic question is a political question.[35] If cultural and artistic practices have a central function in the formation, configuration and reconfiguration of our common sense and our conception of reality, artistic practice is political in that it takes or can take part in reproducing "the way it is" or in dissenting from the established order. The political, on the other hand, is aesthetic in that it has to do with the symbolic ordering of social relations and our coexistence.[36] Stiegler uses the term "aesthetics" in a broad sense, that is, as sensation in general, not only "perceptibility." but taste, feeling, and sensibility in general. This understanding of aesthetics is an invitation to the art world to comprehend its role politically. He is not saying that the artists should "engage" themselves; he is saying that their work is engaged fundamentally in the question of the sensibility of the other. The political question is in essence the question of the relation to the other in a common or shared sensing (*sentir ensemble*), a kind of sympathy.[37] Perception, sensation, feeling, taste, are not only individual but immediately social phenomena. The political problem is to know how to be and to live together beyond our singularities and our conflicts of interest. Politics is the art of securing the unity of the city, the polis, in its desire for a common future, its individuation and its singularity as becoming-one. Such a desire supposes a common aesthetic ground, a common aesthetic medium or milieu. Being together is sensuous, and a political community is thus — in agreement with the Kantian idea of *sensus communis*, i.e., our shared ability to have feelings in common — a community of sensing.[38] If we are not able to appreciate, or love, things like countrysides, cities, objects, artworks, language etc. together, we are not able to love ourselves. This, Stiegler claims, is the sense of "philia" in Aristotle, and to love oneself is to love other things than oneself together with others.

But human aesthetics are anything but stable, they develop historically in an endless transformation of the sensible. Even though Édouard Manet's break with painterly traditions gave, for instance, rise to a multiplication of aesthetic conflicts in the middle of the nineteenth century, these conflicts are nevertheless a process of the construction of aesthetic sympathies. Creative gestures such as Manet's have the potential to transform the world by facilitating new, common forms of sensibility, supporting the construction of a new common sense and understanding of reality, and therefore contributing to the formation of a coming aesthetic community.

The problem today, according to Stiegler, is that a large part of the population is excluded from any aesthetic experience and subjected to the alienating aesthetic conditioning of the culture industry that deprives them of the capacity for connecting aesthetically to singularities and singular objects and makes them passive consumers of symbols.[39]

Rancière agrees with Stiegler that we live in an epoch in which art has, to a large extent, become separate from politics, and where a large part of the population is excluded from participation in the aesthetic or the symbolic. Rancière locates the connection between aesthetics and politics in the partition of the sensible, *le partage du sensible*, in the possibilities of sense and its distribution in terms of sensible forms and practices.[40] He distinguishes politics from the exercise of power that belongs to the police order. The police determines the social configuration, "the partition of the sensible," and administrates the emotional life of citizens, regulating the composition of society and its ways of living, on which it tries to establish *consensus*. Political action, on the other hand, is an action of *dissensus*, where someone tries to be heard or seen even though, or perhaps rather *because*, they are not allowed to speak: "Political subjectivity thus refers to an enunciative and demonstrative capacity to reconfigure the relation between the visible and the sayable, the relation between words and bodies: namely, what I refer to as 'the partition of the sensible.'"[41] Art has the capacity of creating a critical break with the established, consensual common sense, opening up the possibility of a new commonality of sense. Such politically "active" art changes the conditions for what we see and what we speak about; it challenges the borders between the visible and the invisible, between the sayable and the unsayable. It is thus partly through art that the world can be articulated in new ways, and through art that this political reconfiguration of the police order's configuration of the relationship between the visible and the sayable, between words and bodies, this making the unheard heard and the invisible visible, can take place.[42]

According to Rancière, artistic "means" are "the means of participating in the configuration of a specific milieu." In a text entitled "What Medium Can Mean," Rancière discusses two modernist approaches to the concept of medium: on the one hand the medium as the intermediary between an idea and its realization, that is, as a means to an end; and, on the other hand, the Greenbergian idea of the medium as the specific materiality defining the essence of art, where the medium is no longer a means to an end but that which prescribes this end — when art is freed from the tasks of representation and exclusively becomes the execution of its own idea in its own specific materiality.[43] He then tries to synthesize these two contradictory approaches by claiming that art is art "when its productions belong to a sensory milieu in which the distinction is blurred between that which is and that which is not art. In short, the 'means' [*le moyen*] is also a means to achieve something other than its own end. It is also the means of participating in the configuration of a specific milieu."[44] Like Stiegler, Rancière thus considers the medium as milieu: "The milieu in which the performances of a determined artistic arrangement come to be inscribed, but also the milieu that these performances themselves contribute to configuring."[45] Endowed with a relative autonomy, art can participate in the reconfiguration of the established milieus of experience; it can work against the dissociation and expropriation of the milieu in which we communicate, of language and images.

V

By way of conclusion, I would like to return to Jaar and Hirschhorn in order to give a few examples of works of art that, in different ways, oppose and criticize the way in which the image circulation of the mass media functions. Two of them were presented at the 2012 Paris Triennale curated by Okwui Enwezor, at the then newly converted and extended Palais de Tokyo, namely Thomas Hirschhorn's *Touching Reality* (2012) and Alfredo Jaar's *May 1, 2011* (2011), while the other two works by Jaar are a bit older: *Lament of the Images* (2002) was made for Enwezor's documenta 11 and was also included in the Berlin retrospective, whereas *The Sound of Silence* was first exhibited in 2006.

Their common point of departure might be summed up by Rancière's observation that the widespread idea that there is an excess of images, seducing and anesthetizing us, is a cliché marketed by the masters of the machinery of power that lies behind these images:

> Whatever people say, our news bulletins present us with very few images of the wars, violence, or distress that characterize the present on our planet; hardly any violent, mutilated, or suffering bodies. What we see mainly are the faces of those who "make" the news, the authorized speakers: presenters, editorial writers, politicians, and experts, specialists at explaining or debating matters. The "images" on the screen are "their" images.[46]

The task of the artist is not to get rid of the excess of images, but to draw attention to their absence, "the absence of certain images in the selection of what those in charge of the distribution of images consider to be interesting to show."[47]

Hirschhorn's video installation *Touching Reality* features a hand scrolling through images with its fingertips on a touchscreen. The images are photographs of corpses and destroyed human bodies. They go by quickly and every now and then the hand stops to zoom in for detail or to select a portion to enlarge. In relation to the piece, Hirschhorn clarifies: "Why it is important — today — to show and look at images of destroyed human bodies?" With reference to former US Secretary of Defense Donald Rumsfeld's formulation: "Death has a tendency to encourage a depressing view of war," he claims that the invisibility of destroyed bodies in the news media is not innocent, but a strategy of supporting the war effort, by eschewing "discouraging" images and thereby making it acceptable.[48] "I want to see with my own eyes. Resistance to today's world of facts is what makes it important to look at such images."[49]

Thus, I would claim that Hirschhorn — although he balances dangerously on the border of spectacle and, sometimes, seems to tip over — reconfigures the partition of the sensible in the milieu of the news media by making the mutilated bodies that are excluded or left out by the news bulletins visible — while also, through the hand touching the images, addressing our individual *relation* to, or *association* with, these images.

Before turning to Jaar's artistic practice, I would like to make an excursion to philosopher and media theorist Boris Groys's analysis of the topology of contemporary art and use it to spell out the differences between modernist and contemporary image politics.

As Groys points out, creativity was the central notion of modern art.[50] In order to be creative the artist "was supposed to effectuate a radical break with the past, [...] to destroy the past, to achieve a zero point of artistic tradition" with a view to a new future — in line with Peter Osborne's understanding of modernity as a qualitative, not a chronological category, and modernist art as characterized by being "dependent for its intelligibility upon a temporal logic of negation [whereby] it makes its claim on the present, through its negation of past forms, in the name of a particular, qualitatively different future."[51] Groys continues:

> It is also no accident that the vocabulary constantly used by the historical avant-garde is the language of iconoclasm. Abolishing traditions, breaking with conventions, destroying old art, and eradicating out-dated values were the slogans of the day. The practice of the historical avant-garde was based on the equation — "negation is creation" — already formulated by Bakunin, Stirner, and Nietzsche. Iconoclastic images of destruction and reduction were destined to serve as the icons of the future.

Thus, the genuine creativity of the artist depends on how far they can reduce and destroy the traditional image, how radical and iconoclastic their work is. But to recognize the iconoclasm of a certain image, it has to be compared with the supposedly traditional images it purports to erase or negate. This means that recognition of the iconoclastic gesture, of the creative destruction yielding new orders, requires a constant comparison with tradition and with the past. Whatever new it brings about can only be recognized on the basis of the history and the tradition with which it breaks. "A creative act," Groys observes,

> [...] if it is understood as an iconoclastic gesture, presupposes a permanent reproduction of the context in which the act is effectuated. [...] The Modern artwork is re-presented and re-cognized before it is produced. It follows that modernist production by negation is governed by just this reproduction of the means of comparison — of a certain historical narrative, of a certain artistic medium, of a certain visual language, of a certain fixed context of comparison.[52]

This understanding of the modernist iconoclastic gesture, with its concomitant goal of revealing the mediality and the materiality of the artwork, leads me to *contemporary* artistic practices and how they may be said to differ from modernist practices.

With reference to Walter Benjamin's famous essay "The Work of Art in the Age of Its Technological Reproducibility," in which Benjamin introduces the concept of "aura" to analyze the difference between original and copy, Groys stresses that, according to Benjamin, "the loss of aura" is a loss of the fixed, constant and affirmable context of an artwork. According to Benjamin, the artwork in the age of its technical reproducibility leaves its original context and begins to circulate anonymously in networks of mass communication. While high modernist art negates the repetition of traditional images but leaves its art historical context intact, the new forms of low art reproduce these images while negating and destroying their original context of comparison. What is happening in today's art, which primarily operates with new media and techniques of reproduction, however, has more to do with *the emergence* of aura than with the loss of aura, Groys claims. The difference between original and copy can be seen as a topological difference between a fixed, well-defined, auratic place or context and a profane, placeless, unmarked space of anonymous mass circulation. This not only implies that the original can be dislocated and deterritorialized, but also that the copy can be *re*located and *re*territorialized:

> We are not only able to produce a copy out of an original by a technique of reproduction but we are also able to produce an original out of a copy by a technique of topological relocation of this copy — that is, by a technique of installation. Installation art [...] operates as a reversal of reproduction. The installation takes a copy out of an allegedly unmarked, open space of anonymous circulation and puts it — even if only temporarily — in a fixed, stable, closed context of a topologically well-defined "here and now." This means that all the objects placed in an installation are copies.

> Artworks in an installation are originals for one simple topological reason: it is necessary to go to the installation to see them. [...] What differentiates contemporary art from previous times is only the fact that the originality of a work in our time is not established depending on its own form, but through its inclusion in a certain context, in a certain installation, through its topological inscription.[53]

In contemporary culture images permanently circulate from one medium to another medium, from one defined context to another defined context. Traveling through different networks of communication, these images are transformed by their different framings and contextual settings. "By circulating through different contexts a copy becomes a series of different originals," Groys argues. Every change of context and medium can be regarded as a negation of the status of the copy as a copy. While it may remain a copy, it becomes different originals with each new context. Whether a certain image is recognized as an original or as a copy is dependent on the context in which we see it. Groys therefore contends that the installation — with its demonstration of a certain logic of inclusion and exclusion — is the leading art form of contemporary art:

> Modern art was working on the level of individual form. Contemporary art is working on the level of context, framework, background, or of a new theoretical interpretation. That is why contemporary art is less a production of individual artworks than it is a manifestation of an individual decision to include or to exclude things and images that circulate anonymously in our world, to give them a new context or to deny it to them. [...] The installation reveals precisely the materiality of the civilization in which we live, because it *installs* everything that our civilization simply *circulates*. The installation thus demonstrates the material hardware of civilization that would otherwise go unnoticed behind the surface of image circulation in the mass media.[54]

VI

This detour through Groys's distinction between modernist iconoclasm and contemporary installation art as a kind of occasional re-emergence of aura through artistic contextualization — or reframing of the images circulating unnoticed in the mass media — provides a useful interpretative framework for Jaar's artistic practice.

Jaar is in no way trying to do away with images or to destroy the image. Rather, he constructs sensory arrangements that restore the powers of attention itself and try to create other spatiotemporal arrangements; he tries to oppose other light boxes to the dominant light box.[55] In an interview he states:

> I still believe images are more necessary than ever. But I also believe that the political and corporate landscape of our times is full of control mechanisms that will not allow certain images to exist in their proper context. As artists are producers of meaning, we need to contextualize images properly. We must create a framework for their political efficiency.[56]

Jaar's installation *The Sound of Silence* is an example of such a contextualization of images — and of the crucial importance of *editing* in his arrangements or installations.[57] Jaar has removed an image from its context of constant circulation and asks us to spend eight minutes of our time on this particular image (instead of the average three seconds that a visitor spends in front of an artwork in a gallery or a museum): in other words, he transforms the image circulating as a copy in a detached media spectacle into an original demanding our attention. He has dedicated a whole theater, 300 cubic meters of space, to *one* image: the photograph that won the South African photographer Kevin Carter a Pulitzer Prize in 1994. The photograph depicts a starving little Sudanese girl crawling on all fours while being observed by a vulture. The installation is a *mise-en-scène* that interweaves three stories: that of the photojournalist, that of the subject of his photograph, and that of the photograph itself. Shaped by the space of the small theater, the external structure of the work is open to visitors on one side, while the opposite side presents a face illuminated by a dazzling array of white neon lights.[58] Access to the theater is signaled by a green light announcing the start of the screening so that visitors see the whole of the projection — visitors are meant to wait while the projection is running and the light is red. Inside, a text in white letters on a black ground scrolls past slowly in the darkness of the small projection room. The text tells the story of Kevin Carter, committed to documenting and exposing the brutality of apartheid, and who became famous for his picture of the starving girl dragging herself along the ground under the gaze of the vulture taken in Sudan in 1993. The text is interrupted only once, by four violent flashes of light that let the famous picture appear on the screen, but in such a fleeting manner that it is perceived as an after-image. Carter committed suicide two months after receiving the Pulitzer Prize and the controversies aroused by his photograph, leaving behind these words: "I am really, really sorry. I am haunted by the vivid memories of killings and corpses and anger and pain... of starving or wounded children... The pain of life overrides the joy to the point that joy does not exist." The text ends by describing the fate of his picture, the rights to which are managed by the Corbis Group, owned by Bill Gates, and which controls close to a hundred million images, making it the largest photographic agency in the world. “No one knows what happened to the child,” the text concludes, and the words resound in silence when the visitors come back out into the blinding white light of the neon lamps.

As Rancière remarks, Jaar constructed a spatio-temporal viewing apparatus removed equally from the newspaper and the hanging of large-format photographs in museums; a device that involves an exceptional sensory experience: the closed space of the theater performance, which has to be followed for the eight minutes of its duration. Jaar has configured a space and a time suitable for allowing the image to resonate in silence.[59] He has *installed* it in a new context; made it undergo what Groys calls a “topological inscription.”

On the night of May 1, 2011, the image of then president Barack Obama and his political and military team in the White House Situation Room during the killing of Osama bin Laden by US Navy SEAL Team 6 was transmitted throughout the world.[60] The image of the scene in the Situation Room, documented by official photographer Pete Souza, came to play a central role in the image politics of the “war on terror.” In his installation, *May 1, 2011*, Jaar uses the official photograph from the White House. The image had been visibly retouched to disguise sensitive information before being disseminated. The execution of the operation was broadcast live to the White House by cameras physically mounted on the Navy Seals who conducted the mission. No trace of the body of bin Laden, and no image of him, was shown to the media. Jaar has adapted the image of the group at the White House and juxtaposed it with a blank screen, representing the absent, never-authorized image of the act that was said to have taken place. The non-image occupies the position of the invisible screen, on which all the imaginative imagery conjured up by the iconic press photograph can be projected. The caption to the right of the photo of the White House identifies all the political figures in the press image, while on the left side next to the white screen there is no one to be identified.

In my reading, Jaar thematizes how the media image is a staging of the visible, a particular configuration of the visible and what it says, and of the language and what it makes apparent for us.[61] He does not produce another image, but reconfigures the existing one by contextualizing our encounter with, and reflection upon, the encounter with this omnipresent media image.[62]

May 1, 2011 echoes another blank screen in Jaar's work, namely the blank screen of the *Lament of the Images* installation. The first part of this piece consists of a dark space with three blocks of texts describing paradigmatic cases of images lacking, or being removed, from public space: the first recounts that there are no photographs that show Nelson Mandela crying when he was released after twenty-eight years of detention under the apartheid regime. "It is said that the blinding light from the lime [he was forced to labor in a limestone quarry on Robben Island, JL] had taken away his ability to cry." The second describes how Bill Gates's company Corbis is about to bury the Bettmann and United Press International archive, comprising around seventeen million historical photographs — including a photograph of Mandela in prison, in an old limestone mine — following which they will be inaccessible, and only digital scans of will be available for sale (at the time, less than two percent had been scanned, which, at that rate of progress, meant that it would take 453 years to digitize the entire archive). The third describes the US airstrike against Afghanistan and the Department of Defense's purchase of exclusive rights to all available satellite images of Afghanistan and its neighbors from the private company Space Imaging Inc. just before the attack. According to Space Imaging's CEO: "They are buying all the imagery that is available." The text concludes: "There is nothing [i.e. no effects of the bombing, JL] left to see." After reading the texts, the visitor walks through a dark corridor, roughly twenty-five meters in length, before turning left and entering a huge room filled with blinding light emitting from a cinema-size white screen.

In one of his comments on *Lament of the Images* Jaar emphasizes:

> Images are important. Very important. In creating this work I was trying to lament their loss, mourn their absence. In doing so, I ended up creating a new image, which is unavoidable. An image of an intense, blinding light that could possibly become the blank screen on which we project our fears and our dreams. [...] I was trying to create perhaps the ultimate pensive image. A space of resistance. A space of hope.[63]

Jaar's aesthetics of resistance reveals the invisible and exhibits the milieu and the media through which we comprehend the world, stressing the need to re-establish association with this image-milieu.

In concluding, I would claim that the artistic practices of Thomas Hirschhorn and Alfredo Jaar are examples of the ways in which putatively damaged or empty common media and symbolic milieus are being renegotiated in contemporary art, whereby senses of community may begin to be reinstalled.

A
Iñigo Manglano-Ovalle
Phantom Truck, 2007

B–E
Thomas Hirschhorn
Touching Reality (video still), 2012

F–H
Alfredo Jaar
The Sound of Silence, 2006

I
Alfredo Jaar
May 1, 2011, 2011

J–K
Alfredo Jaar
Lament of the Images, 2002

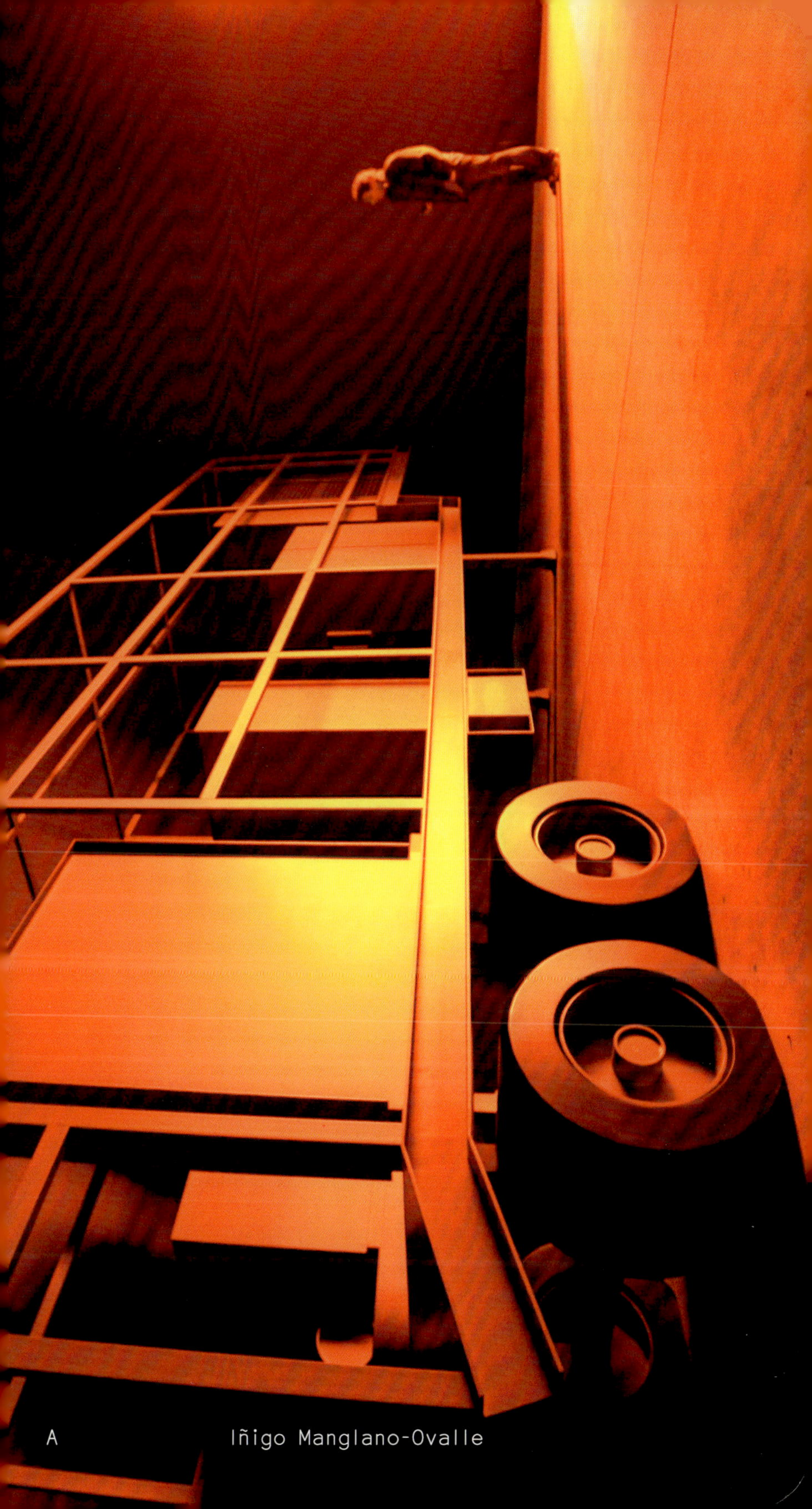

A Iñigo Manglano-Ovalle

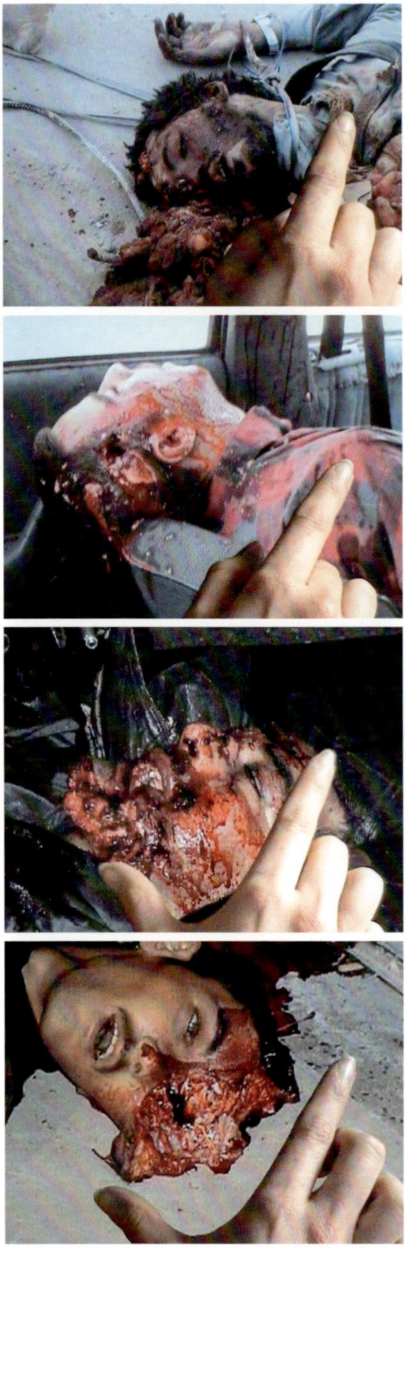

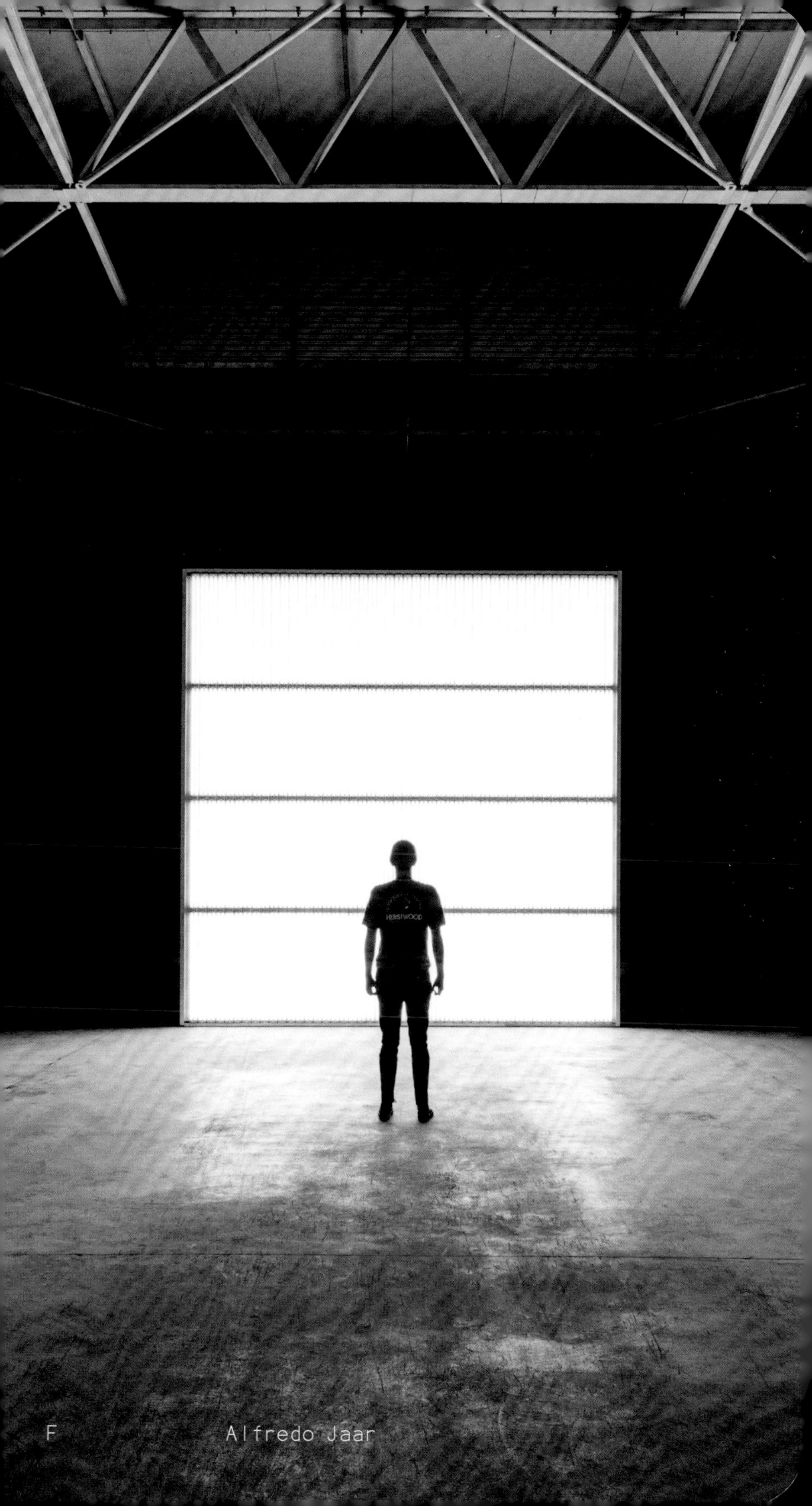

F Alfredo Jaar

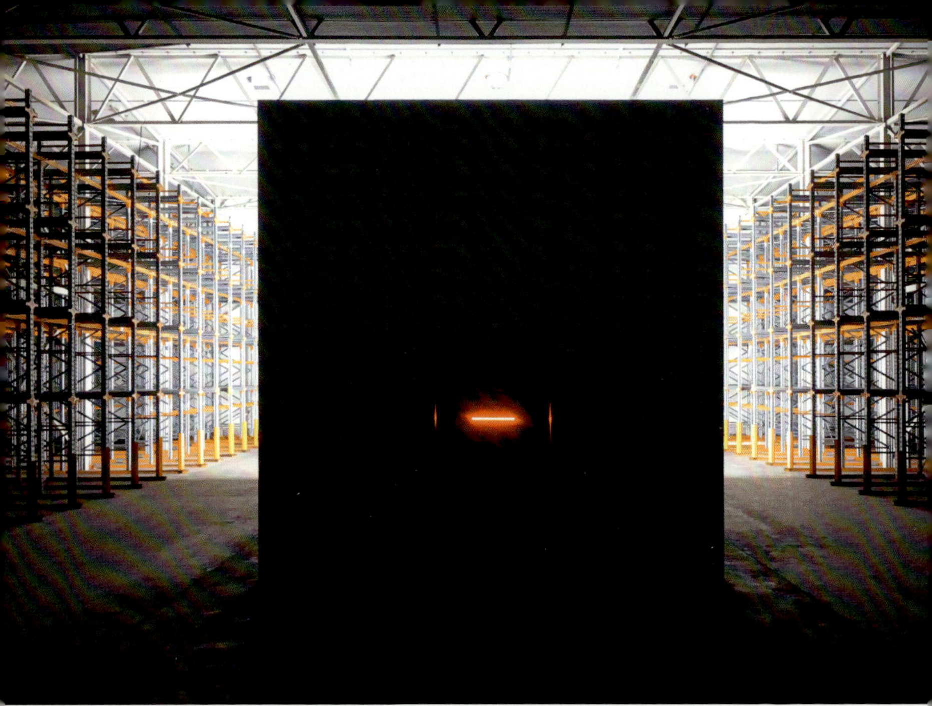

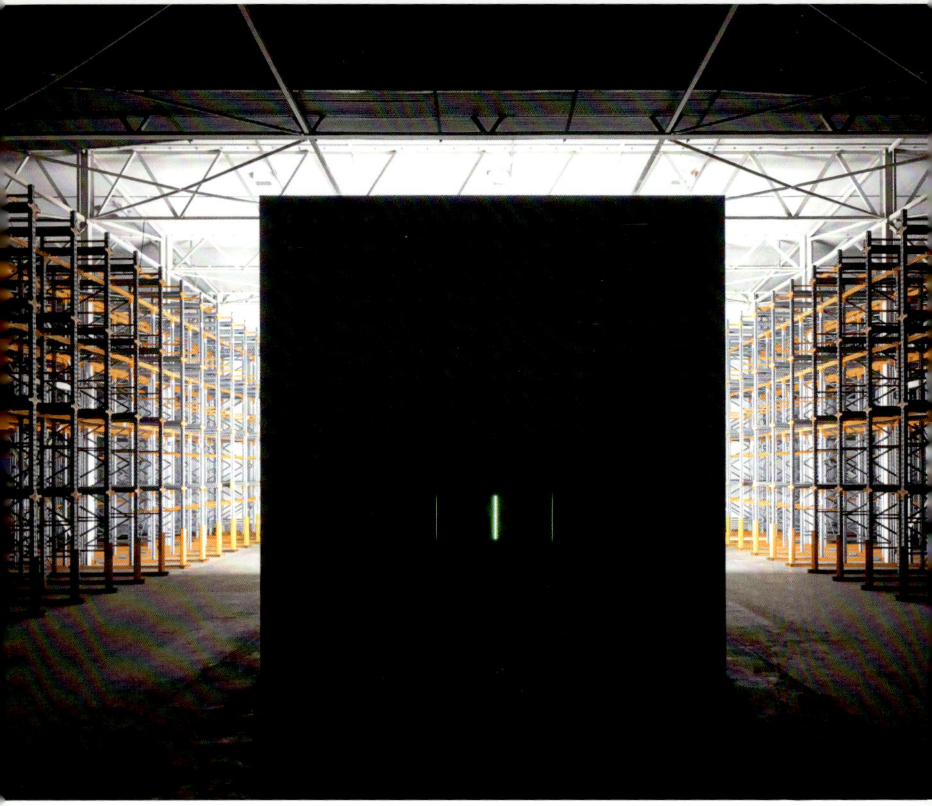

G-H Alfredo Jaar

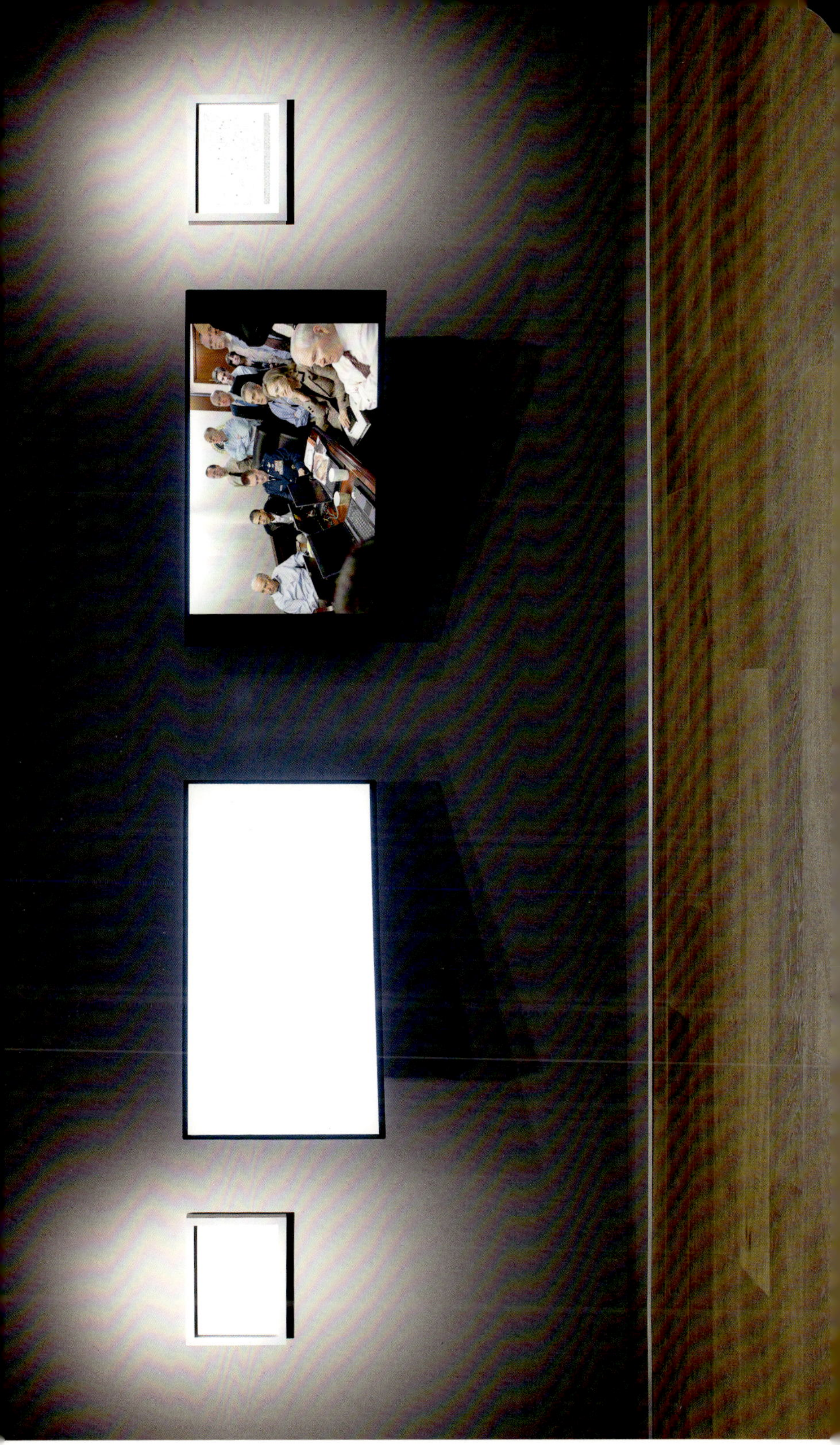

| Alfredo Jaar

J Alfredo Jaar

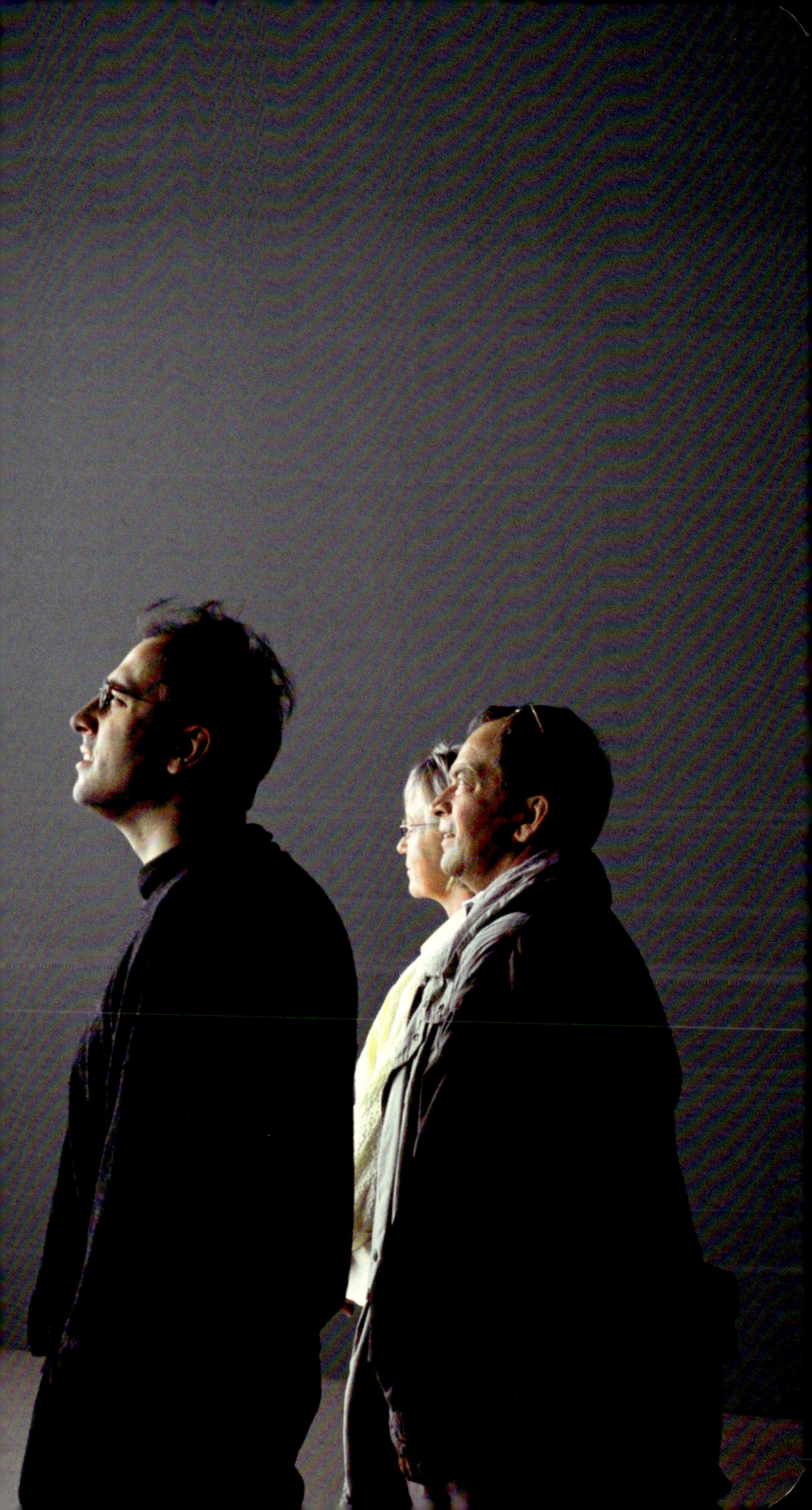

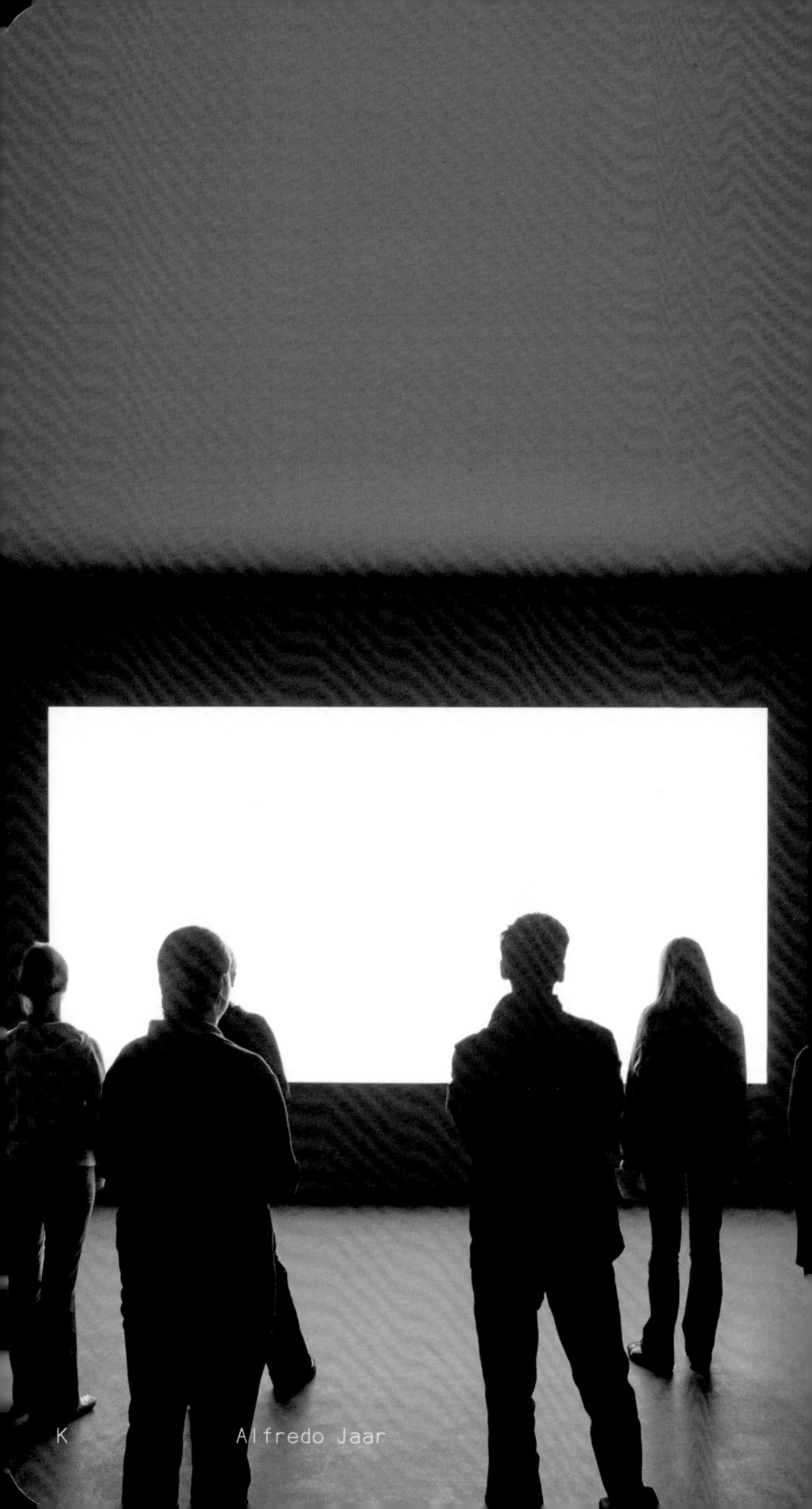
K
Alfredo Jaar

Notes

1 The exhibition was shown at the Neue Gesellschaft für Bildende Kunst, Berlinische Galerie, and at Alte Nationalgalerie, June 15–August 19 / September 17 / September 16, 2012 respectively.

2 Cf. Chantal Mouffe, "Alfredo Jaar: The Artist as Organic Intellectual," in *Alfredo Jaar. The way it is: Eine Ästhetik des Widerstands/An Aesthetics of Resistance*, ed. Jan Ketz (Berlin: NGBK, 2012), 266–282: 266.

3 Alfredo Jaar, quoted in Claire Bishop, "The Social Turn: Collaboration and Its Discontents" [2006], in *Artificial Hells: Participatory Art and the Politics of Spectatorship* (London: Verso, 2012), 292, note 48.

4 Noël Carroll, *Engaging the Moving Image* (New Haven, CT: Yale University Press, 2003), 6. "Forget the Medium!" is the title of the first chapter.

5 W.J.T. Mitchell, *What Do Pictures Want? The Lives and Loves of Images* (Chicago: University of Chicago Press, 2005), 215.

6 Wolfgang Welsch, "Aesthetics beyond Aesthetics," in *Rediscovering Aesthetics: Transdisciplinary Voices from Art History, Philosophy, and Art Practice*, eds. Francis Halsall et al. (Stanford, CA: Stanford University Press, 2009), 178–192: 182f.

7 "Between Baudrillard and the Cave: Alfredo Jaar and Simon Critchley in Conversation," *Mute online*, March to May 2011, accessed January 6, 2022, http://www.metamute.org/editorial/articles/between-baudrillard-and-cave-alfredo-jaar-and-simon-critchley-conversation.

8 Welsch, "Aesthetics beyond Aesthetics," 183.

9 Ibid.

10 Cf. the description of the work in the exhibition catalogue *Documenta Kassel: 16/06 – 23/09 2007, 12*, eds. Roger Buergel and Ruth Noack (Cologne: Taschen, 2007), 280.

11 Cf. Bernard Stiegler, *La technique et le temps, 1: La faute d'Epiméthée* (Paris: Galilée, 1994).

12 Cf. Bernard Stiegler, "How I Became a Philosopher," in *Acting Out*, trans. David Barison et al. (Stanford, CA: Stanford University Press, 2009), 3f.

13 Ibid.

14 Cf. Bernard Stiegler and Irit Rogoff, "Transindividuation," *e-flux journal*, #14 (March 2010), 01/06, accessed January 6, 2022, http://www.e-flux.com/journal/transindividuation.

15 Cf. Bernard Stiegler, "Technics, Media, Teleology. Interview with Bernard Stiegler," in *Theory, Culture & Society*, vol. 24 (7–8) (2007), 334–341: 335.

16 Stiegler, "How I Became a Philosopher," 5.

17 Paolo Virno, *A Grammar of the Multitude: For an Analysis of Contemporary Forms of Life*, trans. Isabella Bertoletti et al. (Los Angeles: Semiotext(e), 2004), 78f.

18 Stiegler, "How I Became a Philosopher," 14.

19 The standard reference on structural oblivion to the medium is, of course, Marshall McLuhan's seminal study *Understanding Media: The Extensions of Man* (New York: McGraw Hill, 1965), 32, where he likens his own position to that of Louis Pasteur, who told the doctors that their biggest enemy was invisible, and as yet not even recognized.

20 Aristotle, quoted by Stiegler, "How I Became a Philosopher," 14.

21 Ludwig Wittgenstein, *Philosophical Investigations*, trans. G.E.M. Anscombe (New York: Macmillan, 1953), §309.

22 Cf. Giorgio Agamben, "The Idea of Language," in *Potentialities*, trans. Daniel Heller-Roazen (Stanford, CA: Stanford University Press, 1999), 46.

23 Stiegler, "How I Became a Philosopher," 14.

24 Ibid. Stiegler became a philosopher while incarcerated for five years, from 1978 to 1983, for armed robbery.

25 Bernard Stiegler, "The Tongue of the Eye: What 'Art History' Means," in *Releasing the Image: From Literature to New Media*, eds. Jacques Khalip and Robert Mitchell (Stanford, CA: Stanford University Press, 2011), 222–235: 230f.

26 "Exhausted States: Alfredo Jaar and Simon Critchley in Conversation," *Mute online* (March to May 2011), accessed January 6, 2022, http://www.metamute.org/editorial/articles/exhausted-states.

27 Giorgio Agamben, "Marginal Notes on *Commentaries on the Society of the Spectacle*," in *Means without End: Notes on Politics* [1996], trans. Vincenzo Binetti and Cesare Casarino (Minneapolis: University of Minnesota Press, 2000), 85.

28 Giorgio Agamben, "Notes on Gesture," in *Means without End*, 58.

29 Ibid., 59.

30 Bernard Stiegler and Irit Rogoff, "Transindividuation," 04/06.

31 Ibid.

32 Ibid., 05/06.

33 Bernard Stiegler, "Suffocated Desire, or How the Cultural Industry Destroys the Individual: Contribution to a Theory of Mass Consumption," *Parrhesia,* no. 13 (2011): 52–61, 53. Cf. also Jonathan Crary, *24/7: Late Capitalism and the Ends of Sleep* (London: Verso, 2014).

34 Patrick le Lay in *Les dirigeants face au changement: Baromètre 2004*, eds. Les associés d'EIM (Paris: Éditions du Huitième jour, 2004). Cf. also Bernard Stiegler, *De la misère symbolique, 2: La catastrophè du sensible* (Paris: Galilée, 2005), 85.

35 Bernard Stiegler, *De la misère symbolique, 1: L'époque hyperindustrielle* (Paris: Galilée, 2004), 16; and Bernard Stiegler, "De la misère symbolique," *Le Monde* (October 10, 2003).

36 Cf. Mouffe, "Alfredo Jaar," 269.

37 Cf. Stiegler, "De la misère symbolique," *Le Monde*.

38 Cf. Daniel Ross, "Politics and Aesthetics, or, Transformations of Aristotle in Bernard Stiegler," in "Bernard Stiegler and the Question of Technics," *Transformations,* no. 17 (2009), accessed January 6, 2022, http://www.transformationsjournal.org/wp-content/uploads/2017/01/Ross_Trans17.pdf.

39 Cf. ibid. Interestingly, Jaar divides his work into three main areas: "Only one third of my time is dedicated to working within the so-called art world [...] where we address a limited audience which is a very priviledged one, a small elite. It is because of this that I have dedicated another third of my time to create what I call public interventions, works that try to address real life issues in places and communities far removed from our little art world. Finally the last third of my time is spent teaching, directing workshops and seminars around the world [...]. By directly addressing the elite, I may be able to affect change in those that have the power to actually trigger those changes. By working on my public interventions I try to expand the limited outreach of the art world and reach much wider audience, in a context where I can be much more radical, without the normal constraints of institutional spaces. And by teaching I try to lead the new generations towards a more radical kind of practice, one that is responsive to the needs of our times and more particularly to the context in which it takes place." Alfredo Jaar, "Interview with Luigi Fassi," *Klat*, Winter 2009–2010, 73f., quoted in Mouffe, "Alfredo Jaar," 274.

40 Cf. Jacques Rancière, *Le partage du sensible: Esthétique et politique* (Paris: La fabrique, 2000).

41 Jacques Rancière & Davide Panagia, "Dissenting Words — A Conversation with Jacques Rancière," *Diacritics*, 30:2 (2000): 113–126, 115.

42 Cf. also Jacques Rancière, "From Politics to Aesthetics?," *Paragraph*, 28:1 (2005): 13–25.

43 Jacques Rancière, "What Medium Can Mean," *Parrhesia*, no. 11 (2011): 35–43, 35.
44 Ibid.
45 Ibid., 36.
46 Jacques Rancière, "Theater of Images," in *Alfredo Jaar: La politique des images,* ed. Nicole Schweizer (Lausanne: Musée cantonal des beaux-arts, 2007), 71–80: 73.
47 Ibid., 72.
48 Thomas Hirschhorn, "Why it is important — today — to show and look at images of destroyed human bodies?" in *Le Journal de la Triennale #2*, ed. Émilie Renard (Paris: Centre national des arts plastiques (CNAP), February 2012), 62–67: 64.
49 Ibid.
50 Boris Groys, "The Topology of Contemporary Art," in *Antinomies of Art and Culture: Modernity, Postmodernity, Contemporaneity*, eds. Terry Smith et al. (Durham, NC: Duke University Press, 2008), 71–80: 71ff.
51 Peter Osborne, "Non-places and the Spaces of Art," *The Journal of Architecture,* vol. 6 (Summer 2011): 183–194, 183.
52 Groys, "The Topology of Contemporary Art," 72.
53 Ibid., 74.
54 Ibid., 76.
55 Cf. Jacques Rancière, "Theater of Images," 76 and 79.
56 Alfredo Jaar, quoted in Alfredo Jaar, *Let One Hundred Flowers Bloom* (exh. cat.) (Rome: Museo d'arte contemporanea Roma & Electa, 2005), 68.
57 Cf. Georges Didi-Huberman, "Emotion does not say 'I': Ten Fragments on Aesthetic Freedom," in *Alfredo Jaar: La politique des images* (exh. cat.), ed. Nicole Schweizer (Lausanne: Musée Cantonal des Beaux-Arts & Zurich: JRP Ringier, 2007), 57–70.
58 The following description draws heavily upon Alfredo Jaar, *It is difficult,* vol. 2 (exh. cat.) (Verona: Edizioni Corraini, 2008), 171f.
59 Rancière, "Theater of Images," 80.
60 This description of Jaar's work draws heavily upon the catalogue text, *Intense Proximity: An Anthology of the Near and the Far. La Triennale 2012*, eds. Okwui Enwezor et al. (Paris: Palais de Tokyo, 2012), 100, and a description by Leonie Radine for SCAD Museum of Art, accessed January 6, 2022, http://www.scadmoa.org/art/exhibitions/may-1-2011.
61 Cf. Rancière, "Theater of Images," 74.
62 Cf. Griselda Pollock, "Not-Forgetting Africa," in *Alfredo Jaar: La politique des Images*, ed. Nicole Schweizer (Lausanne: Musée cantonal des beaux-arts, 2007), 113–135: 132.
63 "Between Baudrillard and the Cave."

From Embodied to Mediated Memory

Chapter 2

How are we to transmit, and represent, the traumatic events collected under the designation "the Holocaust" *today*? How can its events be represented without being transformed into abstractions, and in a way in which we, who had not yet been born when they took place, can relate to them? How can that specific past be actualized and re-membered in the present so that we do not forget, or simply file the genocide of the European Jews away in the archive as completed and consigned to the past?

Paris-based artist Esther Shalev-Gerz's installation works *Between Listening and Telling: Last Witnesses, Auschwitz 1945–2005* (2005) and *MenschenDinge/The Human Aspect of Objects* (2006) constitute, in different ways, specific acts of remembering the Holocaust, while, at the same time, investigating the very workings and nature of remembering.[1] These two works provide the framework of this chapter, in which what I find to be some of the main issues involved in current debates on the representation and actualization of the Holocaust are analyzed and discussed.

I

The act of remembering necessitates that some things and events are brought out of the indifference of the archives and given value, while others are left and forgotten. According to Aristotle, remembering is "some kind of search," that is, an activity, a process.[2] Re-membering or re-collection, that is, the active and intellectual process of re-calling, *anamnesis* in Greek, is a vital human activity that forms our relations to the past, and the ways in which we remember are a decisive part of defining who we are in the present. Thus, it could be claimed that remembering, in a certain sense, is a re-presentation that belongs to *the present*.[3]

How do these general characteristics of remembering relate the Holocaust and our endeavors to re-present and thus remember it? The introductory questions about the representation of the Holocaust above become even more urgent as the generation of witnesses and survivors is passing away, and we, the post-generations, are beginning to accept the fact that our access to the events of the Holocaust is necessarily mediated. It could even be claimed that the function and the purpose of the representation of the Nazi crimes has changed. The primary purpose and function of testimonies and representations is no longer to establish specific knowledge of the historical facts. Within the last couple of decades, representations have become more a question of inscribing, maintaining and actualizing these past events in the present. In other words, contemporary representations and memories often have the function of being a means of communicating and transmitting the experience of Auschwitz to the post-Holocaust generations; a way of working against oblivion, instead of merely consigning what has happened to the archive. The Holocaust is becoming what American scholar of Holocaust memory James E. Young has called a "vicarious past," or "received history," and the question is, within the artistic context of this chapter, how today's artists are supposed to represent and "remember" events they did not experience directly.[4] This means that post-Holocaust representations of the Holocaust, that is, Holocaust representations made by artists belonging to the generations who were not alive at the time, are often representations of relations to the past rather than representations of the past itself, while also thematizing themselves as acts of remembering.

Thus, the question is no longer just about remembering, but also about how and what to remember, *how* the object of memory is evoked and how the mode and medium of this calling forth influences *what* is called forth. The past is not simply there in memory, it has to be formed and articulated, stressing the importance of the very mode of representation and mediation, of how we try to re-present the Holocaust through images, words, sounds, silences and gestures.

II

Esther Shalev-Gerz's work is emphatically of the present; it takes its point of departure in the here and now when addressing and articulating the past, not in "history as it happened." Based on different forms of collaboration and exchange with the audience, her works are instigations of dialogue,[5] shapings of *interlocutory situations* through which meaning and signification are configured and re-configured,[6] variants of what art historian Grant H. Kester has coined *dialogical aesthetics*.[7] Predominantly, they involve specific interlocutors. With the terminology of linguist Émile Benveniste, one could say that their mode of enunciation is *discursive* rather than *historical*, meaning that what is said is closely connected to the time and space of the speaking persons. Their use of deictic markers such as "I," "you," "here," and "now," refer to the time, space and participants of the act of communication — instead of, as in historical enunciation, being disconnected from the present via a narrative mode articulated in the past tense, in which events seem to narrate themselves, without recourse to the productive act behind the narrative. In an historical enunciation, the speaker does not interfere with what is narrated, and the events are, in a certain sense, objectified by being detached from the present, situated in a past that lies outside the person who nevertheless narrates them. Contrary to the always *personal* and *subjective* discursive discourse, the historical discourse tries to objectify and authorize itself by excluding the marks of enunciation, by negating the enunciative apparatus from which it inevitably arises.[8]

Shalev-Gerz's dialogical aesthetics, on the other hand, brings this "enunciative apparatus" to the fore. Letting herself be guided by the contributions of the participants, she usually starts by presenting her idea within a shared space, where the work is exposed to the interventions of others and to their approval. Her objective, she states, is to produce a work form that is not tied to the ego of the artist, but rather one that is oriented toward the construction of a space for memory through active participation by the audience:

> the moment when the supposed spectator becomes a participant by writing his name, using his voice or sending in his photo. Thanks to the traces left during these acts, the participants keep the memory of their own participation in the work's procedure, which also bears witness to their responsibility to their own times.[9]

In consequence, her works are dependent upon memories and narratives that are constructed and changed by the participants: "As an artist, it is very important for me to trust the participants — whom I approach (right away) as equals, and whose contributions are an element of the project."[10] The work is conditioned by her "trust in the other person's intelligence"; she neither defines the aesthetic parameters of the work in advance, nor begins forming it until she has received the participants' contributions in the shape of narratives or stories, bringing a distinct, dynamic character to her artistic practice that sets it apart from the so-called relational aesthetics theorized by Nicolas Bourriaud, which are far more internal to the art world.[11]

III

Shalev-Gerz's work is made up of specific, present acts of remembering, while, at the same time, investigating the very workings of the act of remembering, thereby placing itself at the centre of recent debates around the representation of the Holocaust. I will now move on to argue that Shalev-Gerz's installations attest to a phase of transition between first-hand, embodied memory based on and preserving the traces of sense-perception, and a so-called vicarious post-memory, the situation in which the vast majority of us find ourselves today.[12] Thus, I claim that these works can be seen to represent both *gestures of testifying to experience of the Holocaust,* and *the gesture of witnessing and actualizing the remnants of these events* — the former testifying to the passing of the generation of survivors, the latter to the post-generation.

The installation *Between Listening and Telling: Last Witnesses, Auschwitz 1945–2005* was exhibited at the Hôtel de Ville in Paris in 2005 to mark the 60th anniversary of the liberation of Auschwitz-Birkenau. The project was chosen from three proposals for presenting the testimonies of sixty survivors living in the Paris area, who had been invited by the mayor of Paris and the Holocaust memorial in Paris, Mémorial de la Shoah. Shalev-Gerz's installation consisted of sixty unedited, newly recorded interviews with survivors, conducted by four teams comprising a sound engineer, a cameraman, and a journalist who were to ask the survivors to talk about their lives before, during, and after the war.[13] The audience could watch and listen to the testimonies at four long, winding, red tables furnished with small DVD monitors and headphones. The duration of the interviews — which can now be consulted at the Mémorial de la Shoah — was between two and nine hours each. Each of the interviews was projected onto three large screens hung side by side at the end of the spacious exhibition room with a seven-second time lapse. The faces of the survivors, filmed in slow motion and close up, were shown in silence, their expressions captured between words, between a question and their articulation of an answer.

In this manner, the spectators become the witnesses' witnesses; witnesses to the act of testifying of the last witnesses. The work is very much about silence, about showing silence, and allowing silence to take part in the formation of signification, about showing the gesture of testimony. It is a silence, however, that differs substantially from the sublime aesthetics of silence and of the unpresentable that philosopher Jean-François Lyotard sees in the gestures of the witnesses depicted in philosopher and filmmaker Claude Lanzmann's nine-hour film *Shoah* (1985). Lyotard famously claims that Auschwitz defies images and words, that it cannot be represented without slipping away, without being missed and forgotten again, but:

> Claude Lanzmann's film *Shoah* is an exception, maybe the only one. Not only because it rejects representation in images and music but because it scarcely offers a testimony where the unpresentable of the Holocaust is not indicated, be it but for a moment, by the alteration in the tone of a voice, a knotted throat, sobbing, tears, a witness fleeing off-camera, a disturbance in the tone of the narrative, an uncontrolled gesture.[14]

In Lyotard's thinking, the sublime art of the unpresentable is the only art adequate — and ethically proper — to Auschwitz, and he is looking, therefore, for the gestures that indicate the unpresentable, so as to verify his aesthetics of the sublime, according to which Auschwitz is an unsayable and unimaginable event that evades any realistic or figural representation. Within the last couple of decades, however, this ethics of silence that puts a ban on images and words has, rightfully, been problematized, not least by Jacques Rancière, who points out, echoing historian Hayden White's theory of emplotment, that the unrepresentable does not exist as a property of an event: "An event in itself neither imposes nor prohibits any specific artistic means. And neither does it impose any duty on art to represent or not to represent it in this or that way."[15] From Rancière's perspective, Lanzmann's *Shoah* does not confirm Lyotard's thesis, but refutes it. One of the most important aspects of the film, according to Rancière, is that it demonstrates that the question of the representable/unrepresentable relationship is first and foremost a question of means.[16]

Lanzmann's film — and the transcription of its narratives, which was published under the title *Shoah: An Oral History of the Holocaust* — is, to a great extent, about gesture in testimony.[17] It shows survivors and witnesses recounting their experiences to Lanzmann, and the camera, and thus is also emphatically about the time of narration, the very time of enunciation and the very act of testifying, and not only about *the text* or content of the testimony, that is, the narrated past events to which they try to bear witness. The documentation and testimony to the *Shoah* is an act and gesture of the present. Hence, the first words of the film: "The story begins in the present."

In *Between Listening and Telling*, Shalev-Gerz stresses this gestural aspect even more by giving time and attention to the survivors' gestures before speech, before the words endow what was experienced with a certain meaning. It is not, however, a gesture indicating sublime unpresentability, but, rather, the very moment of *articulation* and signification, of configuration and reconfiguration of meaning, in which singular experiences connect to collective communication in an actualization of language. Thus, the installation by Shalev-Gerz is not about silence as such. It is not a matter of rejecting words and images. Her extraction and subsequent montage of the silent moments of the interviewed survivors is not an endeavor to isolate the silences, but rather to confront them with the words spoken in order to *show* the silences as a decisive part of the process of signification. As Georges Didi-Huberman observes in a text written for the catalogue of Shalev-Gerz's retrospective in the Musée des Beaux-Arts in Lausanne in 2012–13: "The gaps are really there — not only as absences, but as fundamental *gestures* — and that is what the work of Esther Shalev-Gerz shows."[18] The projected montage of silences appears as a collection of transitory moments between articulation and non-articulation. Even though they are shown in slow motion, each gesture pertaining to these breaks in speech is quickly replaced by the next, giving the viewer an impression of visual discontinuity while the silences persist.

Between Listening and Telling makes these moments between articulation and non-articulation, these silent, fundamental gestures of testimony *visible*. These gestures do not, however, indicate a sublime unpresentability, and they should not be seen as dissociated from the language or discourse that they punctuate. Rather than non-linguistic elements, they are closely tied to language in the way in which Giorgio Agamben understands gesture as a forceful presence in language itself, a presence that is more originary than conceptual expression: "[I]f speech is originary gesture, then what is at issue in gesture is not so much a prelinguistic content as, so to speak, the other side of language, the muteness inherent in humankind's very capacity for language, its *speechless* dwelling in language."[19] Following the Aristotelian definition of the human being as *zoon logon echon* (the animal who has language), Agamben sees the human as the living being who has language, but this human "having of language" also implies that the human subject is capable of *not* having language, that it is capable of its own *infancy* or wordlessness, and that it therefore becomes the site where language can or cannot be realized, or actualized, in discourse, that is, the possibility that language does not take place.[20] Furthermore, "man" (understood as the human being), is, according to Agamben, "the living being who, in language, separates and opposes himself to his own bare life and, at the same time, maintains himself in relation to that bare life in an inclusive exclusion."[21] In that sense, the silent embodied memory of the survivors is tied to their "bare life" as well as to their experience of the Nazi attempt to desubjectify them and reduce them to such bare life, to so-called *Muselmänner* without language. The survivors' gestures of silence interrupt the medium of language in its very being-medium, and thus they come to exhibit the mediality of language as such, including their own relation to this medium of expression. Shalev-Gerz makes their gestures between articulation and non-articulation as gags visible:

> [I]n its essence gesture is always a gesture of a non-making of sense in language, it is always a gag in the strict meaning of the term, indicating in the first instance something that is put in the mouth to hinder speech, and subsequently the actor's improvisation to make up for a memory lapse or some impossibility of speech.[22]

Thus, silence is not necessarily non-communicative, and, in some cases, it can be more telling than words; actually, we often hear survivors and witnesses talk and talk without end, sometimes frenetically, in order, consciously or unconsciously, to cover up the experiences they are talking about or perhaps even omitting. As Rancière has remarked, silence in Shalev-Gerz's work "is never an empty space ... it is primarily thought at work inside the bodies: thought trying to speak, trying to understand, and forcing us to do so as well, even in the course of reflection."[23] Giving testimony is about sharing experiences. The montage and linking together of the moments of silence in *Between Listening and Telling* may be said to form a community of breaks of speech that makes what cannot be put into words *visible*, to form an image addressed to us, an image of silence as part of the communication of the survivors' experiences and of the pain associated with this communication.

Didi-Huberman calls the breaks in the survivors' speeches "emanations of suffering that come, so to speak, to poison their will to tell their story ... imprisons them mutely in the unbearable nature of a remembered image that fails to be unraveled in words."[24] The projected, slow-motion close ups display the spaces between words, when memory is still internal, alive dynamically in the minds of the testifying subjects, before what is remembered is verbalized and thereby fixed in a particular image or idea. Aesthetics, framing and formal elements in general are conventionally downplayed in audio-visual testimonies as they are thought obtrusive, as distracting attention from the enunciation of testimony, which is often painful, precarious and elliptical. According to this logic, formal elements should not interfere with the audience's receptivity, its ability to listen openly, but, as has also been argued by documentary film scholar Michael Renov, the close-up framing is also the composition best suited to engaging the viewer.[25] Seen in close up, without, or between, words, our attention is drawn to the faces of the survivors, their mouths and their eyes in the act of remembering. The involuntary responses and gestures of their bodies — rendered sensible to our eyes and ears — come to the fore as a multimodal expression of memory and suffering that is incommensurate with words alone. Without knowing what is being remembered, we become witnesses to their inward search for memory. In Shalev-Gerz's composition, their gestures and facial expressions display a capacity to convey memory and suffering outside of, beyond, or on the other side of language, rendering visible an excess of emotion and embodied memory that exists apart from what is narrated. Were there to be only written transcripts of the testimonies, the tearful eyes and the failing voices would escape the process of signification.[26] This is the reason why the book *Shoah: An Oral History of the Holocaust. The Complete Text of the Film* captures only a fraction of Lanzmann's filmed testimonies. *Between Listening and Telling* allows us to become witnesses to the survivors' search for adequate words to verbalize their memory, to their inability to find such words, and to the suffering their memories now re-inflict on them.[27] In many cases, we seem to be made attentive to their struggles with their buried selves, with their "deep memory" in the terminology of scholar of Holocaust literature and testimony Lawrence L. Langer.[28] Through the framing and installation of close ups of remembering faces — the camera distance, and our position in relation to the projections — Shalev-Gerz succeeds in not turning us into voyeurs. The gaze of the camera appears curious, open-minded or "listening." engaging without being interrogative, without indulging in overidentification with the survivors' suffering and victimization, demonstrating her respect and "trust in the other person's intelligence."[29]

As I have just argued, however, the close ups in *Between Listening and Telling* should not be considered as replacements for language, but rather as its important supplements, indeed, the close ups are of speaking subjects captured between words, demonstrating the inextricability of the process of enunciation with what is being actually said.[30] It is, in Benveniste's terminology, a discursive mode of enunciation in which what is said is closely connected to the time and space of speaking — or, in accordance with Agamben's understanding of gesture, non-speaking — persons. The silences of the survivors imply that something is addressed to us without its being uttered. They are events of speech, authentic events in the testimonies of the survivors, but testimony is not only silence. Silence is part of it, but cannot stand alone any longer — if it ever could. Today, we also need to know what the silence refers to. Otherwise, we, who were born after, may run the risk of losing sight of the historical events, of turning them into abstractions, of not having an idea of what it is that cannot be represented and put into words and images. This danger of losing sight of the actual historical event — of the extermination of European Jewry — would be my objection to architect Peter Eisenman's Memorial to the Murdered Jews of Europe in Berlin, had it not been supplemented by an information centre, that "guides," so to speak, the abstraction above from underground. And that is why — at least in my reading — the edited silence in Shalev-Gerz's installation is contextualized by the unedited actual testimonies in which each survivor relates their experiences of the camps and describes their life before, during, and after internment.

The articulation and externalization of the survivors' experiences in words and images implies a depersonalization, while, at the same time, they also provide a necessary support for memory. The work of memory takes place in a dialogical exchange with the media of words and images. Memory and representation are interdependent. As, among others, cultural critic Andreas Huyssen has argued, all representation is inescapably based on memory. Re-presentation always comes after, despite the endeavor of some to let the media appear as pure presence. Memory, on the other hand, leads neither to any authentic origin nor does it constitute a verifiable access to the real; memory, in its belatedness, is conditioned by representation: "The past is not simply there in memory, but it must be articulated to become memory."[31] The testifying subject experiences, however, in the very articulation of their past, a loss of singular, personal, inner memories and images. In order to be communicated they are in a sense expropriated, are no longer only theirs. It is indicative, in this perspective, that one of the witnesses retracted his recorded testimony just before the completion of Shalev-Gerz's project. He had told neither his family nor his friends about his internment, and, at the last moment, he took his testimony back into his own possession, reappropriated it, unable to disclose it.[32] The testifying subject experiences that such 'inner memory' or image is not static, and that memories about the past are constructed and reconstructed, configured and reconfigured in the present rather than simply and "purely" relived and recollected from the past.

IV

In line with this "constructivist" understanding of memory, this interdependency between memory, images and words, Shalev-Gerz states that she believes "images are, actually, the reality of our past. When we reflect at what happened before, we depend on images and stories."[33] This leads us to another of Shalev-Gerz's works, *MenschenDinge/The Human Aspect of Objects* (2006), an installation representing the gesture of witnessing and actualizing the remnants of the events of the Holocaust, depicting the post-generation.

In 2006, Shalev-Gerz completed a two-year long process of developing an installation for the Buchenwald Memorial. The installation, *MenschenDinge/The Human Aspect of Objects*, comprises videos and photographs that represent objects found in the soil of the former concentration camp. Among the many objects she chose only those that had been modified, engraved, repurposed and personalized by the detainees during their imprisonment. The objects — a ruler comb, a pewter broach, a pair of cloth and cardboard slippers, an aluminium mirror, and a wire ring, for instance — are presented, slightly out of focus, in film and photographs. Five videos show representatives of the memorial — the director, a historian, an archaeologist, a conservator and a photographer — relating their understanding of the objects and describing their professional, personal and imaginary relationships with these traces of the past while addressing them with their hands, voices and bodies. The historian, Harry Stein, for example, sits by the desk in his office with a range of found objects — bowls, spoons, knives, dishes, etc. — picking up different bowls in his hands, turning them around and investigating them while talking:

> Those are really badly dented bowls, they look awful and half eaten away by rust; they're no longer of any use. And the aspect that had been so fascinating for us, namely that something was coming from history itself, as a trace, that in some cases people had expressed themselves — like here on this bowl [he picks up a bowl from the desk], which is inscribed in Russian: Take yours and not mine! And then it is signed Zigan. So you can say that maybe he went by the name of Zigan. But if you keep translating, it means: Take yours and not mine — you gipsy. This means in other words that the bowl tells a story. There were very few bowls. A bowl was a very valuable possession, because with a bowl you could go get food for yourself, and accordingly people stole each other's bowls. Here someone wrote his initials on it; we weren't able to decipher them, but it said: This is mine ... [H]ere is someone who says: Take yours and not mine, mine is important for my life. A statement like that, in that situation...[34]

Archaeologist Ronald Hirte gives another example of the endeavors to make the objects communicate. At one point he picks up an object, which presumably functioned as an improvised iron, made from a French army mess tin and scraps of different material that could be found in the camp:

> And what we have is an iron, which you can heat accordingly and then iron with it. But the question remains, what sense does ironing make in the camp, what sense does ironing make in the Small Camp, since that's where the iron was found. Sooner or later, by reading a lot, searching the archives a lot, you hit on something ... [T]here was a description of how inmates in the Small Camp or in Buchenwald sub-camps disinfected their clothing to guard against body lice. You can kill body lice by ironing ... And that immediately makes sense — that at Buchenwald's most extreme site, where there were always pathogens going around, you somehow simply find a way of

> protecting yourself against these pathogens. Dishes were generally very rare in the camp, and anyone who had a dish was already a bit privileged. Apparently it was possible to sacrifice this one, though. In order to construct an iron for himself, someone gave up this mess tin.[35]

In the video recordings, Stein and Hirte pick up a number of things, try to interpret and endow them with meaning, but the actual objects were not part of the installation. They appear only through the perception of the people who work with and actualize them, through *re-presentations*. Focalizing the objects through people alive today makes their *relation* to the past part of the content of the work — this interest in our relationship to the past is emphasized in the video with the photographer Naomi Tereza Salmon:

> Essentially my concern is not with the things, in other words it's not with a fetish. It's not about touching them and developing a relationship to them, but my concern is about our relationship to the past, the way it then simply comes to light through these objects. I leave that to the viewer, essentially his thoughts, his feelings ... And there are no texts.[36]

With reference to Walter Benjamin, Shalev-Gerz sees the objects as "dialectical images" through and between which historical truth appears: "They are time-interfaces because they connect the present with the past, like indices, material traces that trigger other images and open up new imaginary spaces," she says.[37]

Even though Buchenwald was not a death camp, 56,000 people lost their lives there. The exhibition, however, is not a representation of, or a testimony to, their suffering and mass murder, but is dealing with the memory work of the living, with the endeavor to actualize the objects in the present. As Stein remarks in the video: "When I tell these stories, I also always tell a little of myself."[38] It is more about the construction of memory and the handling of the past in the present than about narrating history as it happened. The absence of testimonies and the absence of the people who created the objects leaves a silence which points to the need for translation and activation by post-generations. What Shalev-Gerz is trying to stage is exactly "the process of translation ... interpretation, the constant flux of rethinking history starting from the object and the absences that are inherent."[39]

V

MenschenDinge/The Human Aspect of Objects suggests that we need to supplement the subjective linguistic testimonies of survivors — very soon there will be no survivors left — with what architect and founding director of the research agency Forensic Architecture Eyal Weizman has called a forensic sensibility or "forensic aesthetics," which implies an attention to the communicative capacity, agency and power of things, an object-oriented culture that is immersed in matter and materialities.[40] Christian Boltanski's many "inventories," such as *Inventaire des objets ayant appartenu à une femme de Bois-Colombes* (Inventory of objects that belonged to a woman of Bois-Colombes, 1974), may, for instance, be seen in the light of such forensic aesthetics and, furthermore, might thus be put in relation with Shalev-Gerz's work — Boltanski claims that: "All my work is more or less about the Holocaust" — but without people engaging in interpretation as an integral part of it, as we see in *MenschenDinge*.[41] The so-called era of the witness has, according to Weizman, been saturated with representation of testimonies of trauma: written, recorded, filmed, archived and exhibited. As the creative resistance represented by the objects of *MenschenDinge* implies, this primacy of trauma as a site of history also runs the risk of turning into a depoliticized "politics of compassion," focusing too much on victimization — something that Shalev-Gerz also delicately avoids in the presentation of the recorded survivor testimonies in *Between Listening and Telling*. The risk of such a one-sided focus on victimization may be countered by a forensic sensibility. Derived from the Latin *forensis*, the root of the word forensics refers to "forum." Forensics deals with the presentation of scientific findings and the making of an argument before a gathering, a forum. Part of making such argument involves having objects that do not speak for themselves address the forum. In order for this to be possible, the things need to be translated, mediated or interpreted.[42] Such forums are not fixed, but dynamic and contingent. They are gathered around disputed things, emerging around found evidence. The *MenschenDinge* installation can be considered as just such a gathering, a forum where the objects found at the site of the former concentration camp are being translated and interpreted. It is a forensic aesthetics, understood as

> an arduous labor of truth construction, one employing a spectrum of technologies that the forum provides, and all sorts of scientific, rhetorical, theatrical, and visual mechanisms. It is in the gestures, techniques, and turns of demonstration, whether poetic, dramatic, or narrative, that a forensic aesthetics can make things appear in the

> world. The forums in which facts are debated are the technologies of persuasion, representation, and power — not of *truth*, but of *truth construction*.[43]

VI

Between Listening and Telling represents the gesture of testifying to the experience of the events of the Holocaust, including the significance of non-linguistic, gestural elements, while *Menschen-Dinge* represents the gesture of witnessing and actualizing remnants of these events. The two installations by Esther Shalev-Gerz function as acts of remembrance, and as "truth constructions" of the present. Taken together, they measure the ongoing transition from embodied first-hand memory to mediated post-memory. In these different actualizations, Shalev-Gerz moves beyond the sublime aesthetics of silence and makes visible the ways in which memory is not simply *re*-presentation and *re*-collection of the past, but rather presentation, an act in and of the present. The installations thematize the activity of remembering, constructing space for different subject positions in this activity, of the survivors and the post-generations in particular in these works, positions which could, of course, be differentiated further. The participants appear as emancipated individuals, "intelligent persons," who have to create their own relation to the past by interpreting, translating and endowing it with meaning. The works analyzed above respectfully make the embodied memory of the last witnesses trying to communicate their past experiences visible as well as the post-generations' necessarily mediated relation to this past and their need — and right — to establish their own relation to this past, their need to "open up new imaginary spaces."[44]

A–B
Esther Shalev-Gerz
Between Listening and Telling: Last Witnesses, Auschwitz 1945–2005, 2005

C–D
Esther Shalev-Gerz
MenschenDinge/The Human Aspect of Objects, 2006

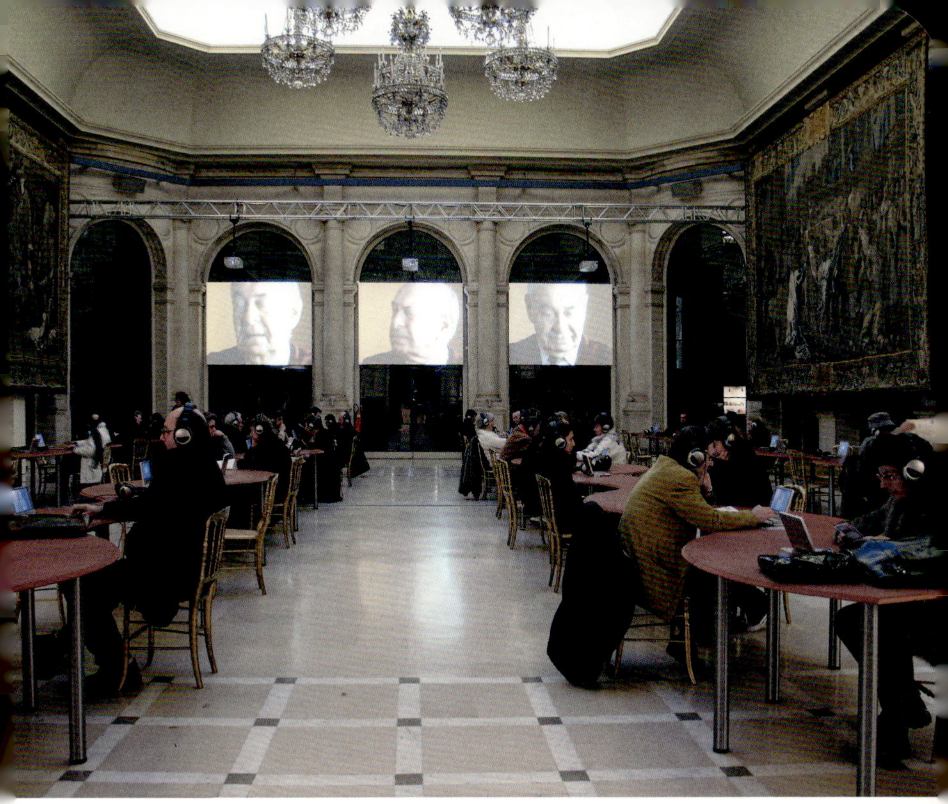

A Esther Shalev-Gerz

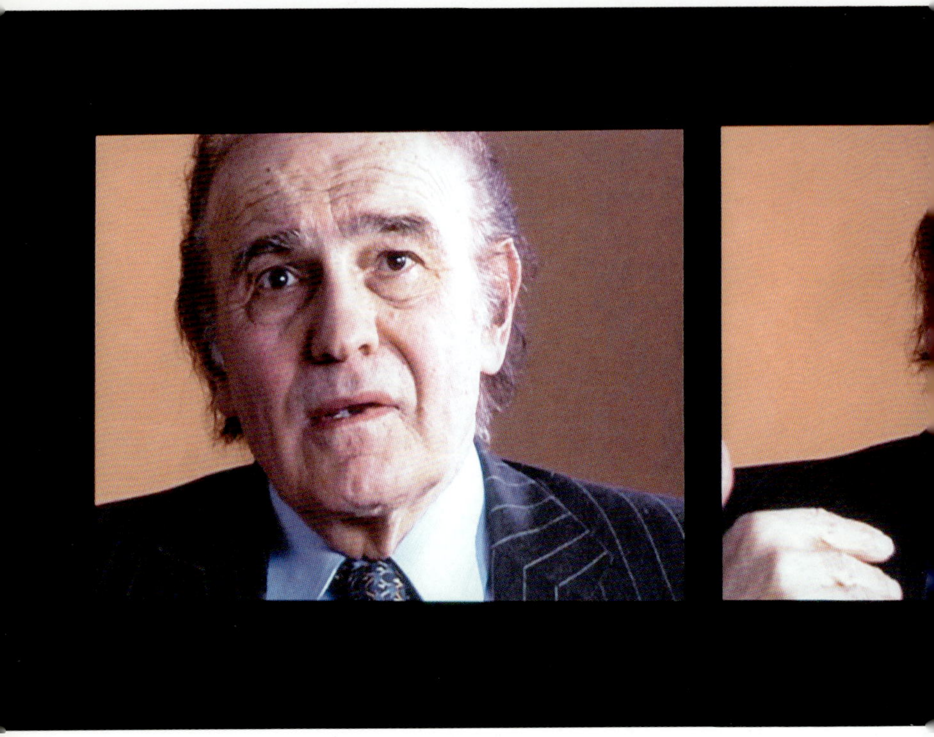

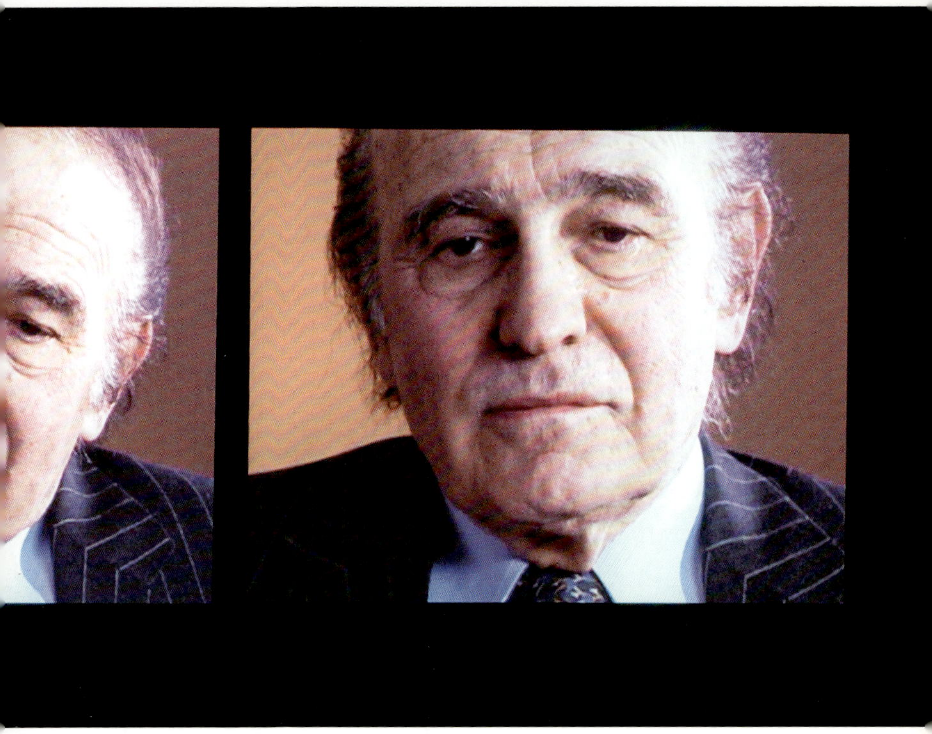

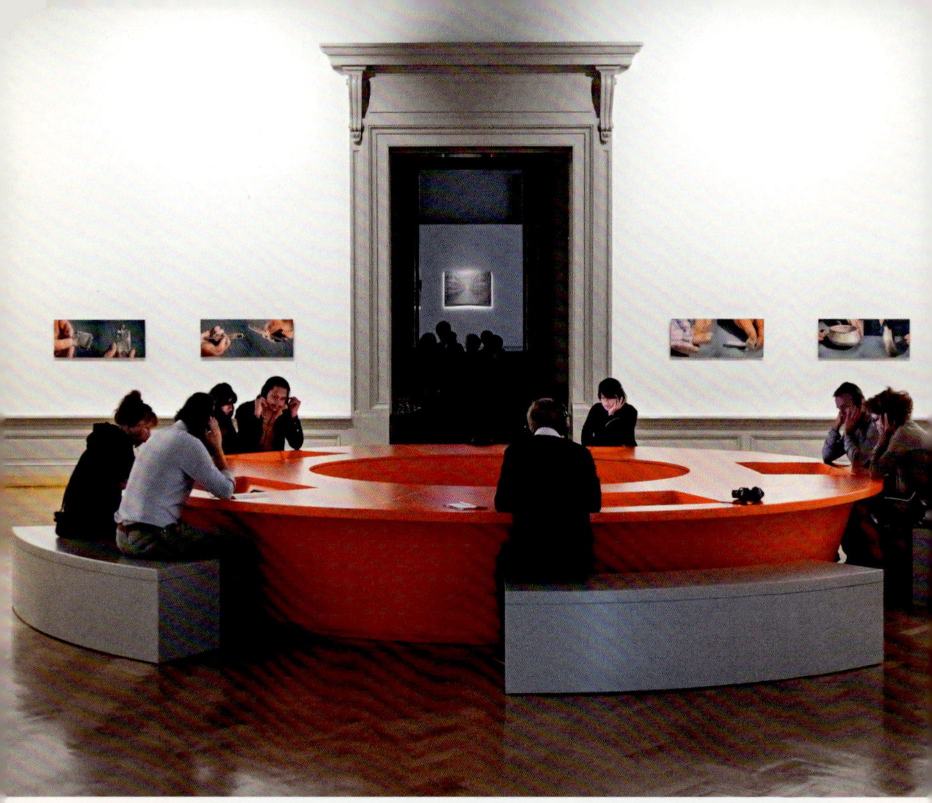

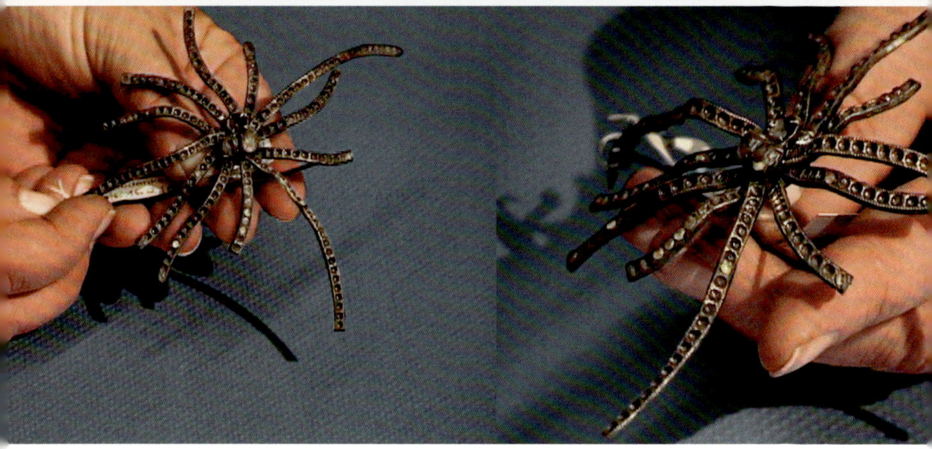

C-D Esther Shalev-Gerz

Notes

1 Esther Shalev-Gerz, *MenschenDinge/The Human Aspect of Objects*, exh. cat. (Weimar: Stiftung Gedenkstätten Buchenwald und Mittelbau-Dora, 2006).

2 David Bloch, *Aristotle on Memory and Recollection: Text, Translation, Interpretation, and Reception in Western Scholasticism* (Leiden: Brill, 2007)

3 Andreas Huyssen, *Present Pasts: Urban Palimpsets and the Politics of Memory* (Stanford, CA: Stanford University Press, 2003).

4 James E. Young, *At Memory's Edge: After-Images of the Holocaust in Contemporary Art and Architecture* (New Haven, CT: Yale University Press, 2000).

5 Sinziana Ravini, "Dialogisk estetik och den relationella estetikens uppgång och fall" [Dialogical Aesthetics and the Rise and Fall of Relational Aesthetics] *Paletten: tidskift för konst*, 264.2 (2006): 4–9.

6 Georges Didi-Huberman, "The 'Blancs Soucis' of Our History," in *Esther Shalev-Gerz: Between Telling and Listening - Entre l'écoute et la parole*, exh. cat., ed. Nicole Schweizer (Zurich: JRP Ringier, 2012), 57–62.

7 Grant H. Kester, *Conversation Pieces: Community and Communication in Modern Art* (Berkeley: University of California Press, 2004).

8 Émile Benveniste, "Les relations de temps dans le verbe français," in *Problémes de linguistique générale I* (Paris: Gallimard, 1966), 237–50.

9 Cf. Esther Shalev-Gerz, *Est-ce que ton image me regarde?/Geht dein Bild mich an?/Does your image reflect me?*, exh. cat. (Hannover: Sprengel Museum, 2002). For more on the construction of a space for memory through active participation by the audience in Shalev-Gerz's work, cf. Ravini, "Dialogisk estetik och den relationella estetikens uppgång och fall."

10 Cf. Esther Shalev-Gerz, *Esther Shalev-Gerz*, exh. cat. (Paris: Fage éditions du Jeu de Paume, 2010).

11 Cf. Esther Shalev-Gerz's comprehensive website for descriptions, images and videos of her work: http://www.shalev-gerz.net, accessed January 28, 2022. For a description and critique of participatory art and "the social turn," cf. Claire Bishop, *Artificial Hells: Participatory Art and the Politics of Spectatorship* (New York: Verso, 2012). In "Antagonism and Relational Aesthetics," Claire Bishop criticizes Bourriaud's micro-utopian, undifferentiated relational aesthetics for not considering the quality of the human relations established by pointing out: "if relational art produces human relations, then the next logical question to ask is what *types* of relations are being produced, for whom, and why?" Claire Bishop, "Antagonism and Relational Aesthetics," *October* 110 (2004): 51–70, 65.

12 Marianne Hirsch, *The Generation of Postmemory: Writing and Visual Culture after the Holocaust* (New York: Columbia University Press, 2012).

13 Shalev-Gerz described these circumstances, as well as how the installation came about, to me in a personal correspondence of July 24, 2013.

14 Jean-François Lyotard, *Heidegger and "the jews,"* trans. Andreas Michel and Mark Roberts (Minneapolis: University of Minnesota Press, 1990).

15 Jacques Ranciére, "S'il y a de l'irreprésentablé," in *L'art et la mémoire des camps: Représenter exterminer*, ed. Jean-Luc Nancy (Paris: Seuil, 2001), 81–102.

16 Cf. Jacques Ranciére, "The Aesthetic Revolution and Its Outcomes," in *New Left Review*, no. 12 (March–April 2002), 133–51.

17 Claude Lanzmann, *Shoah: An Oral History of the Holocaust. The Complete Text of the Film* (New York: Pantheon Books, 1985).

18 Cf. Didi-Huberman, "The 'Blancs Soucis' of Our History," 58.

19 Giorgio Agamben, "Kommerell, or On Gesture," in *Potentialities: Collected Essays in Philosophy*, trans. Daniel Heller-Roazen (Stanford, CA: Stanford University Press, 1999), 77–85: 78.

20 Cf. Giorgio Agamben, *Remnants of Auschwitz: The Witness and the Archive*, trans. Daniel Heller-Roazen (New York: Zone Books, 1999), 146.

21 Cf. Giorgio Agamben, *Homo Sacer: Sovereign Power and Bare Life*, trans. Daniel Heller-Roazen (Stanford, CA: Stanford University Press, 1998), 8.
22 Cf. Giorgio Agamben, *Infancy and History: On the Destruction of Experience*, trans. Liz Heron (London: Verso, 2007), 156.
23 Cf. Jacques Ranciére, "Die Arbeit des Bildes / The Work of the Image," in Shalev-Gerz, *MenschenDinge / The Human Aspect of Objects*, 8–25: 10.
24 Didi-Huberman, "The 'Blancs Soucis' of Our History," 61.
25 Michael Renov, "The Facial Closeup in Audio-Visual Testimony: The Power of Embodied Memory" (2013), 1–8: 3, accessed January 28, 2022, http://www.preserving-survivors-memories.org/media/presentations/Michael_Renov_The_Facial_Closeup_in_Audio-Visual_Testimony.pdf?1354623339.
26 Ibid.
27 Cf. James E. Young, "Spaces for Deep Memory: Esther Shalev-Gerz and First Counter-Monuments," in *Esther Shalev-Gerz: Between Telling and Listening — Entre l'écoute et la parole*, ed. Schweizer, 79–82: 82.
28 Lawrence L. Langer, *Holocaust Testimonies: The Ruins of Memory* (New Haven, CT: Yale University Press, 1991).
29 Cf. Shalev-Gerz, *Esther Shalev-Gerz*.
30 Cf. Renov, "The Facial Closeup in Audio-Visual Testimony," 6.
31 Cf. Andreas Huyssen, *Twilight Memories: Marking Time in a Culture of Amnesia* (New York: Routledge, 1995), 2.
32 Shalev-Gerz told me about this survivor's silence about his captivity in a personal correspondence on July 24, 2013.
33 Cf. Esther Shalev-Gerz, "Esther Shalev-Gerz in conversation with Ulrich Krempel," in Shalev-Gerz, *MenschenDinge/The Human Aspect of Objects*, 100.
34 Cf. Shalev-Gerz, *MenschenDinge/The Human Aspect of Objects*, 75.
35 Ibid., 91.
36 Ibid., 84.
37 Cf. Shalev-Gerz, "Esther Shalev-Gerz in conversation with Ulrich Krempel," 100.
38 Cf. Shalev-Gerz, *MenschenDinge/The Human Aspect of Objects*, 79.
39 Cf. Shalev-Gerz, "Esther Shalev-Gerz in conversation with Ulrich Krempel," 101.
40 For more on Forensic Architecture, see chapter 8.
41 Steinar Gjessing, "Christian Boltanski — An Interview, November 1993," *Terskel,Threshold*, 11 (1994): 41–50, 43.
42 Thomas Keenan and Eyal Weisman, *Mengele's Skull: The Advent of a Forensic Aesthetics* (Berlin: Sternberg Press, 2012), 28.
43 Ibid., 67.
44 Cf. Shalev-Gerz, "Esther Shalev-Gerz in conversation with Ulrich Krempel," 110.

Filmic Montage as an Aesthetics of Contemporaneity

Chapter 3

Toward the end of his prodigious film essay *Histoire(s) du cinéma*, Jean-Luc Godard declares himself an "enemy of our times," an enemy of "the totalitarianism of the present as applied mechanically grows every day more oppressive on a planetary scale," and of the "faceless tyranny that effaces all faces for the systematic organization of the unified time of the moment. This global, abstract tyranny, which I try to oppose from my fleeting point of view."[1] The argument of this chapter is that *Histoire(s) du cinéma* can indeed be seen as what Godard calls "a thinking form," one that tries to resist the synchronizing, standardizing time of global capital, resist the pervasive uniformity of the global super present of today's televisual and digital communications, which threatens to trivialize different processes of memory and history, as well trivializing art and culture in general — instead of allowing for a contemporaneity of difference.[2] According to Bernard Stiegler, the final stage of capitalism is the control and synchronization of what Patrick le Lay, called "available brain time":

> Our era is characterized by synchronization. The program industries attempt to synchronize the activities of everyone's consciousness; to control the life of souls through marketing and television, establishing the psycho power characteristic of our time. [...] From now on, wherever you go, you have the same modes of production and distribution. Such globalization comes at the price of a synchronization of modes of life and thought. Today, this is being extended to all aspects of our lives, destroying the singularity of existence through consumerism, liquidating ways of knowing how to live well [*les savoir-vivre*].[3]

I argue that Godard's work opposes such control, opposes the synchronization of our minds through *an aesthetics of contemporaneity.* Furthermore, I reflect on the ways in which an aesthetics of contemporaneity relates to the memory of the genocide of the European Jews during World War II.

As has been remarked by Giorgio Agamben and others, one of the principal concerns of Godard's work is the constitutive link between history and cinema. Godard — following up on a question posed initially by fellow post-World War II filmmaker Guy Debord — addresses the historical task of cinema.[4] What interests me here, therefore, is also related to the question of the image, history, and our relation to images. Thus, the new forms of image production and image circulation in contemporary media culture, not least on the Internet, bring the issue of circulation, or what filmmaker and theorist Hito Steyerl terms "circulationism," to the fore. Circulationism is connected not with the art of making images, but with the postproduction, release, and acceleration of images — and with the social relations of images across networks that both establish and tear "communities loosely linked by shared attention deficit" apart.[5] How is it possible for contemporary artistic practice to react critically to circulationism, to the uniform time of the global super present and its concomitant attention deficit? How might the events referred to as the Shoah or Holocaust still be actualized and remembered in our historical present?

I

Recent studies in the aesthetics of memory have been occupied with changes in our conception of memory. They suggest that a model of recall — or what has been called the model of original plenitude and subsequent loss, which sees memory as something formed fully in the past, and which is thus assumed to have been experienced once in its completeness, as something that therefore subsequently needs to be maintained and kept alive — has been replaced by a more constructivist understanding of the work of memory.[6] The latter stresses — among other things — the fact that memory is always an act of the present. Our relations to, and images of, the past are always conditioned by the present, indeed our point of departure is always the present, not the past in itself.

In the following, I would like to turn my attention to the quality of this present, to the quality of *our* present, as I would claim that the current present differs from past presents — so the present from which *we* try to remember the Holocaust differs from that from which our forebearers tried to remember it. It differs from Primo Levi's presents of 1946 and 1986, when *If This Is a Man* and *The Drowned and the Saved* were published; it differs from Anselm Kiefer's present of the '80s as well, when his paintings explicitly addressed the Holocaust, and, maybe, also from his presents of the '90s and '00s, where his work became more abstract meditations of a generic mythological nature. Here, I explore some of the qualities of the global present through a reading of Godard's film.

One crucial difference, of course, is the difference between the living memory of firsthand witnesses, and the so-called post-memory of the second and subsequent generations, but I think that this generational change within Holocaust memory should also be seen in relation to a broader change in the temporal quality of the present, if we want to understand Holocaust remembrance today.[7] Not least when the topic is Holocaust remembrance in contemporary art — and how the Holocaust might relate to our very understanding of the contemporary. In relation to memory, the temporality of the survivors is necessarily different from that of the post-generations. As firsthand witnesses — i.e. as contemporaries with the historical events, in the quotidian sense of the word — the survivors occupy a different temporal register, one which has its own internal differences of gender and language, and, among others, of being a victim, perpetrator, bystander. Therefore, contemporary art dealing with the aesthetics of memory in relation to the Holocaust needs to try to thematize or reflect this condition of contemporaneity between different temporal registers, their co-existence.

The change of the temporal quality of the present has to do with the general condition of our everyday life and of artistic production today being one of contemporaneity, where the urgent question of being with time, or being genuinely "contemporary," is a matter of grasping a coexistence of different temporalities and various "ways of being in relation to time."[8] It should, of course, be noted here that the historical origins of the current, perpetual present are debatable: did our — or perhaps more objectively *the* — present begin when WWII ended, with "68," the fall of the Berlin Wall, 9/11 or some other time? And how do its prehistories appear when seen from the Global South?

Thus, before turning to the question of the aesthetics of memory and discussing Jean-Luc Godard's video work *Histoire(s) du cinéma* as a contemporary artistic work of Holocaust memory, I would like to begin with some general reflections on the quality of *our* present understood as being defined by *contemporaneity*, that is, the confluence and clash of different times, and the temporal complexity that follows from the coming together in the same cultural space of heterogeneous clusters generated along different historical trajectories, across different scales, and in different localities. As an integral part of the shift from modernity and postmodernity to contemporaneity, cultures and art worlds have become global phenomena in the sense that they have become interconnected and contemporaneous with each other, forming global networks. As Peter Osborne and Terry Smith observe, the idea of contemporaneity as a *condition* is new, and Osborne stresses:

> what seems distinctive and important about the changing temporal quality of the historical present over the last few decades is best expressed through the distinctive conceptual grammar of con-temporaneity, a coming together not simply "in" time, but *of* times: we do not just live or exist together "in time" with our contemporaries — as if time itself is indifferent to this existing together — but rather the present is increasingly characterised by a coming together of *different but equally "present"* temporalities or "times", a temporal unity in disjunction, or a *disjunctive unity of present times*.[9]

Such global contemporaneity means that new communication technologies and social and mass media play a decisive role both in shaping the field of art and culture and in the ways in which art and culture themselves function and create meaning. The Internet, in particular, has produced an extreme spatial and temporal compression, altering the ways in which we experience places, events and time, as everything happens as if contemporaneously. This geopolitical condition of contemporaneity not least occasions negotiations of identity, subjectivity and community on a range of different levels as it becomes increasingly evident that our being is networked and connective — which also raises the important question of the praxis of memory within the condition of contemporaneity.

The shift from the modern to an era of contemporaneity is connected to the Benjaminian realization that time is not an empty duration, unaffected by the events that fill it; that time itself has a history. Time is constructed, multiple and asymmetrical, neither homogeneous nor blank, and there are many different coexisting ways of being in time and belonging to it. "The contemporary" points to an awareness of what it is to be in the present whilst being attentive to the presence of other kinds of time. It designates a multi-chronicity and a thickening of the present in contemporary experience, an extension of the present beyond the immediate instant back and forward in time and across the globe. "Contemporaneity," Terry Smith claims, "consists precisely in the constant experience of radical disjunctures of perception, mismatching ways of seeing and valuing the same world, in the actual coincidence of asynchronous temporalities, in the jostling contingency of various cultural and social multiplicities, all thrown together in ways that highlight the fast-growing inequalities within and between them."[10]

Thus, the idea of contemporaneity undermines the modern orientation toward a particular future and the concomitant understanding of history as a linear teleological development in time. As Osborne has argued, modernist art must be understood according to "a temporal logic of negation [whereby] it makes its claim on the present, through its negation of past forms, in the name of a particular, qualitatively different future."[11] The temporal logic of modernity is oriented toward a qualitatively different future and thus implies an idea of historical linearity.

What we seem to be witnessing is an extension of the present without orientation toward any particular all-encompassing future. As the editors of the *e-flux journal* remark, "The phase of contemporary art has [...] been characterized [...] as a reformatting of time into a perpetual present. The contemporary is the now that never ends, the art that circles itself at the tail end of history looking back on defunct ideologies, archiving and polishing them for a future that never arrives."[12] One could argue, with Terry Smith, that we live in a time of unsettlement in which the modern sense that all societies were moving toward a better future has been irrevocably lost (Auschwitz made that very clear); and that we have come to realize that we are all living in a condition of permanent transition, facing uncertain, unclear futures. Our highly differentiated and multidirectional contemporaneity within this shared uncertainty is what makes us no longer modern. Contemporaneousness is "the pregnant present of the original meaning of *modern*, but without its subsequent contract with the future."[13] Contemporaneity, Smith remarks, includes within it many revived pasts and wished-for futures that are all being lived out in the present. They are all possible, and, as distinct from the modern era, there is no overriding narrative to decide which is which — a world-picturing that thereby also runs the risk of becoming too permissive in its affirmation of pluralism.

This global, or planetary, uncertainty about the future (and having entered the so-called Anthropocene, such uncertainty includes the planet itself) is one of the main reasons for the recent upsurge in memory and memory culture. Historian Pierre Nora speaks of "the age of commemoration," which he sees as intersecting with two major historical phenomena: a temporal "acceleration of history" and a social "democratization of history."[14] The democratization of history is related to the marked emancipatory trend "of all those forms of memory bound up with minority groups for whom rehabilitating their past is part and parcel of reaffirming their identity."[15] The acceleration of history, which is the most important notion in our context, signals that the most continuous or permanent feature of the contemporary world is no longer continuity or permanence, but change, which is an increasingly rapid change, "an accelerated precipitation of all things into an ever more swiftly retreating past."[16] A condition of permanent transition, as Smith calls it. This development has broken the unity of historical time, whose straightforward linearity traditionally bound the present and the future to the past. In modernity, it was a particular image or idea of the future that determined what different communities needed to remember of the past to prepare that imagined future. The imagined future gave meaning to the present, which was merely a link between the past and that future, which could either take the shape of a restoration of the past, the shape of progress, or of revolution. Today, we are uncertain as to which shape the future will take and we no longer use such interpretations of the past to organize history to the same degree. Because of this uncertainty about the future and our inability to anticipate it — and thus to anticipate what coming generations need to know about us in order to understand their own lives — the present puts us under an obligation to remember any phenomenon, trace or sign that might be significant. "In other words, it is the end of any kind of teleology of history — the end of a history whose end is known — that places on the present this urgent 'duty to remember' [...] that is so much talked about," Nora remarks.[17] The historical and temporal continuity of modernity has been broken and the present no longer functions as a bridge between the past and the future. The present has emerged as an autonomous category for understanding our own lives — which is why memory, as an act of the present, a re-presentation belonging to the present, has become so important.

An intensified global temporal and cultural interconnectivity and changing perceptions of time and space also affect the status and memories of the events to which we refer to as the Holocaust. As Andreas Huyssen observes:

> memory of the Holocaust as image reservoir, cipher of ultimate suffering, and model for working through the past [has] migrated into other historical contexts: Latin America after the military dictatorships, South Africa after apartheid, and Asia in relation to past and present-day instances of massive violence such as the Indian partition, the Korean comfort women, and the recent Hindu pogroms on Muslims in India. Today, the history of the violent twentieth century is being commemorated in very diverse artistic works across the globe.[18]

The idea of contemporaneity as an intensified global interconnectedness of different times is therefore inseparable from the circulation of images and the role of images in global spectacle. The world is becoming "uniform" or "common" not least because of the global circulation of images.

Against the background of this general diagnosis of the historical present, of its contemporaneity (understood as the coming together of different times, which at the same time are subjected to synchronization and standardization), and the ways in which this conditions how the Holocaust can be remembered, I will now return to Jean-Luc Godard's *Histoire(s) du cinemá* as a work of Holocaust memory.

II

In continuation of Osborne's observation: "To claim something is contemporary is to make a claim for its *significance in participating in the actuality of the present*," we might ask how the Holocaust may be said to be made contemporary in Godard's *Histoire(s) du cinéma*?[19] How does the temporality of the Holocaust appear as active in the historical present? How does the time of the Holocaust come together with other times in the present contemporaneity?

Histoire(s) du cinéma is a 264-minute video essay on the history or histories of cinema and its relation to the 20th century. It was first released in 1998, making it, at a stretch, still somewhat contemporary: Godard may be said to have had an intuition of the changes in current experiences of time. The *Histoire(s)* consists of four chapters, each divided into two parts, making for a total of eight episodes, and originates from an experimental series of improvised talks and lectures Godard gave at the Montreal Film School in the late '70s. Rather than delivering traditional lectures, Godard proposed a form of historical cinematic montage, where he showed one of his own films along with clips from a range of other films, as a basis for reflections on the history of cinema and on his own place within it.[20] The opening two long episodes were eventually broadcast on French television in 1988 and 1989, and the subsequent six episodes were screened at festivals and museums in 1997 and 1998. In 1998 the entire work was released, complete and re-edited on VHS, and came out on DVD in 2008. Made for TV, and later VHS, the work is meant to be seen in the everyday environment of the viewer: on their TV (and today, perhaps, laptop), where they encounter, are bombarded, with a dizzying number of images every day — where their brain is massaged into availability by what Bernard Stiegler refers to as the program industries.

The video essay weaves together clips of old films and newsreels, photographs, stills, images of paintings, new footage, advertisements, music, sound and voice recordings, textual citation, narration and commentary, primarily by Godard himself, but also by the actors Juliette Binoche and Julie Delpy, and writers like André Malraux, Ezra Pound, and Paul Celan. Every now and then we also see Godard at his desk with his books and his typewriter, smoking a cigar while orchestrating it all. In an experimental form, which abandons the linear development of narrative cinema in favour of, as I will argue in the following, a kind of contemporaneity, the work layers, superimposes and juxtaposes all the filmic, musical, textual, voice over, and art historical citations, which deal with a broad swathe of subjects, ranging from film and politics to globalization, memory, genocide, art and God.[21]

The work is characterized by an emphatic use of iconic images, many from the liberation of the concentration camps and the cinematic representation of the Holocaust. Speaking of cinema as a fallen medium, Godard remarks, "the fact of the concentration camp, that it was not shown [by cinema], it wasn't answered."[22] It was, of course, in fact recorded on film — by George Stevens, for example, to whom I shall return, and also by Samuel Fuller and Alfred Hitchcock — but it was not *shown* by cinema in Godard's understanding. Thus, a recurring accusation in *Histoire(s) du cinéma* concerns the failure of cinema to fulfill its duty to be 'present' at the Nazi death camps, and he famously claims that, "cinema did not manage to fulfill its role":

> Naïvely, it was thought that the New Wave would be a beginning, a revolution. Well, it was already too late. Everything was over. It ended the moment the concentration camps were not filmed. At that very instant, cinema totally failed in its duty. Six million people were killed or gassed, principally Jews, and cinema was not there. Yet, from *The Great Dictator* to *La règle du jeu*, it had announced the entire drama. By not filming the concentration camps, cinema gave up completely. It is like the parable of the good servant who died from not having been used. Cinema is a means of expression in which the expression has disappeared. It has remained the means.[23]

"Forgetting extermination is part of extermination," as he says in chapter 1A, and the video-essay is to a large extent an endeavor to think critically about the images, writings, histories and the lack thereof that have reflected and commemorated the Holocaust.[24] Abandoning traditional narrativity, he explores cinema as a way of rethinking time, memory and history when fractured by atrocity.

Godard's history writing is based on a plural concept of history that reflects conditions of contemporaneity. Unified, big history is unachievable, but the innumerable potential histories contained within it are not. They are all possible histories that are not presented as the only possible one, but merely as possible.[25] The parenthetical "s" in the title *Histoire(s) du cinéma* in itself indicates the contemporaneity of a number of different histories: there is no *one* history — and there is also an ambivalence inherent to the genitive form, whereby the histories of cinema are also history through, or *as*, cinema. Furthermore, the title of chapter 1A, "*Toutes les histoires*" (All the Stories), suggests not only that history, like public memory, is constituted by multiple histories from a variety of competing perspectives, but also that history must include all perspectives and voices, including the voices of Hitler, Himmler and a number of other perpetrators.[26] I can therefore understand Jacques Rancière to a certain extent when he criticizes Godard for linking heterogeneous elements into a homogeneous layer of mystery, "where all yesterday's conflicts become expressions of intense co-presence," and for "constructing the world of 'images' as a world of general co-belonging and inter-expression."[27] I would argue, however, that this co-presence is not to be deplored, but to be appreciated as a possible actualization of different temporalities and pasts, and of different relations to these temporalities and pasts. By juxtaposing documentary footage and photographic evidence with fiction film, pornographic movies, popular songs, propaganda, recorded voices and testimony, and by mixing texts, soundtracks, music and double exposures, by not hesitating to expose the historical archive to the artistic repertory of global cinema, the assemblages of *Histoire(s) du cinéma* invite us to reflect upon how to distinguish “a just image” (*une image juste*) from “just an image” (*juste une image*) of different pasts, not least of the Holocaust.

III

One of the references to the filmic representation of the Holocaust is the use of two clips from Claude Lanzmann’s nine-hour documentary *Shoah* from 1985. In accordance with the author of *The Postmodern Condition*, philosopher Jean-François Lyotard’s claim that the Holocaust defies images and cannot be represented without slipping away, Lanzmann’s film rejects representation in images and music in favor of the unfolding of the memories of the survivors and witnesses in the present. Thus, all archival images are excluded and the sublime art of the unpresentable is the only art adequate and ethically proper to the Holocaust.[28]

The first citation from *Shoah* in the *Histoire(s)* is the monumental image of the railway tracks leading to Auschwitz, itself a reference to Alain Resnais’s *Nuit et brouillard* (*Night and Fog*) from 1955. The image signifies all that cannot be seen: the millions of victims that Lanzmann’s survivors testify to, and the destruction of evidence of the genocide, of which the image has become an icon. Godard’s second citation from *Shoah* is the recycling, in extreme slow motion, of the image of Henryk Gawkowski — a retired Polish train driver, hired by Lanzmann to drive a locomotive to Treblinka — leaning out of the locomotive making a gesture by drawing his finger across his throat to symbolize the imminent death of the passengers who were to arrive in Treblinka. Godard dissolves Lanzmann’s ban on images by installing the very image used to advertise the film *Shoah* into a sequence of archival images of the very kind that Lanzmann refused to show. He emphasizes the ambiguity of Gawbowski’s gesture between an image of the past, a reanimation of the past, and a reenactment of the past even more strongly by mounting the image from *Shoah* between two iconic photographs of the Holocaust and two movie clips of Hitler. The first photograph framing the image from *Shoah* is taken from the liberation of Bergen-Belsen and shows survivors waiting for their ration of soup. The second photograph shows a line of naked women holding onto their infants before being murdered by the Einsatzgruppen — taken either during the massacre of the Jewish population of Kiev in September 1941, or during the massacre of the Jews from the Mizocz Ghetto, then in Poland, today in Ukraine, in October 1942.[29]

Through the montage of Lanzmann's film, photographs of the Holocaust, and movie clips of Hitler, Godard implies that the ban on images imposed by Lanzmann and Lyotard among others in the 1980s is *not* an adequate way of representing and actualizing the Holocaust. The ethics of silence and the sublime aesthetics of the unpresentable, which was an important contribution to the debates on the representation of the Holocaust at that point in time, cannot stand alone any longer. Today, if we do not actualize the images that do exist in spite of all — to use the title of a seminal book by Georges Didi-Huberman — the generations born afterward run the risk of losing sight of the actual historical events and of not being able to imagine what it is that cannot be represented and put into words, music and images.

There is thus an important temporal-historical dimension to the difference between the writing of history and the Holocaust memory work of Lanzmann and Godard. The present of the 1980s is different from the current present, both because of the distance in time to the events, and the loss of living memory of them, and because of the changing status of the Holocaust, which has migrated into other historical contexts and has been supplemented by a number of other genocides and war atrocities, adding greater complexity to what might be called the prehistories of the present. For instance, this situation is depicted in a sequence in chapter 3A of Godard's *Histoire(s)*, where images of the Holocaust are juxtaposed with images of the Vietnam, Bosnian and Gulf wars, while elsewhere images of the Rwandan genocide appear.

One of the most widely discussed sequences in *Histoire(s) du cinéma* occurs in the last minutes of chapter 1A, when Godard declares: "and if George Stevens hadn't used the first sixteen-millimetre color film at Auschwitz and Ravensbrück, Elizabeth Taylor's happiness would never have found a place in the sun." The fragment involves the superimposition, within a single frame, of Stevens's images of Holocaust victims, a stop-start sequence from Stevens's later film *A Place in the Sun* (1951), featuring a swimsuit-clad Taylor, and the Mary Magdalene of Giotto's *Noli me tangere* (1304–6). Giotto's painting is tilted ninety degrees, so that it looks as if Mary Magdalene is descending like an angel to draw Taylor up toward the heavens. Godard's voice accompanies two images from Goya's *Disasters of War* series of etchings (1810–20), pausing before the line about Elizabeth

Taylor's happiness. During the pause, the screen fades to black, and a color image of bodies of Holocaust victims piled in railway wagons at Dachau appears out of the darkness, while the black-and-white image of Taylor caressing Montgomery Clift's head in *A Place in the Sun* is gradually superimposed over it. The head of one of the victims seems to rest, along with Clift's, on her arm, close to her chest. Color bleeds into the image of Taylor, while Clift's image disappears. Rather than suggesting the substitution of the figure of the victim with Clift, or vice versa, this fading in and out offers a shocking contrast, of the connection of these images within the history of cinema.[30] Commenting upon the historical connection between the two recordings in 1988, Godard explained: "[W]hen I learned that Stevens had filmed the camps and that for the occasion Kodak had lent him the first rolls of 16-millimeter color film, I couldn't figure out how he was then able to make the great shot of Elizabeth Taylor radiating a kind of somber happiness."[31]

In this way Godard uses montage — what he calls "*mon beau souci*," my beautiful worry — as a technique for articulating the past. According to Godard, only montage can produce historical connections because history is always a matter of juxtaposing one thing with another. Time-based audio-visual media like film and video thus produce specific modes of historical articulation through techniques of the movement, decomposition and superimposition of images.[32] By incorporating both moving and still images, Godard creates a complex assemblage of perspectives from different temporal strata. Painting and photography, in particular, are often perceived as a slice of time, of time suspended, or at a standstill, while film, as a time-image, is linked to a temporality that endures, to a time that reproduces the flow of "real time." By basing his video essay on photographs, paintings and film, Godard blurs these apparently opposite economies of time for the benefit of a contemporaneity of multiple, heterogeneous temporalities that compete and overlap with each other, suggesting a notion of a fractured, layered, multiple temporality.[33]

IV

As in other works and texts, Godard draws upon Walter Benjamin's critique of the historicist conception of time as the merely abstract form of an "empty, homogeneous continuum," which the historian needs simply fill with a succession of facts, thereby producing a "history of events." The problem with this abstract notion of time, and the historicist notion of history as a linear development, is that once time is divided into a chronological series of instants, any moment in the past becomes unreachable as it is irrevocably severed from the present by an infinite number of instants.[34] It becomes a dead object of knowledge, something that can be accumulated without end, but which will never form what Benjamin calls the "true picture of the past." "The true picture of the past flits by," Benjamin writes in his "Theses on the Philosophy of History":

> The past can be seized only as an image which flashes up at the instant when it can be recognized and is never seen again. [...] For every image of the past that is not recognized by the present as one of its own concerns threatens to disappear irretrievably. To articulate the past historically does not mean to recognize it "the way it really was" (Ranke). It means to seize hold of a memory as it flashes up at a moment of danger.[35]

Godard's artistic practice in *Histoire(s)* is defined by montage, by the bringing together of elements that are not otherwise predisposed to be linked in the first place. This creates singular images, connecting well-known but previously unconnected elements and images. Godard thus uses montage as an experimental method for the production of historical intelligibility, to construct what Benjamin called "the image in the now of its recognizability." As Benjamin writes in one of the notes for his *Arcades Project*:

> Every present day is determined by the images that are synchronic with it: each "now" is the now of a particular recognizability. In it, truth is charged to the bursting point with time. [...] It is not that what is past casts its light on what is present, or what is present its light on what is past; rather image is that wherein *what has been comes together in a flash with the now to form a constellation*. In other words: image is dialectics at a standstill. For while the relation of the present to the past is purely temporal, the relation of what-has-been to the now is dialectical: not temporal in nature but figural [*bildlich*]. Only dialectical images are genuinely historical [...]. The image that is read [is] the image in the now of its recognizability.[36]

Historical knowledge only comes about through the "now," i.e. through some conjunction in our experience of the present through which a moment of memory and intelligibility emerges from amongst the immense archive of texts, images and testimonies of the past.[37] According to Benjamin, this critical moment appears as an *image*: a dialectical image in which "what has been comes together in a flash with the now to form a constellation," i.e. a coming together of times, a contemporaneity of past and present.

By speaking of images that are read and recognized, Benjamin — whose thinking on history and memory, in a pre-globalized time, has obviously paved the way for the understanding of the idea of contemporaneity that I am trying to outline here — points not only to the formal aspects of the image, but also to the time of its reading and recognition, to the recognizing spectator. This understanding of the image as something that develops out of the spectator's relation with the image is also made explicit in Godard's comments on his practice of montage:

> But an image doesn't exist. This is not an image, it's a picture. The image is the relation with me looking at it dreaming up a relation at someone else [*sic*]. An image is an association.[38]

The spectator animates the image, so to speak. The montage and interruptions that allow the true picture of the past to flash up for an instant, before it disappears irretrievably, are a spacing of time and an opening in which memory can emerge. According to Godard's conception, images only exist in the plural. Without reducing their difference, or provoking a fusion, the image only appears in intermediate spaces, between two images, located either in the many instances of black screens, or in intervals of superimposition, precisely in the difference between images co-present on screen. Godard comments: "The basis is usually two, always to present from the start two images rather than one, that is what I call image, the one made of two."[39] In this way, montage appears as a narrative into which the spectator can "enter" — a spatialization of time in which temporal connections are *felt* or *sensed*. With reference to the recurring sentence "*une forme qui pense*" (a form that thinks), montage can be regarded as an epistemological and dramaturgical space in which various kinds of temporality may be produced or shown to coexist.[40]

It is thus not only about the time of the images. Godard *shows* us these images and movie clips. They are addressed to us as viewers, which means that *our* time, *our* present, is involved — our historical present (the first decades of the twenty-first century) and our "phenomenological present," the duration of our watching and listening to the film, four and a half hours. This adds another dimension to the time structure of the work, especially when we are concerned with memory, and not merely detached historical material. The temporality of the viewer, who — to use the vocabulary of reception aesthetics — concretizes the artifact of the video essay and gives it an individual form, plays an active part in the constellation of the dialectical image. In the *Histoire(s)*, montage is productive of historical knowledge.

This, however, does not imply a form of knowledge production where the work of the spectator is controlled. The potential readings and recognitions of Godard's complex montage images are incalculable, and the product of their combination cannot be predicted, as it only appears in the here and now of each particular vision, that is, in each concretization of the visual artifact, which gives it an individual form each time. *Histoire(s) du cinéma* demonstrates that memory is something that has to be made, not just received. It testifies to the fact that memory is an activity, a praxis, involving the spectator in the actualization of different temporalities.

Godard's fleeting point of view and non-chronological movements through time and space bring together things and times "that have not been brought together before, and do not seem disposed to be brought together at all," as the title cards reads in chapter 4B, *Les signes parmi nous* (The Signs among Us), thereby reconfiguring the material and media through which we remember the Holocaust in hitherto unseen images that come to participate in the actuality of our present. In this sense he is a true contemporary according to Agamben's different — because personalized rather than historical — understanding of the contemporary as a person who, among other things, is "the one who, dividing and interpolating time, is capable of transforming it and putting it in relation with other times."[41] *Histoire(s)* exhibits the globally circulating images of our everyday, including the images of Dachau and of the Warsaw ghetto, while establishing a relation to these images and making the coexistence of their different temporalities, their contemporaneity in the historical present, *felt* — it is an *aesthetics of contemporaneity* in opposition to "the systematic organization of the unified time of the moment. This global, abstract tyranny."

A–D
Jean-Luc Godard
Histoire(s) du cinéma, 1998

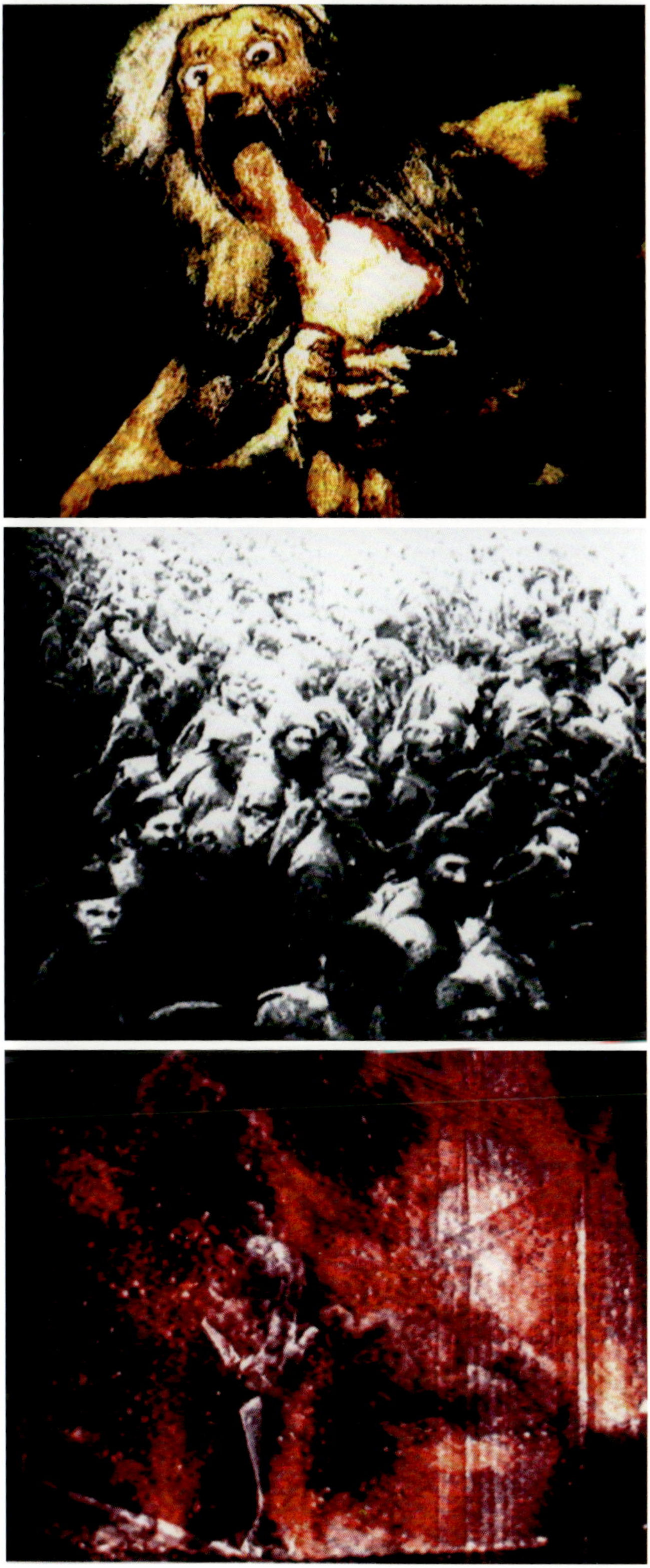

A Jean-Luc Godard

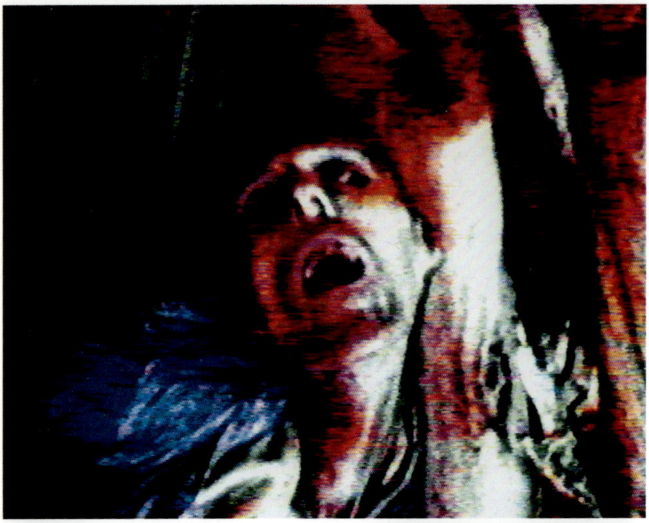

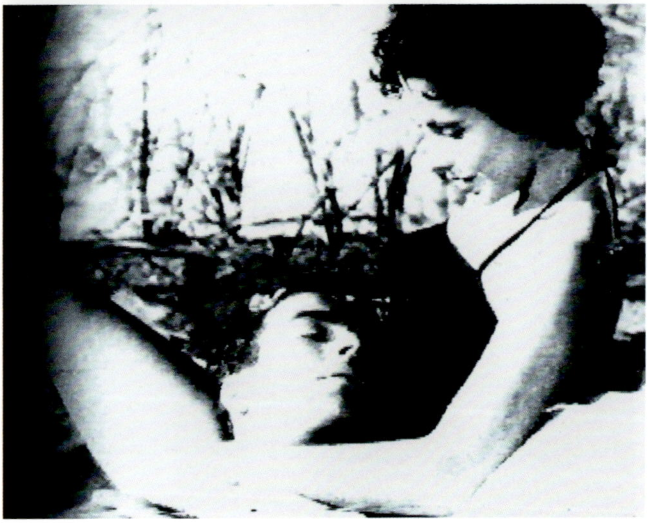

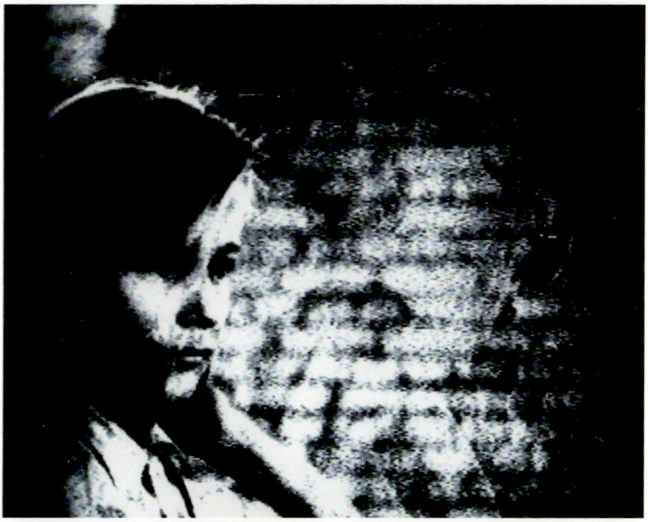

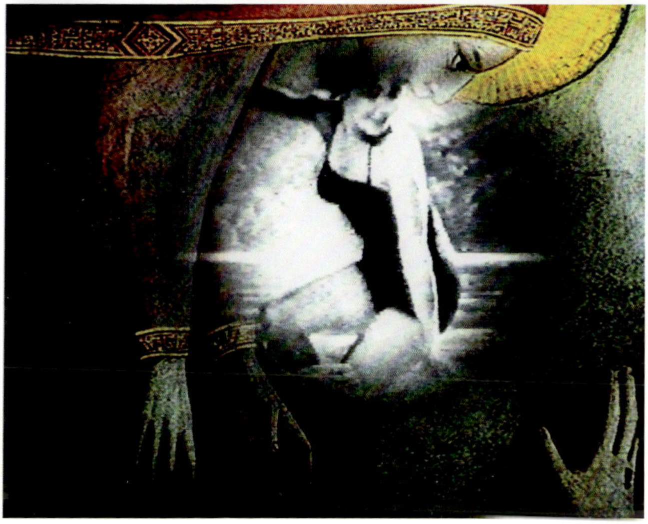

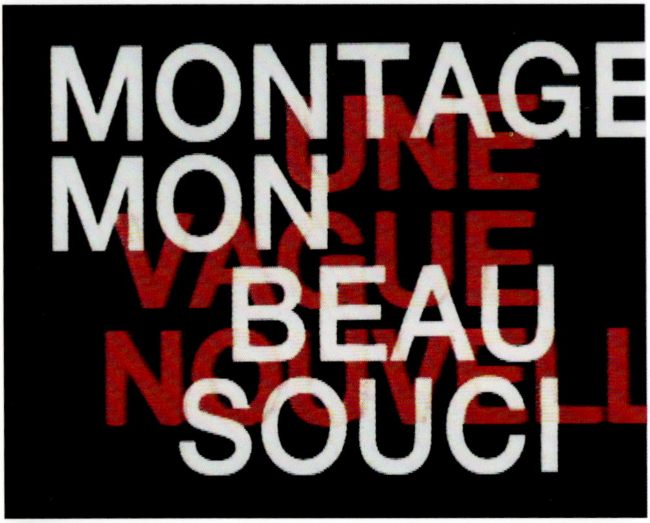
MONTAGE
MON
BEAU
SOUCI
UNE
VAGUE

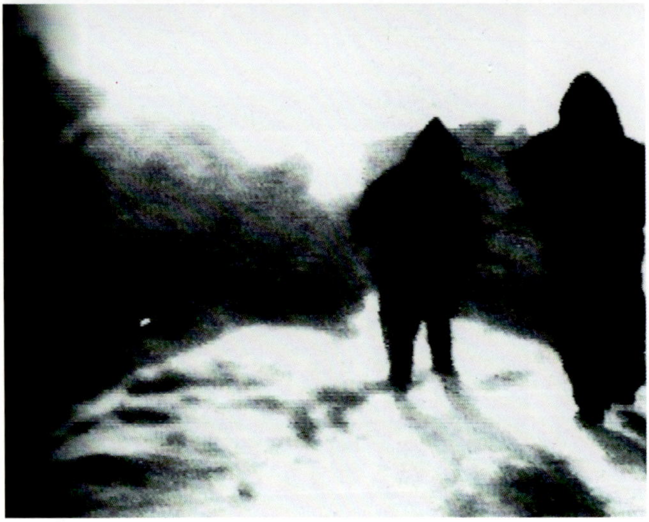

Notes

1 Jean-Luc Godard, *Histoire(s) du cinéma* [1998], DVD (Paris: Gaumont, 2008), chapter 4B.
2 Cf. James S. Williams, "Histoire(s) du cinéma," *Film Quarterly*, vol. 61, no. 3 (Spring 2008), 10–16: 16.
3 Bernard Stiegler, "Dans la vacance, on cherche à retrouver la consistance dans son existence," *Philosophie magazine*, no. 21 (2008), accessed August 8, 2021, http://www.philomag.com/les-idees/bernard-stiegler-dans-la-vacance-on-cherche-a-retrouver-la-consistance-dans-son-existence. See chapter 1 on Stiegler's theory of media.
4 Giorgio Agamben. "Cinema and History: On Jean-Luc Godard," trans. John V. Garner and Colin Williamson, in *Cinema and Agamben*, eds. Henrik Gustafsson and Asbjørn Grønstad (New York: Bloombury, 2014), 25–26: 25.
5 Hito Steyerl, "Too Much World: Is the Internet Dead?," *e-flux journal*, #49 (November 2013): 1–10, 7, accessed January 26, 2022, http://www.e-flux.com/journal/too-much-world-is-the-internet-dead/
6 Cf. Ann Rigney, "Plenitude, scarcity and the circulation of cultural memory," *Journal of European Studies*, 35:1 (2005): 11–28.
7 See chapter 2 for an analysis of changes within Holocaust memory.
8 Cf. Terry Smith, *What Is Contemporary Art?* (Chicago: University of Chicago Press, 2009), 3.
9 Peter Osborne, *Anywhere or Not at All. Philosophy of Contemporary Art* (London: Verso, 2013), 17.
10 Terry Smith, "Contemporary Art and Contemporaneity," *Critical Inquiry* 32 (Summer 2006): 681–707, 703.
11 Peter Osborne, "Non-places and the Spaces of Art," *The Journal of Architecture* vol. 6 (Summer 2011): 183–194, 183.
12 Julieta Aranda, Brian Kuan Wood, and Anton Vidokle, "Editorial — 'The End of the End of History?' Issue Two," *e-flux journal*, #57 (2014), accessed January 26, 2022, https://www.e-flux.com/journal/57/60387/editorial-the-end-of-the-end-of-history-issue-two/.
13 Smith, "Contemporary Art and Contemporaneity," 703.
14 Pierre Nora, "Reasons for the current upsurge in memory," *Transit — Europäische Revue* 22 (2002), 1–9, January 26, 2022, https://www.eurozine.com/reasons-for-the-current-upsurge-in-memory/.
15 Ibid., 5.
16 Ibid., 4.
17 Ibid.
18 Andreas Huyssen, *The Shadow Play as Medium of Memory in William Kentridge and Nalini Malani* (Milan: Edizioni Charta, 2013), 5.
19 Osborne, *Anywhere or Not at All*, 2, my italics.
20 Cf. Michael Witt, "Introduction. Jean-Luc Godard: *Histoire(s) du cinéma* (1988–1998)," *Screen*, 40:3 (Autumn 1999): 304–305.
21 Cf. Dimitrios S. Latsis, "Genealogy of the Image in *Histoire(s) du Cinéma*: Godard, Warburg and the Iconology of the Interstice," *Third Text*, 27:6 (2013): 774–785, 778.
22 Gavin Smith, "Interview: Jean-Luc Godard," *Film Comment* (March–April 1996), accessed January 26, 2022, http://www.filmcomment.com/article/jean-luc-godard-interview-nouvelle-vague-histoires-du-cinema-helas-pour-moi.
23 Godard, quoted in Georges Didi-Huberman, *Images in Spite of All*, trans. Shane B. Lillis (Chicago: University of Chicago Press, 2008), 140; French original: Jean-Luc Godard, *Jean-Luc Godard par Jean-Luc Godard*, II: 1984–1998 (Paris: Cahiers du cinéma, 1998), 336.
24 Cf. Kriss Ravetto-Biagioli, "*Noli me tangere*. Jean-Luc Godard's *Histoire(s) du cinéma*," in *A Companion to Jean-Luc Godard*, eds. Tom Conley and T. Jefferson Kline (Malden, MA: Wiley Blackwell, 2014), 456–487: 457.
25 Cf. Monica Dall'asta, "The (Im)possible History," in *For Ever Godard*, eds. Michael Temple et al. (London: Black Dog Publishing, 2004), 350–363: 352.

26 Cf. Ravetto-Biagioli, "*Noli me tangere*," 461.
27 Jacques Rancière, *The Future of the Image*, trans. Gregory Elliott (London: Verso, 2007), 62 and 63.
28 Jean-François Lyotard, *Heidegger and "the jews,"* trans. Andreas Michel and Mark Roberts (Minneapolis: University of Minnesota Press, 1990), 26.
29 Cf. Ravetto-Biagioli, 465 and 482, note 36.
30 My description of this fragment draws heavily upon Ravetto-Biagioli, 472, and Williams, "Histoire(s) du cinéma," 14.
31 Jean-Luc Godard, "*Histoire(s) du cinéma*: Godard fait des histoires. Entretien avec Serge Daney" (1988), in *Jean-Luc Godard par Jean-Luc Godard*, II: 1984–1998, 172, quoted from Didi-Huberman, *Images in Spite of All*, 147.
32 Cf. Trond Lundemo, "Godard as Historiographer," in *A Companion to Jean-Luc Godard*, 488–503: 496.
33 I draw here upon the description of photofilmic time economies in the program for the conference *Photofilmic Images in Contemporary Art and Visual Culture*, accessed January 26, 2022, http://photofilmic.com/photofilmic-images-in-contemporary-art-and-visual-culture-conference/.
34 Cf. Dall'asta, "The (Im)possible History," 353.
35 Walter Benjamin, "Theses on the Philosophy of History," in *Illuminations*, trans. Harry Zohn (New York: Schocken Books, 1969), 255.
36 Walter Benjamin, *The Arcades Project*, trans. Howard Eiland & Kevin McLaughlin (Cambridge, MA: Belknap Press of Harvard University Press, 1999), 462f., my italics.
37 Cf. Georges Didi-Huberman, "Opening the Camps, Closing the Eyes: Image, History, Readability," trans. Katie Tidmarsh in *Concentrationary Cinema: Aesthetics as Political Resistance in Alain Resnais'* Night and Fog *(1955)*, eds. Griselda Pollock and Max Silverman (New York: Berghahn Books, 2011), 83–125: 87.
38 Smith, "Interview: Jean-Luc Godard."
39 Jean-Luc Godard & Youssef Ishaghpour, *Archéologie du cinéma et mémoire du siècle* (Tours: Farrago, 2000), 27.
40 Cf. Terry Smith's description of contemporary exhibition curating, in *Thinking Contemporary Curating* (New York: Independent Curators International, 2012), 29–31.
41 Giorgio Agamben, "What Is the Contemporary?," in *What Is an Apparatus? And Other Essays*, trans. David Kishik and Stefan Pedatella (Stanford, CA: Stanford University Press, 2009), 39–54: 53.

Untimeliness in Contemporary Times

Chapter 4

No contretemps ... without the promise of a now in common, ... the desired sharing of a living present.
— Jacques Derrida[1]

“Today, we are stuck in the present as it reproduces itself without leading to any future,” remarks Boris Groys.[2] Sharing Groys’s concern (and that of many other thinkers as well) that we have lost the future as a political object, this chapter discusses the temporal complexity of our current situation — indeed of the extent to which it makes sense to speak of *our* situation. The loss of a futural moment, and thus of another temporal horizon than the present, is connected to a sense of an ever-expanding present, defined by a capacity for only short-term perspectives. The present is no longer a hinge between the past and the future but has rather — in the felicitous phrasing of historian François Hartog — become omnipresent. Such presentism, the sense that only the present exists, is a crisis of time.[3]

The loss of the future as a political object has been theorized — among many others — by cultural critic Fredric Jameson, who famously sees the postmodern as “some weakness in our imagination,” insofar as it is easier for us (Jameson lectured on this in 1991) to imagine the deterioration of the earth and of nature than the breakdown of capitalism.[4] This has been analyzed more recently by Peter Osborne. Rather than investigating when the present — the omnipresent present, when, in fact, the present is all there is, is a lack of a present — began, Osborne calls for the present to begin again, the present as the time of action and the time of the production of a qualitatively different future.[5]

Against this background, the aim of this chapter is to provide a critical reading of the notion of *untimeliness*, particularly in Giorgio Agamben’s influential text “What Is the Contemporary?” (2009), as a decisive aspect of being contemporary. In an oft-quoted passage, Agamben makes the Nietzschean claim that:

> Those who are truly contemporary, who truly belong to their time, are those who neither perfectly coincide with it nor adjust themselves to its demands. They are thus in this sense irrelevant. But precisely because of this condition, precisely through this disconnection and this anachronism, they are more capable than others of perceiving and grasping their own time. [...]
>
> Contemporariness is, then, a singular relationship with one’s own time, which adheres to it and, at the same time, keeps a distance from it. More precisely, it is *that relationship with time that adheres to it through a disjunction and an anachronism*. Those who coincide

> too well with the epoch, those who are perfectly tied to it in every respect, are not contemporaries, precisely because they do not manage to see it; they are not able to firmly hold their gaze on it.[6]

Untimeliness is about temporal disjunction and anachronism. Agamben writes of "their time," "their own time," "the epoch," but what is *our* own time and *our* epoch? Who in the post or decolonial situation actually takes part in the possessive determiner "our"? I will argue that it is becoming increasingly difficult to identify a hegemonic "cultural" time in relation to which one can be untimely; that the current contemporaneity makes it practically impossible to be untimely, and thus avant-garde in the traditional sense. Claiming that under contemporary conditions — of an intensified global interconnection of different times and social narratives — it is no longer useful to employ Agamben's conception of *untimeliness* when trying to engage with the present in order to reinstall a futural moment — or to install other temporal horizons than the one in which we live — this chapter will try to indicate how a contemporary kind of untimeliness, characterized by operating in relation to several times at once, and thus differentiating the presentist present, may be seen to appear in the poetics and artistic practice of Kader Attia.

I

Today, it seems redundant to criticize the linearly progressive and teleological understanding of history that is often associated with Western modernity. As indicated above, however, the farewell to this idea of history also has consequences for the ways we may conceive critical relationships with the times in which we now live, and thus for what it might mean to be untimely, if indeed (the idea of) linear unified homogeneous history has become obsolete. Such consequences seem less clear and therefore worth pursuing.

To get a sense of what we have left behind, let us nevertheless begin by returning to the concept of untimeliness — what philosopher Jacques Derrida might call *contretemps* or "countertime" — and what it can be seen to criticize.[7] As indicated above, Agamben takes his cue from Friedrich Nietzsche, reading the second *Untimely Meditation*, "On the Uses and Disadvantages of History for Life,"[8] as a claim for contemporary relevance based on a disconnection from his own time, on an out-of-jointness.[9] One might say that Nietzsche's contemporariness is due not only to his thinking being independent from, and out of joint with, the dominant thinking of his time, but also to the content of his thinking, which was an explicit critique of then dominant historicist understandings of time and history.

Without wanting to go into a detailed reading of Nietzsche's untimely revaluation of history (*Historie*) as life's teacher (*historia magistra vitae*) in favor of an understanding of history in the service of life (*historia ancilla vitae*), I think it is important to note that this revaluation includes a rejection of some of the philosophical-historical axioms that had appeared over the same period to ground the modern concept of history. Most prominent in this context is his denial of any historical teleology able to grant meaning to history, and of any historical necessity capable of injecting a meaning into history that would ultimately exclude human agency.[10]

Agamben, furthermore, introduces a supplementary definition of contemporariness, which can be seen to elaborate on the abilty to see one's own epoch in the passage quoted above. Agamben continues: "The contemporary is he who firmly holds his gaze on his own time so as to perceive not its light, but rather its darkness."[11] Through an analogy to our perception of the sky at night, where remote galaxies move away from us faster than the speed of the light emanating from them, he defines the quality of being contemporary as "being able not only to firmly fix your gaze on the darkness of the epoch, but also to perceive in this darkness a light that, while directed toward us, infinitely distances itself from us. In other words, it is like being on time for an appointment that one cannot but miss."[12] Thus, the present that the contemporary perceives cannot reach him or her:

> The appointment that is in question in contemporariness does not simply take place in chronological time: it is something that, working within chronological time, urges, presses, and transforms it. And this urgency is the untimeliness, the anachronism that permits us to grasp our time in the form of a "too soon" that is also a "too late"; of an "already" that is also a "not yet."[13]

The untimeliness of contemporariness is an urgency that takes place within chronological time, while at the same transforming it. In this way, Agamben's analysis shares some structural similarities with Derridean deconstruction and the insight that there is no outside (no outside-text; *il n'y a pas de hors-texte*). It also operates, however, with *one* more or less unified epoch, with one identifiable hegemonic temporality and shared chronological time in which contemporariness takes place and which contemporariness transforms. This concept of time in the singular is a very Western — and male — one: its history includes Nietzsche, Barthes, Pericles, Robespierre, Sade, Mandelstam, Paul, Messiah, Foucault, and Benjamin, and takes place in Paris, Athens, New York, and so on. It is therefore in a certain sense an undivided or undifferentiated time, which should be historicized in the light of the present conditions of globality to which cultures all over the planet have arrived, or been subjected, via different historical trajectories. Interestingly, Agamben makes a last qualification of his conception of the contemporary: it is not only someone who perceives a light that cannot reach its destination; the contemporary "is also the one who, dividing and interpolating time, is capable of transforming it and putting it in relation with other times."[14] I would claim, however, that today these other times should relate not only to the past — and perhaps the future — on the axis of Western chronological time, but also to other cultural times formed along other trajectories.[15] Today, chronological recomposition, including Hartog's notion of "regimes of historicity" as changing articulations of the structure of past, present, and future, are too reductive for understanding the temporal complexity of the contemporary condition.[16] As I will try to show later, such a complex inclusion or entanglement of different cultural times in the constitution of the present may be said to take place in the work of Kader Attia.

II

As indicated above, Nietzsche's second *Untimely Meditation* should not be read as a critique and rejection of historicism in itself — defined by "the basic thesis that every aspect and expression of human life is unavoidably conditioned by history" — but rather of the teleology and necessity with which it is often associated.[17] Walter Benjamin's reflections on the concept of history (*Geschichte*), written in 1940 and posthumously published in 1942, develop this critique of historicism.[18] As Peter Osborne explains, the use and notion of historicism criticized by Benjamin is that associated with the Historical School in Germany, which developed in the latter part of the nineteenth century in direct opposition to Hegel's philosophy of history.[19] For Hegel, time is self-motivated and unfolds in the form of the workings of the spirit as it moves toward itself through the ages of history.[20] The version of historicism that Benjamin addresses is thus a form of consciousness of historical time, characterized not only by supposed objectivity, of knowledge of the past "'the way it really was,' (Ranke)," but also by the idea of history as progress.[21] According to Benjamin, the historicist conception of history as progressing through "a homogeneous, empty time" involves a naturalization of chronological, continuous history and is oblivious to the constitutive role of the present in any time-consciousness as the point from which history is given direction.[22] For Benjamin, history is, in Osborne's formulation, "an economy of violence dissembling as progress"; needless to say, Benjamin regarded the idea of progress with contempt.[23] He was looking for a "different, *qualitative* experience of the 'now' as an *historical* present."[24] The instantaneity of the now is thus a historical rather than a merely natural or a priori given form of temporality.

Part of the conceptual prehistory of such a *kairotic* moment, such untimeliness, is to be found in Kant. In the *Critique of Pure Reason*, time, alongside space, forms part of Kant's transcendental aesthetics, where both are regarded as necessary for cognition: they are required in order for anything to appear before us, thereby being sensed, perceived, and known.[25] Time is a basic condition for the realization of any phenomenon, but whereas those phenomena may well disappear again, time itself cannot. Kant famously claims that time "is not an empirical conception," but necessarily "exist[s] as a foundation *a priori*," which makes axioms of time in general, such as "time has only one dimension" and "different times are not co-existent but successive," possible.[26] In Kant's first critique, time is thus an a priori given, independent of our sensory perception.

The concept of contemporaneity challenges, of course, transcendental notions of time and the idea that it is exclusively one-dimensional and that different times can therefore not coexist. But Kant's own analysis of the sublime nine years later, in the *Critique of Judgement*, constitutes a challenge to the transcendental notion of time too.[27] Here, the sublime is not only an ungraspable magnitude that exceeds any individual subjective experience or perception, but also a moment where simultaneity or coexistence is made intuitable. The intuition of coexistence involves a negation of temporality, a movement beyond the capacities of sensation and conceptual determination to the realm of reason, whereby successive apprehension is replaced by instantaneous grasping.[28] Thus, "the unstable form of the sublime is," as Michael Wayne remarks in his book *Red Kant*, "inextricably linked with a new and potentially radical conception of temporality and history."[29]

In the *Critique of Pure Reason*, the imagination is linked to time as the form of inner sense. Its function, relative to understanding, is to synthesize the progressive sequence of representations in time. In the sublime, however, the imagination is related to reason, and, in a reversal of its normal operation, institutes what Kant calls a "regression" (*ein Regressus*) that annihilates the condition of time and makes intuition of coexistence possible:[30]

> Measurement of a space (as apprehension) is at the same time a description of it, and so an objective movement in the imagination and a progression. On the other hand the comprehension of

> the manifold in the unity, not of thought, but of intuition, and consequently the comprehension of the successively apprehended parts at one glance [*in einen Augenblick*], is a retrogression that removes the time-condition in the progression of the imagination, and renders *co-existence* intuitable [*und das Zugleichsein anschaulich macht*]. Therefore, since the time-series [*die Zeitfolge*] is a condition of the internal sense and of an intuition, it is a subjective movement of the imagination by which it does violence to inner sense — a violence which must be proportionately more striking the greater the quantum which the imagination comprehends in one intuition.[31]

The sublime violates the model of linear temporal progression in the ordering of the manifold that Kant mapped out in the *Critique of Pure Reason*, where he emphasized the successive apprehension of percepts in a temporal sequence. The sublime radically shifts to an instantaneous grasping of coexistence. Thus, "comprehending in one instant what is apprehended successively, is a regression that in turn cancels the condition of time in the imagination's progression."[32]

The sublime involves a radical cancellation of ordinary temporal unfolding and disrupts our habitual ways of perceiving and experiencing the world; rather than annihilating time as such, however, the regress of the imagination — the comprehension in an instant of what was successively apprehended — suggests a possible negation of the mathematical or linear form of time.[33]

In this way, Kant's analysis of the sublime might be seen as a tacit model for Benjamin's concept of *Jetztzeit* (translated as now-time or the presence of the now), which describes time at a standstill, where the past, in a flash, enters into constellation with the present, objectively interrupting the mechanical temporal process of historicism.[34] Just as the sublime interrupts successive apprehension as described in the *Critique of Pure Reason*, dialectics at a standstill interrupt and open the linear continuum of history.

For Benjamin, the dialectical convergence of past and present therefore holds a political potential. His ambition is to explode "the continuum of history" in order to make it possible to recompose it.[35] His now-time is a constructive form of temporality in which "the slivers of history," as emphasized by political theorist Isabell Lorey in her recent reading of Benjamin's reflections on the concept of history, "are newly composed, in which history persistently emerges. The now-time is the creative midpoint, not a transition of the past into the future."[36] Unlike the presentism described by Hartog, Groys, and others, Benjaminian now-time is a time full of emancipatory possibilities (rather than mere probabilities): "History is the subject of a structure whose site is not homogeneous, empty time, but time filled by the presence of the now [*Jetztzeit*]," as Benjamin remarks in the famous passage quoted in part above.[37] Time is not an empty, homogeneous duration unaffected by the events that fill it. Time itself has a history and politics. It is mediated, constructed, and multiple, not some blank a priori, and there are many different coexisting ways of being in time and belonging to it. The experience of contemporaneity is, perhaps, sublime in the sense that it is an interruption of unified, linear time; the contemporary condition, however, does not allow us any distance to that which would otherwise elicit an experience of the sublime — today there is no temporal outside to the sublime spectacle, so to speak.

In a chapter entitled "Sharing Responsibility: Farewell to the Sublime," published in the anthology *Reset Modernity!* that accompanied an exhibition of the same name, philosopher and sociologist Bruno Latour remarks that it becomes increasingly difficult for the Western subject living in the Anthropocene to enjoy any feeling of the sublime — in the Anthropocene we humans have ourselves become a geological force and have realized that we are part of the overwhelming nature we used to see as a separate and remote phenomenon:

> To feel the sublime you needed to remain "distant" from what remained a spectacle; infinitely "inferior" in physical forces to what you were witnessing; infinitely "superior" in moral grandeur. Only then could you test the incommensurability between these two forms of infinity. Bad luck: there is no place where you can hide yourselves; you are now fully "commensurable" with the physical forces that you have unleashed; as to moral superiority, you have lost that too![38]

The difficulty, I argue, of experiencing the Kantian sublime today not only concerns the nullification of our distance to that which would trigger experience of the sublime, the loss of a secure position from where to experience something as a sublime spectacle. There is also an important *temporal* aspect, in that we no longer enjoy the comfort of a secure position in relation to a one-dimensional time, from where it would be possible to grasp, or to establish a disjunctive relationship with, time, becoming thereby untimely, as in Giorgio Agamben's definition of the contemporary. Contemporaneity may, of course, be seen as synchronization and standardization of all the world's cultures and time-experiences, in line with a conception of the sublime as "a symptom of the supersensible totality of global capitalism"; but, it can also — as an, in principle, shared present, a globally shared experience of co-presence — be seen to hold the potential to interrupt the mechanical progression, or rather accumulation and repetition, of what is without alternative.[39]

To be untimely *then* (under the modern regime of historicity), was to not coincide with the present time in the singular; to be untimely *now* is to act on present times in the plural and to counter the time of global capital, which is about standardization, synchronization, and accumulation with no other temporal horizon, with no different future, even if imagined. It is therefore urgent to pay attention to, and allow for, cultural difference in the — at a certain level at least — globally shared present, as access to this present is still highly unevenly distributed. Anthropologist Marc Augé describes a new condition of radical contemporaneity between peoples and cultures:

> It is only now, in the rather blinding light of a generalized situation of cultural circulation, that we can become aware of what the eruption of the outside world into their societies has meant for certain peoples. Likewise, it is only today that the conditions of a contemporaneous anthropology are emerging, in the sense that the dialogue between observer and observed is inscribed in a universe where both recognize each other, even though they continue to occupy different and unequal positions. Contemporaneity cannot be decreed; the transformation of the world imposes it.[40]

The speed of cultural, economic, and migratory circulation has inaugurated *a generalized sharing of time*. "The world's inhabitants have at last become truly contemporaneous," Augé states.[41] Due to this circulation, there is now an undeniable coexistence of different temporalities.

The time in relation to which one should be untimely today is the complex temporality of global capital, which subjects all social forms to its standardizing logic. Untimeliness today may consist of differentiating the presentist present, opposing colonizing synchronization by marking or articulating a contemporaneity of difference that permits another kind of what Terry Smith calls "world-making" and "coeval composition."[42]

III

Kader Attia is a contemporary artist in the sense that he — unlike modernist artists who produce new work and carry the progressive history of art forward — is occupied with establishing relationships, or what he calls restitutions and reparations, with the past, allowing it to take part in the present.[43] The pasts that he actualizes are, however, pasts that come from places and cultures that do not share the Western point of view of history. The different — and from a modern Western progressivist perspective hitherto “other,” developmentally “delayed” or non-coeval — cultural temporalities that are brought to the fore and which become visible and audible in Attia’s reconfiguration of “the distribution of the sensible” are not necessarily reduced in their difference.[44] They are not being made to comply with a neocolonial standard set by a Western-dominated notion of art and cultural signification; rather, they enter into relationships while retaining their prehistories and particularities. In Attia’s work they often incorporate, in a certain sense, the otherness of the colonizing cultures — which have, of course, also been the primary motors in the globalization of capitalism — but leave this incorporation or appropriation visible, without covering it up and without wanting to return to an original, “non-contaminated” state of self-identity, to a time and history that is exclusively their own.

Attia’s work thus engages in a global dialogue, intervening in and seeking to replace the Western monologue. It addresses cultural questions and global issues concerning the coming together of Occidental and Oriental (or extra-Occidental) cultures with a focus on politics, on living together — including, in very concrete ways, works that deal with social housing projects. For instance, in the piece *Oil and Sugar #2* (2007), he worked with the materials oil and sugar, important commodities in the global economy that have played decisive roles in the creation of unequal systems of domination, poverty and colonization, letting dark oil dissolve a white cube made of small sugar cubes — figuratively the piece also reads as a dismantling of the white cube central to the ideology of modern Euro-American art. In *Holy Land* (2006), Attia installed almost a hundred mirrors on a beach on the Canary Islands to help African migrants at sea navigate, but also to signal that this is not any holy land as the mirrors were shaped to look like tombstones; just to mention one aspect of this complex piece. His work thus aims not only to criticize colonial history but also, and more so, to criticize current coloniality. As part of this endeavor he opened the cultural space with the telling name la colonie in Paris in 2016. Central to this is the relationship between injury and repair, concretely as well as psychologically and metaphorically. *(Untitled) Ghardaïa* (2009), for instance, is a fragile model of the “functionalist” eleventh-century Algerian city — which inspired modernist architects like Le Corbusier — made from couscous and thus constituting a kind of repair of the relationship between Western modernity and the ancient Mzab culture, reinstalling time and a historical trace:

> Lack of quotation is lack of acknowledgement. Even today, when Le Corbusier's work is the focus of a retrospective, Mozabite architecture is mentioned succinctly, in the best case. During a huge exhibition of his work in London, you could only see two postcards from Ghardaïa. We should try to imagine this conversation in another context, in Algeria or Congo for instance, so you can see how much Algerian or Congolese people could learn about the extent of their own heritage upon the world. Even though colonization is now over, it is still a fact that entire intellectual territories and areas have not been freed yet, or at least "reappropriated" by the traditional cultures representing the very origins of European "sources of inspiration."[45]

Attia's documentary film *Reflecting Memory* (2016), to add another example that deals with establishing relationships with "unacknowledged" pasts in the present, explores the phenomenon of phantom limbs as a way of addressing the phantom limbs of cultural complexes and the hauntings that remain within our consciousness:

> It was by extending to the human psyche the body of my political research on the concept of reparation that I fathomed the importance of the immaterial character of wounds, and the silent cry that they emit between official History and the one lived endlessly in the secret of family and community stories. Mass traumas and injustices or those of simple individuals last far longer than the initial act; they are maintained by the dominant power's stories while the mind imposes, troubles, and hides the necessity of their denunciation. This absolute, quasi-religious conception of science as a factor of modernity dominates the human psyche by the universalism of its conception of progress. This hegemony has led inevitably to the production of opposed reactions.[46]

Repair has thus become a central concept and concern in Attia's poetics and artistic practice.[47] A recent piece, *Le grand miroir du monde* (The grand mirror of the world) (2017), simply consists of a large rectangle of broken mirrors covering the whole floor of the gallery space.[48] Attia — who was trained in philosophy — speaks of the ambiguity of the concept of repair or reparation and opposes, in what he calls a conceptual polarization of civilizations, the way in which it is understood in traditional non-Western civilizations to the way it is understood in modern Western civilizations. The Euro-modern version of repair — of the body as well as objects — tries to erase the traces of the injury and bring the object or body back to its original shape, which involves, according to Attia, a denial of time, as the removing of the injury is also a removal of time, of the history of the object or body. In contrast, in many traditional, so-called primitive societies' understanding, repair preserves the trace of the injury, acknowledging what has happened to the object or body. It therefore adds to the history of the object or body.[49]

Historian, philosopher, and political theorist Achille Mbembe writes of the postcolonial present, where a multiplicity of coexisting times and traditions are interconnected and are being brought to bear on the same present, as "the *time of entanglement*":

> This time of African existence is neither a linear time nor a simple sequence in which each moment effaces, annuls, and replaces those that preceded it, to the point where a single age exists within society. This time is not a series but an *interlocking* of presents, pasts, and futures that retain their depths of other presents, pasts, and futures, each age bearing, altering, and maintaining the previous ones.[50]

Nietzsche's as well as Agamben's contemporary person was a (male) Westerner, someone who is able to establish a disjunctive relationship with his, her or their, *own* time, i.e. with a singular, unified Western progressivist time and history. Attia's work of repair complicates this modern untimeliness by introducing other times, other pasts, and by permitting prehistories hitherto unheard, indeed, silenced, in the Euro-modern present to become audible, to some extent, in an entangled contemporary present. The reparative relationships with different pasts that Attia's artistic practice brings into being somehow interfere with and differentiate a falsely synchronized present — and thereby imply at least a potential for imagining other, decolonized futures where various cultural traditions take part in the constitution of the present.

A
Kader Attia
Oil and Sugar #2, 2007

B
Kader Attia
Holy Land, 2006

C
Kader Attia
Untitled (Ghardaïa), 2009

D
Kader Attia
Reflecting Memory, 2016

E-F
Kader Attia
Le grand miroir du monde, 2017

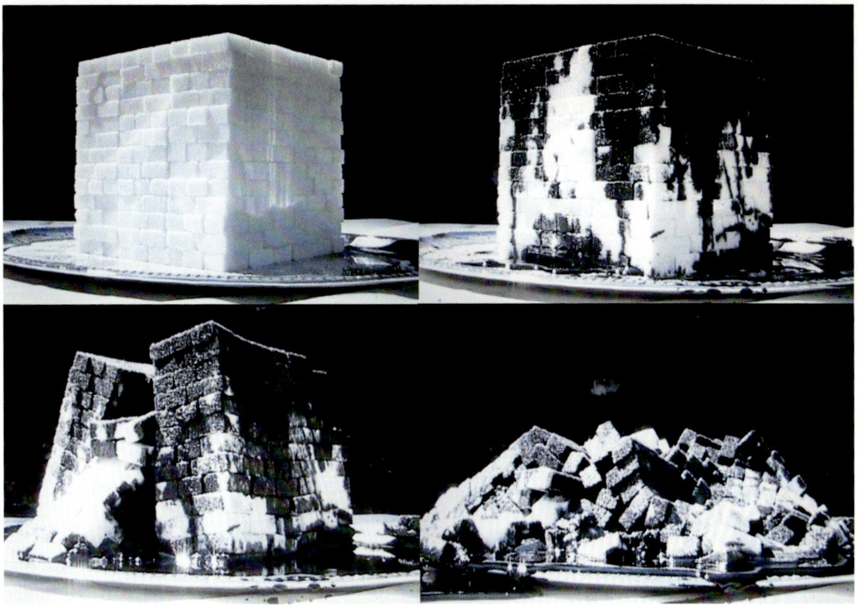

A Kader Attia

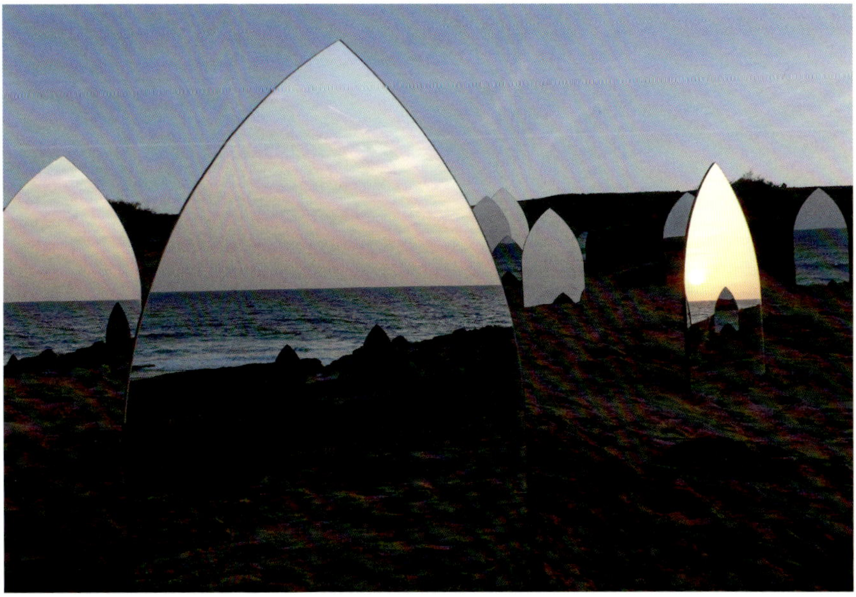

B Kader Attia

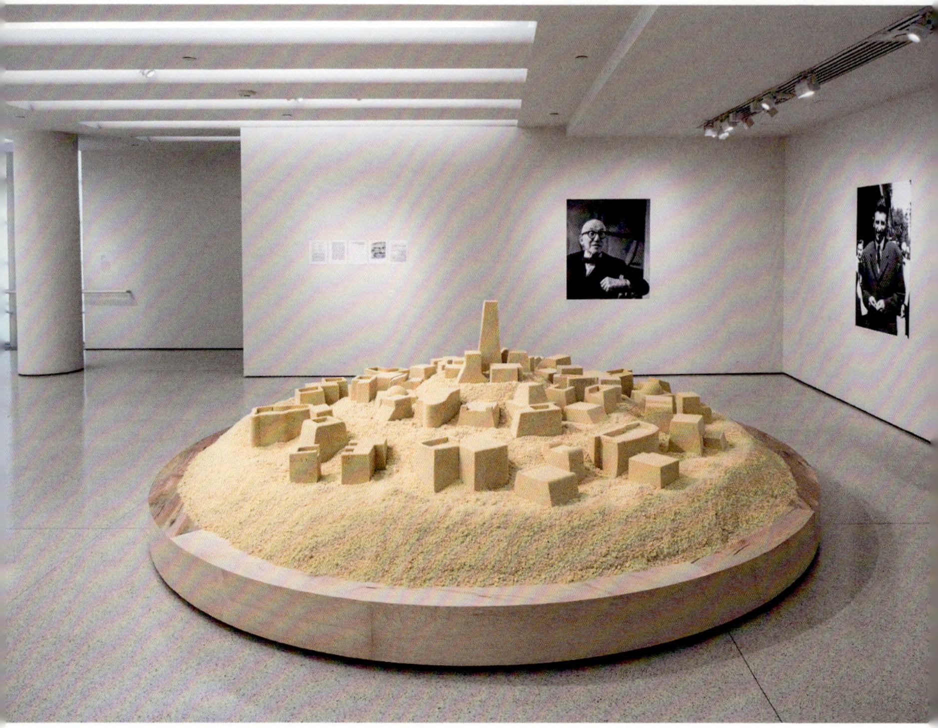

C Kader Attia

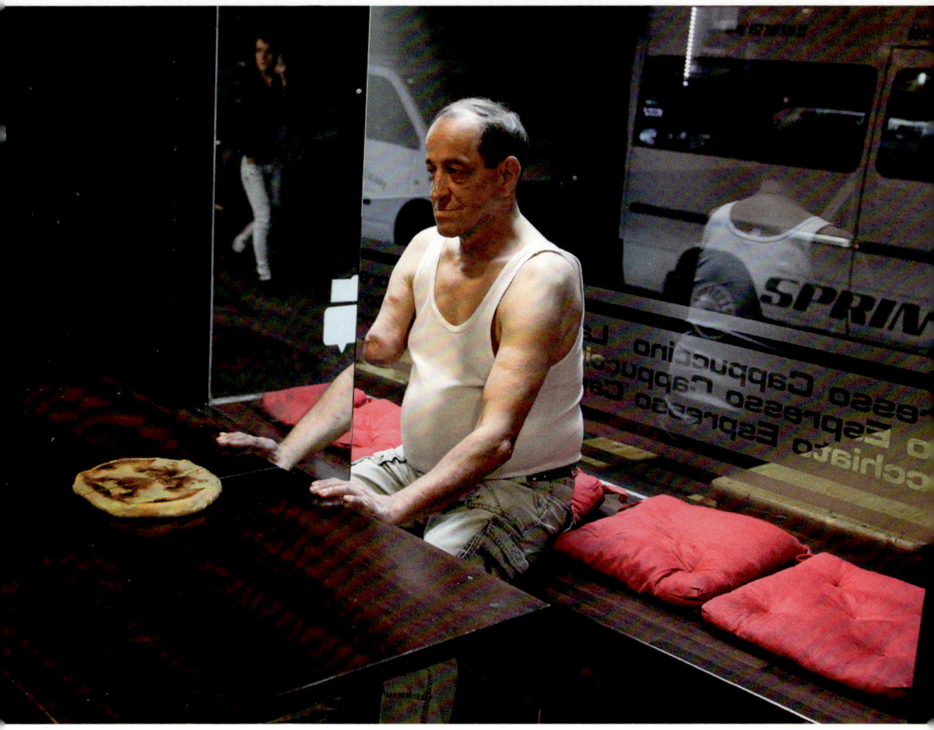

D Kader Attia

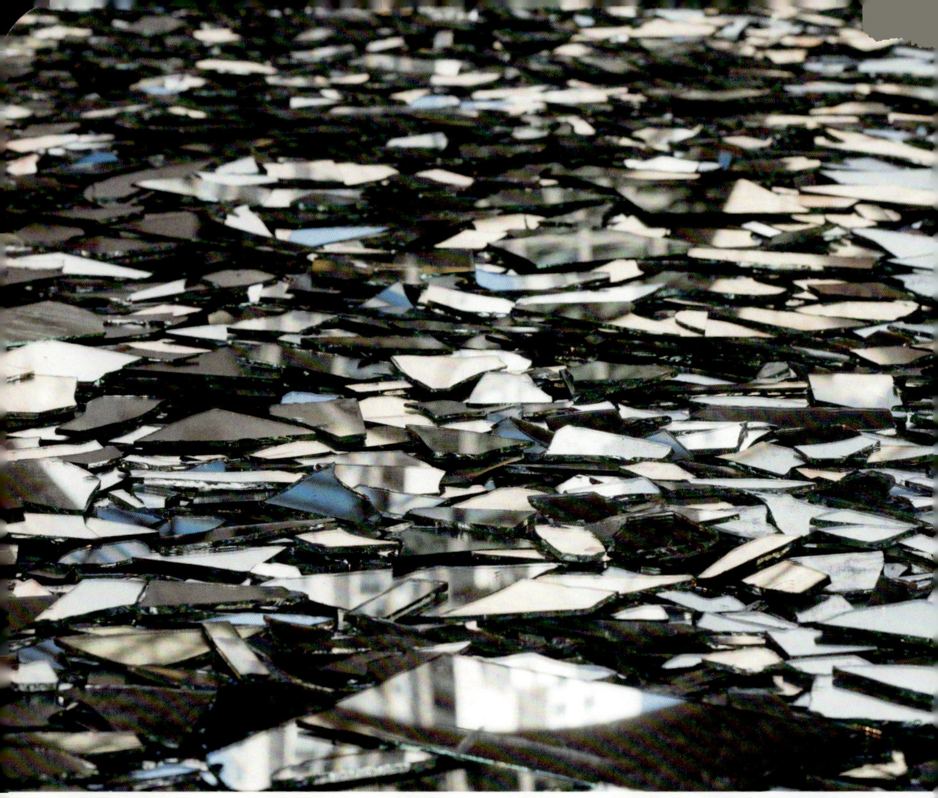

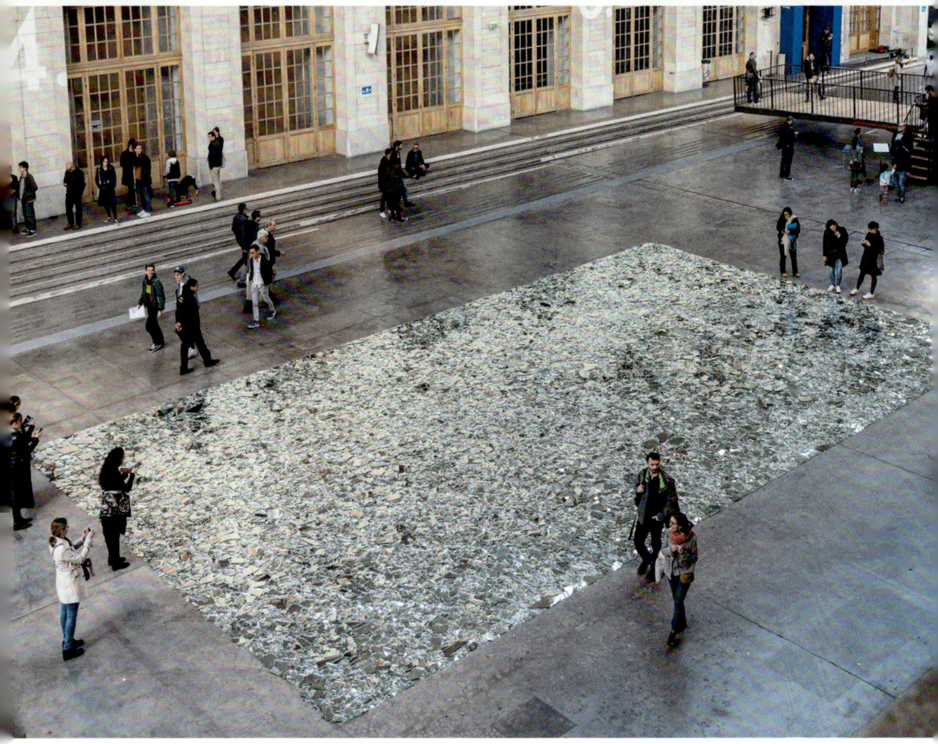

E-F Kader Attia

Notes

1 Jacques Derrida, "Aphorism Countertime," in *Acts of Literature*, trans. Nicholas Royle, ed. Derek Attridge (New York: Routledge, 1992), 414–33: 421.
2 Boris Groys, "Comrades of Time," in *Going Public* (Berlin: Sternberg Press, 2011), 84–101: 90.
3 François Hartog, *Regimes of Historicity: Presentism and Experiences of Time* [2003], trans. Saskia Brown (New York: Columbia University Press, 2015).
4 Fredric Jameson, *The Seeds of Time* (New York: Columbia University Press, 1994), xii.
5 Peter Osborne, "Existential Urgency: Contemporaneity, Biennials and Social Form," *Nordic Journal of Aesthetics,* no. 49–50 (2015): 175–88: 186.
6 Giorgio Agamben, "What Is the Contemporary?," in *What Is an Apparatus? And Other Essays*, trans. David Kishik and Stefan Pedatella (Stanford, CA: Stanford University Press, 2009), 39–54: 40-41.
7 Derrida, "Aphorism Countertime."
8 Friedrich Nietzsche, "On the Uses and Disadvantages of History for Life," in *Untimely Meditations*, ed. Daniel Breazeale, trans. R. J. Hollingdale (Cambridge: Cambridge University Press, 1997), 60–123.
9 Cf. Agamben, "What Is the Contemporary?," 40.
10 Cf. Reinhart Koselleck, "On the Meaning and Absurdity of History," in *Sediments of Time: On Possible Histories*, trans. and ed. Sean Franzel and Stefan-Ludwig Hoffmann (Stanford, CA: Stanford University Press, 2018), 177–96: 189–96. The Nietzschean critique of modern historicism, of course, also inspired Michel Foucault in his development of a genealogical approach in "Nietzsche, Genealogy, History," in *Language, Counter-Memory, Practice: Selected Essays and Interviews by Michel Foucault*, trans. Donald F. Bouchard and Sherry Simon, ed. Donald F. Bouchard (Ithaca, NY: Cornell University Press, 1977), 139–64. Foucault's rejection of "the metahistorical deployment of ideal significations and indefinite teleologies" (140), however, still operates within a "pre-global era" and, thus, within a very Western tradition and cultural sphere. It is therefore — for good historical reasons — unable to take the current condition of contemporaneity into consideration.
11 Cf. Agamben, "What Is the Contemporary?," 44.
12 Ibid., 46.
13 Ibid., 47.
14 Ibid., 53.
15 The art historiographical consequences of what I prefer to call the condition of contemporaneity are explored in a recent anthology, *Time in the History of Art: Temporality, Chronology and Anachrony*, eds. Dan Karlholm and Keith Moxey (New York: Routledge, 2018). See also chapter 6.
16 Cf. Hartog, *Regimes of Historicity: Presentism and Experiences of Time.*
17 Daniel Breazeale, "Introduction," in Friedrich Nietzsche, *Untimely Meditations*, xv.
18 Walter Benjamin, "On the Concept of History," in *Selected Writings*, vol. 4, *1938–1940*, trans. Edmund Jephcott and others, eds. Howard Eiland and Michael W. Jennings (Cambridge, MA: Belknap Press of Harvard University Press, 1992), 389–400.
19 Cf. Peter Osborne, *The Politics of Time: Modernity and Avant-Garde* (London: Verso, 1995), 138–44.
20 Georg Wilhelm Friedrich Hegel, *Aesthetics: Lectures on Fine Art,* trans. T. M. Knox, 2 vols. (Oxford: Clarendon Press, 1975).
21 Benjamin, "On the Concept of History," 391.
22 Ibid., 395.
23 Osborne, *The Politics of Time*, 141.
24 Ibid., 143.
25 Immanuel Kant, *Critique of Pure Reason*, trans. J. M. D. Meiklejohn (London: H. G. Bohn, 1855), 1.1.2.4, 28–29.
26 Ibid., 28.

27 Cf. Immanuel Kant, *Critique of Judgement,* trans. James Creed Meredith, ed. Nicholas Walker (Oxford: Oxford University Press, 2007).

28 Michael Wayne, *Red Kant: Aesthetics, Marxism and the Third Critique* (London: Bloomsbury, 2014), 121.

29 Ibid.

30 Rudolf Makkreel, "Imagination and Temporality in Kant's Theory of the Sublime," *Journal of Aesthetics and Art Criticism*, no. 42 (March 1984), 303–16: 303.

31 Kant, *Critique of Judgement*, 89.

32 Ibid., §27, as translated by Wayne in *Red Kant*, 121.

33 Cf. Makkreel, "Imagination and Temporality," 308.

34 Cf. Benjamin, "On the Concept of History," and *The Arcades Project*, trans. Howard Eiland and Kevin McLaughlin (Cambridge, MA: Belknap Press of Harvard University Press, 2002), 262.

35 Benjamin, "On the Concept of History," 395. Cf. Geoff Cox and Jacob Lund, "Time.now," in *Uncertain Archives: Critical Keywords for Big Data*, ed. Nanna Bonde Thylstrup et al. (Cambridge, MA: MIT Press, 2021), 523–31.

36 Isabell Lorey, "Presentist Democracy: Exodus and Tiger's Leap," trans. Aileen Derieg, *Transversal Texts*, June 2014, n.p., accessed January 27, 2022, http://transversal.at/blog/Presentist-Democracy.

37 Benjamin, "On the Concept of History," 395.

38 Bruno Latour, "Sharing Responsibility: Farewell to the Sublime," in *Reset Modernity!*, ed. Bruno Latour (Karlsruhe: ZKM & Cambridge, MA: MIT Press, 2016), 169.

39 Cf. Wayne, *Red Kant*, 118.

40 Marc Augé, *An Anthropology for Contemporaneous Worlds*, trans. Amy Jacobs (Stanford, CA: Stanford University Press, 1999), 50.

41 Ibid., 89.

42 Terry Smith, "Defining Contemporaneity: Imagining Planetarity," *Nordic Journal of Aesthetics*, no. 49–50 (2015): 156–74, and *The Contemporary Composition*, The Contemporary Condition 2 (Berlin: Sternberg Press, 2016).

43 Arthur C. Danto, *After the End of Art: Contemporary Art and the Pale of History* (Princeton, NJ: Princeton University Press, 1997), 4–5.

44 Cf. Johannes Fabian, *Time and the Other: How Anthropology Makes Its Object* (New York: Columbia University Press, 1983) with regard to non-coevalness, and Jacques Ranciére, *The Politics of Aesthetics: The Distribution of the Sensible,* trans. and ed. Gabriel Rockhill (London: Continuum, 2004).

45 Kader Attia, *Repair*, ed. Léa Gauthier (Paris: Blackjack éditions, 2014), 180.

46 Kader Attia, "The Field of Emotions," Kader Attia's homepage (2018), accessed January 27, 2022, http://kaderattia.de/the-field-of-emotion/.

47 Cf. Attia, *Repair*.

48 The dimensions of the piece vary according to the specific exhibition site.

49 Kader Attia, "Kader Attia Speaks about the Idea of Repair," interview with Judith Benhamou-Huet, YouTube video, 2:38, posted by "Judith Benhamou-Huet Reports," May 22, 2018, accessed January 27, 2022, https://www.youtube.com/watch?v=PBYoL6z4V7Q.

50 Achille Mbembe, *On the Postcolony*, trans. A. M. Berrett et al. (Berkeley: University of California Press, 2001), 16, Mbembe's italics. On the postcolonial present as interconnecting a multiplicity of co-existing times and traditions, see Dipesh Chakrabarty, *Provincializing Europe: Postcolonial Thought and Historical Difference* (Princeton, NJ: Princeton University Press, 2000), 109. On the postcolony as, initially, a reference to a chronological moment that, ambiguously, signaled an end to colonization and the beginning of the establishment of a new nation form, see Harry Harootunian, *Marx after Marx: History and Time in the Expansion of Capitalism* (New York: Columbia University Press, 2015), 197–234.

Dematerialization in the Contemporary Present

Chapter 5

When speaking of the disappearance and immateriality of the artwork, we should take the changing historical context of "dematerialization" into consideration. In the 1960s, works of Conceptual art famously aimed to dissolve their material support and question the traditional media of art; they sought to avoid becoming material objects that could be turned into commodities, in favor of an art whose "material" would be ideas and concepts. In a certain sense, they aimed to become an "art beyond aesthetics," that is to say, an art beyond its immediate sensuous physical qualities. Such artistic conceptuality, however, necessarily requires *some* form of materialization, that is to say, a spatio-temporal, and thus, *aesthetic* presentation — or, as art critics Lucy Lippard and John Chandler remark in their 1968 essay "The Dematerialization of Art": "Dematerialized art is post-aesthetic only in its increasingly non-visual emphases."[1] A concept — or a formula or a mathematical equation — has to be presented, made *present*, and can also always be sensed and experienced aesthetically.

Interestingly, Peter Osborne, a leading specialist in the theory of Conceptual art, suggests that Lippard's notion of dematerialization came not only from "an intuitive sense of the process-based immateriality of the results of the art practices of the mid-1960s," but had its source in the Soviet avant-garde, especially El Lissitzky's 1926 text on "The Future of the Book," which was published in English translation a couple of months before Lippard and Chandler wrote their essay. According to Lissitzky, dematerialization, which he associates with energy, marks the epoch:

> The idea moving the masses today is called materialism, but dematerialisation is the characteristic of the epoch. For example, correspondence grows, so the number of letters, the quantity of writing paper, the mass of material consumed expands, until relieved by the telephone. Again, the network and material of supply grow until they are relieved by radio. Matter diminishes, we dematerialise, sluggish masses of matter are replaced by liberated energy.[2]

The Conceptual art of the 1960s — along with Fluxus and performance etc. — was, to a large extent, motivated by a radical impulse to free art from its institutional confinement (though less so than the historical avant-garde). The relational and socially engaged art of the 1990s and onward, whose agenda or hope was to make art a more democratic and perhaps less material process, may be seen as another opening up of the structures of art toward the spectator and their participation in a "dematerialized," or at least partly dematerialized artwork. It seems, however, that the conditions for these developments, which to a large extent remain within the history of contemporary art, have fundamentally altered. Today, our lifeworld — surrounding and invading the spaces of art, a framework of enunciation that used, perhaps, to grant some relative autonomy — is highly mediated and digitally networked, and has thus seemingly become far more dematerialized, virtual and fluid.[3] Dematerialization now bears on fundamental changes in labor processes, in the economy, and within social relations too; it is not only about de-emphasizing the material aspects of products, artifacts and human activities, but also about substituting digital phenomena for physical things. As historian and media scholar Mark Poster remarks concerning global media,

> networked computing places in the hands of the general population information machines that are linked to their existences in fundamental ways. [...] [T]he assemblage of human and information machine must be accounted for as a phenomenon unprecedented in the array of media technologies, an innovation that is drastically changing the character of culture. For the human/information machine link introduces new configurations of the binaries of space and time, body and mind, subject and object, producer and consumer, indeed all the constituents that form cultures.[4]

And because of this digitization and computerization, of which Jean-François Lyotard already spoke in *The Postmodern Condition* in 1979, media-enabled people all over the globe are now taking part in a new global infrastructure of the senses — an infrastructure that may seem "immaterial," but which is still very much aesthetic, as it decisively informs the ways in which we perceive and experience the world and each other. Today, artistic practices regarding dematerialization have changed from focusing on the development of a critical strategy that reduces commodifiable physical material in favor of ideas and concepts, to critically exploring and disclosing the complexities of the digital society in which we — or at least the large majority of us — live, a society where big data, algorithms and surveillance are put into extensive operation with immense political, social and psychological consequences.

Thus, the conditions for politically engaged art, for questioning the present, have changed, as our present and its temporal quality is not the same. Our experience of the categories of present and presence has changed, and this changing status and experience of presence also affects our relation to artworks and how they operate. Chronological progression has been challenged by anachronic approaches to time that perceive the present as being informed by a multitude of different times and temporalities; not only by the past and the future but also by other times and temporalities on a horizontal or spatial plane, and times and temporalities are now being interconnected at a global scale. "Material" space seems to be overcome by computational technology that, for instance, allows us to talk to each other in so-called real time across vast physical distances, via Skype or FaceTime. The contemporary present is thus composed of a number of interconnected temporalities, "material" as well as "immaterial," and many recent artworks also thematize, or make the material dependency of our seemingly immaterial digital cultures perceptible: server farms, toxic waste, etc.[5]

Our present, or, the contemporary present, is defined by *contemporaneity* — understood as the interconnection of different heterogeneous times, histories and temporalities in the *same* present — and it is defined by contemporaneity as a *condition*.[6] And the formation of our present by an intensified global or planetary interconnection of different times and experiences of time — this condition of contemporaneity — is to be regarded as something historically new; something that makes our present, the present present, qualitatively different from previous presents. Thus, the contemporaneity that the *contemporary* present relates to is not just another period in a narrative of historical development, in which it might be seen as replacing modernity and the modern. Contemporaneity also has to do with changes in our relation to time itself, and changes in the ways in which we exist in time. The plurality of times today not only has to do with a number of times existing at the same time, in parallel to each other, simultaneously. They interconnect, and are brought to bear on, *the same* present, making up a kind of planetary present, and — at least in principle — a globally generalized sharing of time, even though the possibility of taking part in this interconnection and sharing is most unevenly distributed. We seem, therefore, to live in an expanded present in which several temporalities, histories, and times take part in what is perceived as present and as presence.

Our question is how such contemporaneity, and transformations to temporality, are registered and articulated in contemporary art. To be a contemporary work of art is, I suggest, to explore the constitution of the contemporary present, to explore the formation of the present and how something like presence comes into being today. Experiencing something as present now may not necessarily involve its physical or material being-there.

Aspects of contemporaneity may be seen to be thematized in some of the work of Hito Steyerl and Camille Henrot, for instance. Although not in themselves "dematerialized" — but at least technically reproducible — some of the video installations of both artists may be said to negotiate the role of media and computational technologies in the interconnection of times and lifeworlds, and speculate on the impact of the Internet and digitization on the fabric of our everyday lives and our experience of time.[7] Digitization technologies have altered the ways in which images are reproduced and consumed and made a global circulation of images possible. Images — or images of images, as well as texts and sounds — are subject to almost instantaneous global dissemination and access (for instance, via the share functions of various social media sites, accessible on our mobile phones and personal computers). The networked architecture of the Internet, in particular, exposes us to histories and events all over the globe playing out and unfolding in real time. "One may argue that culture is always already mediated (by language). But," as Poster remarked in 2008, "the increasing sophistication, multiplication, and dissemination of information machines change the experience of all culture. Every cultural object now exists in a (potentially) global context."[8]

Thus, "dematerializing" media and computational technology play a highly significant role in shaping the coming into being of contemporaneity, in shaping the temporality of globality itself. Contemporaneity and the role played by digital technology and media are, however, double-edged: what has come, and still comes, into being, is not only a contemporaneity of differences, but also a contemporaneity that allows for synchronization and standardization in the service of globalized capitalism. As material culture scholar Bill Brown remarks:

> The economy shapes our contemporary media landscape, but that economy itself has taken shape — assumed its global spatiality and instantaneity — as a result of new media. Indeed, the psychological, social, and political effects of technological communication have been so profound (and so profoundly internalized by human consciousness) that they often remain imperceptible.[9]

As is well known, Hito Steyerl takes a critical stance toward what circulates as "contemporary art," asserting that: "If contemporary art is the answer, the question is: How can capitalism be made more beautiful?"[10] In the video piece entitled *Duty Free Art* (2015), she speculates on the destruction of time and space and claims that contemporary art functions as a proxy for a common time and space.

The installation thematizes some of the ways in which contemporary art takes part in the global economy. It deals with free-trade zones, where art commodities are bought and sold invisibly and tax free, showing how works of art literally constitute a currency. That art literally constitutes a currency is a point also made by art historian David Joselit in his book *After Art*, where he regards the image explosion of our current globalized — and digitized — society of the spectacle as a *condition* of contemporary art (and architecture), shifting focus from the production and exhibition of artworks to the life and circulation of works outside the closed context of art. That is to say, a shift from discrete individual objects and unique works to their effects in the networks of circulating images, that are working, or at work, in the world. Joselit thus shifts critical attention from the *production* of art to what images *do* when they circulate and enter diverse networks — seeing aesthetic objects as forms crystallizing out of a population of images.

In *Duty Free Art*, the free-trade zones located in, for instance, Geneva, Singapore and Beijing, are presented as the backbone of the transnational art business; they facilitate the redistribution of public property into private hands and are catalysts of global inequality. The piece also makes use of WikiLeaks files to show how the Louvre, British Museum and celebrated architect Rem Koolhaas served the Assad regime as museum planners and gentrifiers in Syria.[11] Like much of her recent work, the video installation *Factory of the Sun*, made for the 56th edition of the Venice Biennale in 2015, for example, can be said to articulate and reflect upon the global circulation of images and the workings of new media realities as well as how digital culture and networked relations, rather than those of place, increasingly mediate social relations and the social imaginary. As Steyerl remarks in a text that is also entitled "Duty-Free Art," the free port art storage facility

> is not only a device realized in one particular location in 3-D space. It is also basically a stack of juridical, logistical, economic, and data-based operations, a pile of platforms mediating between clouds and users via state laws, communication protocols, corporate standards, etc., that interconnect not only via fiber-optic connections but aviation routes as well.[12]

Steyerl is thus trying to articulate how social, human and "analog" layers are interconnected with informational, non-human computational and "digital" layers.

Steyerl draws here upon sociologist and architectural theorist Benjamin Bratton, according to whom smart grids, cloud computing, mobile software and smart cities, universal addressing systems, ubiquitous computing and robotics are not unrelated genres of computation but constitute an aligned and coherent whole, an accidental megastructure in the form of a planetary-scale computing system, which he calls "The Stack."[13] Bratton's notion of the Stack marks the interconnection of all these multiple layers, the interpenetration between digital and analog times, and technological, material and human times — bringing into being a kind of planetary instantaneity, a present in which every*one* and every*thing* takes part. "The Stack" may thus be seen as a way of visualizing the technological infrastructure that enables contemporaneity and the coming together of times on a planetary scale.

The work of Camille Henrot, which anthropologist Haidy Geismar calls an "ethnography of digital experience,"[14] is another artistic example incorporating mediated and digitally networked temporalities, making aspects of digital culture that are often considered to be immaterial aesthetically perceptible — by, for instance, spatially materializing digitally transmitted emails in the large-scale installation *Office of Unreplied Emails* (2016).[15]

Grosse Fatigue, a thirteen-minute video installation, was presented at the 55th Venice Biennale in 2013. The piece tries to tell the story of the universe's creation from a computer desktop — and can be seen as a digital 2-D "immaterial" counterpart to the 3-D installation piece *The Pale Fox* (2014–2015), which comprises a great number of material objects. Based on the collections and databases of the Smithsonian Institute in Washington D.C. and inspired by the concept of "encyclopedia" — "The Encyclopedic Palace" was the title of the 55th Venice Biennale — it forms a dizzying narrative about the universe by mixing scientific histories with creation stories belonging to various religions, traditions and cultures.[16] The work unfolds through a succession of fluid juxtapositions and superimpositions of still and moving images taken and filmed in the Smithsonian's collection, as well as at other locations, or found on the Internet, which appear in a series of pop-ups and open windows on a computer screen. The succession of windows and folders opening and closing on the screen is accompanied by minimal hip-hop electronic percussion music by Joakim and a poetic text written in collaboration with Jacob Bromberg and spoken by Akwetey Orraca-Tetteh.

The rhythmic superimpositions, juxtapositions and associations of images and words constitute an "intuitive unfolding of knowledge" that functions at the same time as a kind of meta-reflection on the desire to universalize knowledge, to grasp and comprehend an infinite mass of information that will necessarily always remain in excess, and the work thus relates the vastness of the universe to the expansive arena of the Internet, signaling the impossibility of any search for universalization or a unifying system of knowledge.[17] The windows upon windows of information and images — all appearing as if found on the Internet — create an apparent *mise en abyme* that questions the status and value of artifacts and objecthood in the age of digitization and dematerialization. The very medium of this breathless excursion through the history — or histor*ies* — of the universe, the medium in which all this information and all these "dematerialized objects" are made virtually present, forms, in itself, an integral and omnipresent part of our everyday environment. The stories and their objects are available at our fingertips, on the screen of any computer, tablet or mobile phone, anytime and anywhere. The piece thus also points to the way in which the assemblage of human and informational machines that Poster, along with Bernard Stiegler, and many others, have theorized, occasions transcendence of bodily or phenomenologically grounded senses of linear temporality.

Interestingly in this context, philosopher of media and communication Marshall McLuhan, with reference to the influence of media on our perception of time and history, declared in 1969 that: "Just as there was no history when there was no linear time sense, so there is post-history now when everything that ever was in the world becomes simultaneously present to our consciousness."[18] According to McLuhan, linear history began with writing and ended with television.

The Internet, in particular, can be seen as a medium of contemporaneity, and in media archaeologist Wolfgang Ernst's development of McLuhan's media theory the temporal message of digital communication media consists in temporal deferral: "from" what he calls "*live on tape* to media content *on demand*."[19] According to Ernst, the immediate, instantaneous accessibility of digital communication media — this media content on demand — implies a "tactilization" of what used to be mass media broadcasting, in the form of "an almost *haptic* access to media time" (there are a lot of hands trying to grasp the things presented in Henrot's video), but, at the same time, in digital communication media any clear perception of the border between what is present and what is past is dissolved, and it becomes almost impossible to distinguish between what is transmitted *live* and what is collected from the archive.[20]

This means that our ideas and experiences of time are increasingly media-based and influenced by the temporal logic of media and communication technologies, that is to say, by an accelerated "mediated time," which creates a sense of planetarily interconnected instantaneity.[21] In that sense, the communication platform the World Wide Web also operates as a kind of time factory. *Real-time web* and communication practices such as *instant messaging* — making use of technologies that permit users to receive information as soon as it is published — constitute a temporal field where the message of the medium is "immediacy serving to create the illusion of a pseudo-co-presence."[22] The Internet, therefore, is not only the space of an enormous global generalized archive, but also of a technical compression of time, because of an extremely accelerated processing of information which creates an experience of what appears as *co-presence*. This means that communication — in Ernst's compelling analysis — is not primarily about exchange of meaning, but about time-sharing, about being present at the same time and sharing the same temporality.

As I already said, these digital communication technologies and the Internet can, of course, pave the way for homogenization of perceptual and temporal experience and synchronization in the service of capitalism,[23] for "creating and tearing apart communities loosely linked by shared attention deficit," as Steyerl puts it.[24] But there is also a potential in this global co-presence and becoming present to each other, this "generalized sharing of time" constituted by the co-presence of differences and otherness. To be contemporary, art today must articulate the condition of contemporaneity — along with the potentials and effects this contemporaneity might bring into being.

I will not — to conclude — pretend to be qualified to enter into nuanced discussion of the differences between art fairs and biennials, but I do think that the biennial form is still able to provide one of the spaces where we can get a sense of contemporaneity, a sense of the temporal complexity occasioned by the coming together of *different* times, temporalities and experiences of time.[25] I do not think we should only deplore the institutions of contemporary art creating a new kind of cultural space, "dedicated," in the words of Peter Osborne, "to the exploration through art of similarities and differences between geo-politically diverse forms of social experience that have only recently begun to be represented within the parameters of a common world."[26] Osborne sees the new international biennials — and I guess this to a large extent pertains to art fairs too — as "emblems of capital's capacity to cross borders, and to accommodate and appropriate cultural differences. Art labor," he claims, "is variable cultural capital."[27] The idea of contemporaneity, understood as the "projection of the temporal unity of the present across the planet," is grounded in the interpenetration of social forms and cultural clusters by capital and their consequent interconnection and dependency, but the experience and cultural significance of contemporaneity cannot merely be reduced to the workings of global capital — and we should also remark that the work of many of the contemporary artists, worthy of the name, also according to Osborne, for instance Walid Raad and Robert Smithson, often appear at biennials.[28] The form of the biennial is often the context in which their work is made public, it is what provides the background from which they stand out.[29]

With the dematerializing endeavors of Conceptual art of the '60s and '70s in mind, one might say that some of the most interesting contemporary art explores the possibilities for installing a social imagination beyond capitalism in conditions of contemporaneity, which, to a large extent, are the consequence of the development of capitalism, without being reducible to it. Perhaps we should take a critical point of departure in the interconnections of the material and the immaterial, rather than letting these be defined exclusively by the logic of capital.

1 In *Art International*, 12.2 (February 1968): 31–36, 33.

2 El Lissitzky, as quoted by Peter Osborne in "The Kabakov Effect: 'Moscow Conceptualism' in the History of Contemporary Art," in *The Postconceptual Condition* (London: Verso, 2017), 167–183: 173.

3 I draw here upon the text accompanying the exhibition "Fluidity" at the Kunstverein in Hamburg, January 30–April 10, 2016, curated by Nina Möntmann et al., accessed January 27, 2022, https://www.kunstverein.de/projekte/fluidity.

4 Mark Poster, "Global Media and Culture," *New Literary History*, 39.3 (Summer 2008): 685–703, 689.

5 Cf. also Christiane Paul, "The Myth of Immateriality: Presenting and Preserving New Media," in *MediaArtHistories*, ed. Oliver Grau (Cambridge, MA: MIT Press, 2007), 251–274: 252, regarding the material components of digital dematerialization: "[I]mmateriality is not a fiction but an important element of new media that has profound effects on artistic practice, cultural production, and reception, as well as the curatorial process. At the same time, this immateriality cannot be separated from the material components of the digital medium. A more productive approach to understanding this tension may be Tiziana Terranova's definition of immateriality as 'links between materialities.'"

6 Cf. Peter Osborne, *Anywhere or Not at All: Philosophy of Contemporary Art* (London: Verso, 2013); Terry Smith, "Contemporary Art and Contemporaneity," *Critical Inquiry* 32.4 (Summer 2006): 681–707, as well as his *What Is Contemporary Art?* (Chicago: University of Chicago Press, 2009), and *The Contemporary Composition* (Berlin: Sternberg Press, 2016).

7 Cf. Nick Aikens, *Too Much World: The Films of Hito Steyerl*, ed. Van Abbemuseum (Berlin: Sternberg Press, 2014). As Hito Steyerl remarks in an essay titled "The Terror of Total Dasein: Economies of Presence in the Art Field," the changes in our technologies of communication also affect our understanding of the value and importance of *human* presence: "In the age of the reproducibility of almost everything physical, human presence is one of the few things that cannot be multiplied indefinitely, an asset with some inbuilt scarcity [...] Interestingly enough, the demand for total presence and immediacy [in the art field] arises from mediation; or more precisely from the growing range of tools of communication, including the internet. It is not opposed to technology but its consequence. [...] The point is that technology gives you tools for remote and delayed presence, so that physical presence is just one option and probably the scarcest one." In *Duty Free Art: Art in the Age of Planetary Civil War* (London: Verso, 2017), 21–30: 23–24.

8 Poster, "Global Media and Culture," 698.

9 Bill Brown, "Materiality," in *Critical Terms for Media Studies*, eds. W.J.T. Mitchell & Mark B.N. Hansen (Chicago: University of Chicago Press, 2010), 49–63: 59.

10 Hito Steyerl, "Politics of Art: Contemporary Art and the Transition to Post-Democracy," in *e-flux journal*, #21 (December 2010), accessed January 27, 2022, http://www.e-flux.com/journal/politics-of-art-contemporary-art-and-the-transition-to-post-democracy/.

11 My descriptions draw heavily upon the sheets made for Hito Steyerl's exhibition "Left to Our Own Devices" at the KOW gallery in Berlin 17 September 17–December 5, 2015.

12 Hito Steyerl, "Duty-Free Art," in *e-flux journal*, #63 (March 2015), accessed January 27, 2022, http://www.e-flux.com/journal/duty-free-art/.

13 Benjamin H. Bratton, "The Black Stack," in *e-flux journal*, #53 (March 2014), accessed January 27, 2022, http://www.e-flux.com/journal/53/59883/the-black-stack/.

14 Haidy Geismar, "On Digital Anthropology," in Camille Henrot, "Days Are Dogs," in *Palais. Le magazine du Palais de Tokyo* (2017), 127–129: 127.

15 In an interview in relation to her recent exhibition "Days Are Dogs," at the Palais de Tokyo in Paris, Henrot remarks: "Digital culture is creating a relationship to time that, even as it is shared on a much greater scale, is also more subjective." Camille Henrot interviewed by Daria de Beauvais, "Dogs are always hungry," in Camille Henrot, "Days Are Dogs," in *Palais. Le magazine du Palais de Tokyo* (2017), 15–18: 15.
16 The collections and databases in question are the Smithsonian Archives of American Art, National Air and Space Museum, and National Museum of Natural History.
17 Cf. Camille Henrot, "The Grasp of Totalizing Systems," in *Art in America* 110:6 (June/July 2013), 44–45.
18 Marshall McLuhan, *Counterblast* (New York: Harcourt, Brace & World, 1969), 122, as quoted by Wolfgang Ernst, "Printed Letters, Acoustic Space, Real Time Internet: The Message of Current Communication Media, Deciphered with (and Beyond) McLuhan," in *SITE* 33 (2013), 197–212: 206.
19 Ernst, "Printed Letters," 202ff. In the following, I paraphrase these pages.
20 Ibid., 202.
21 Cf. Helga Nowotny, "Eigenzeit Revisited," keynote lecture at the conference *100 Years of Now* at Haus der Kulturen der Welt (September 30, 2015), accessed January 27, 2022, https://hkw.de/en/programm/projekte/veranstaltung/ p_119626.php, regarding "media-based Eigenzeit."
22 Ernst, "Printed Letters," 203.
23 In particular through the mass reception of hyperindustrialized temporal objects (audiovisual products, including movies, television programs, popular music, video clips and the like), separating, isolating, and neutralizing individuals who are thus cut off from participating in the exchange of symbols and meaning. Cf. Bernard Stiegler, *De la misère symbolique I-II* (Paris: Galilée, 2004–2005).
24 Hito Steyerl, "Too Much World: Is the Internet Dead?" in *e-flux journal*, #49 (November 2013), accessed January 27, 2022, http://www.e-flux.com/journal/too-much-world-is-the-internet-dead/.
25 Terry Smith spells out the differences between biennials and art fairs in "Biennials/Art Fairs in the Exhibitionary Complex," in *Double Trouble in Exhibiting the Contemporary: Art Fairs and Shows*, eds. Cristina Baldacci et al. (Milan: Scalpendi Editore, 2020), 23–45.
26 Osborne, *Anywhere or Not at All*, 27.
27 Peter Osborne, "Contemporary Art Is Postconceptual Art," Public Lecture, Fondazione Antonio Ratti, Villa Sucota, Como, (9 July 2010), 9, accessed January 27, 2022, https://api.fondazioneratti.org/assets/PDFs/XVI-CSAV_Lectures/Leggi-il-testo-della-conferenza-di-Peter-Osborne-in-PDF1.pdf.
28 Ibid., 7. Osborne mainly focuses on the damaging dimension of contemporaneity, i.e. on synchronization and presentism, whereas Terry Smith, for instance, in his analysis, sees a potential, reserving room for a co-existence of different temporalities and the possibility of "planetary thinking," cf. the references in note 6 as well as Terry Smith, *Art to Come: Histories of Contemporary Art* (Durham, NC: Duke University Press, 2019).
29 In an interview with *artnet* in 2016, founder of the Berlin Biennale and then director of PS1, Klaus Biesenbach, talked about mistaking: "the art market for what art, the art world and art history really is," and defended the continued relevance of biennials, stating: "Perhaps these large shows also are the occasions for which new relevant work is produced and seen in relation to and at the same time with other relevant art work." See https://news.artnet.com/exhibitions/klaus-biesenbach-making-berlin-biennale-506594, accessed January 27, 2022. All the aspects of the experience economy and the celebrity focus of the contemporary art world aside, this is a point of view that I find it difficult to disagree with.

A–B
Hito Steyerl
Duty Free Art, 2015

C–D
Hito Steyerl
Factory of the Sun, 2015

E
Camille Henrot
Office of Unreplied Emails, 2016

F–G
Camille Henrot
The Pale Fox, 2014

H–J
Camille Henrot
Grosse Fatigue, 2013

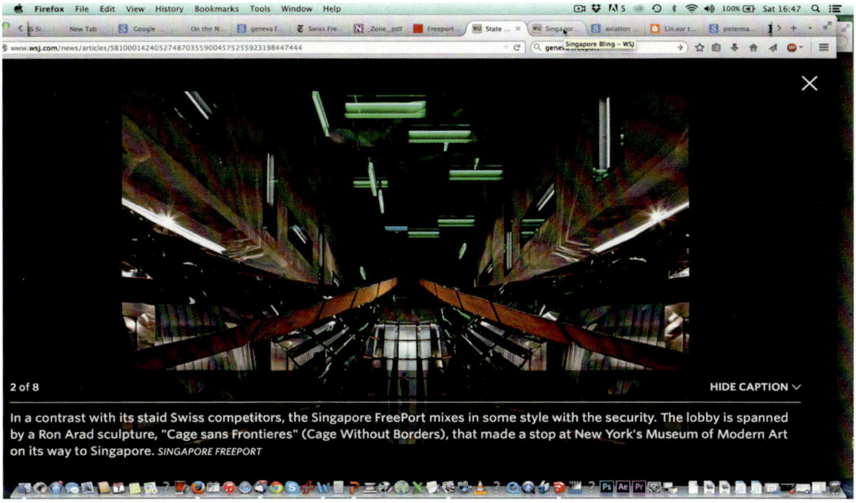
Firefox File Edit View History Bookmarks Tools Window Help
www.wsj.com/news/articles/SB10001424052748703559004575255923198447444
Singapore Bling - WSJ
2 of 8
HIDE CAPTION
In a contrast with its staid Swiss competitors, the Singapore FreePort mixes in some style with the security. The lobby is spanned by a Ron Arad sculpture, "Cage sans Frontieres" (Cage Without Borders), that made a stop at New York's Museum of Modern Art on its way to Singapore. SINGAPORE FREEPORT

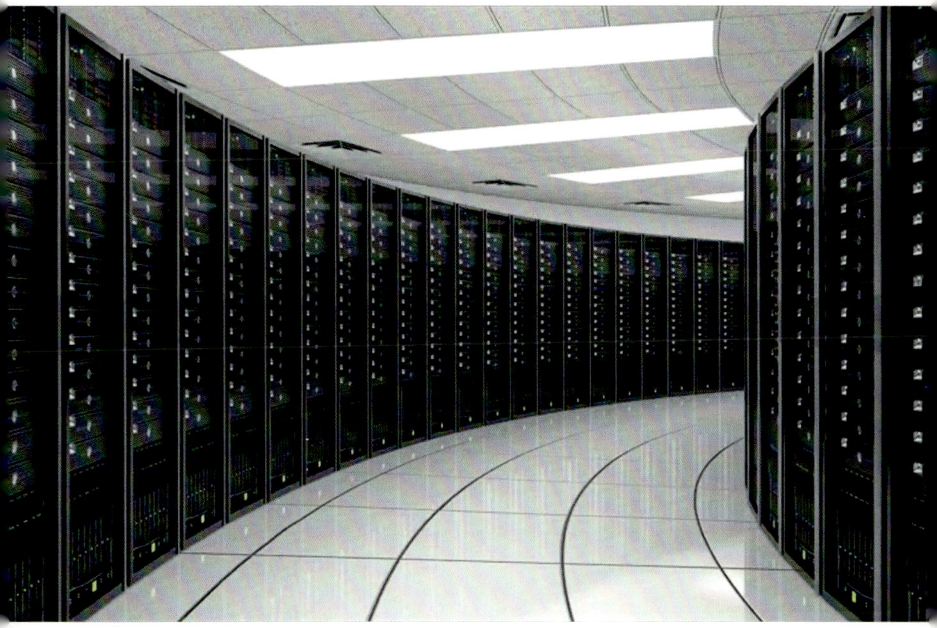

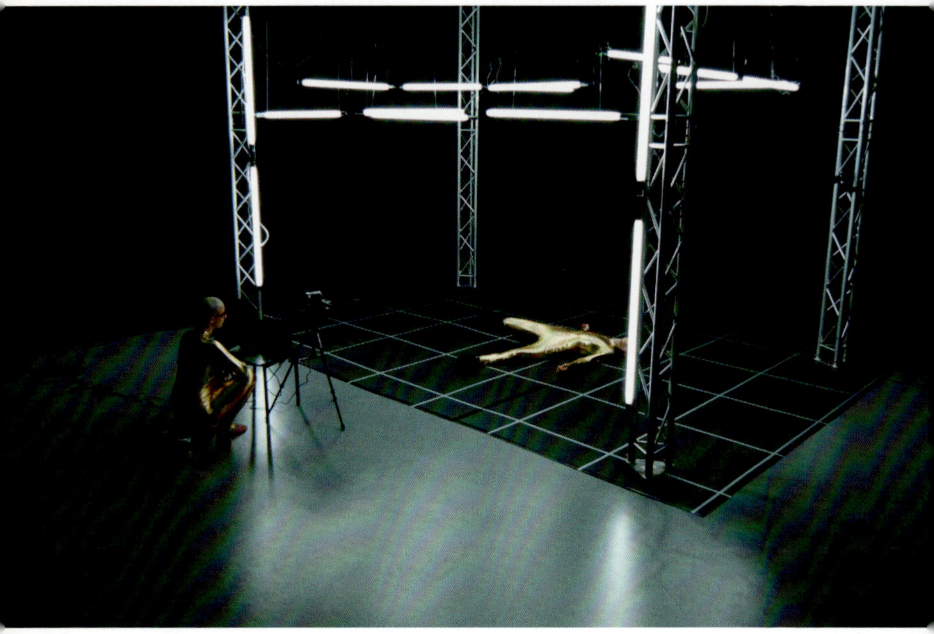

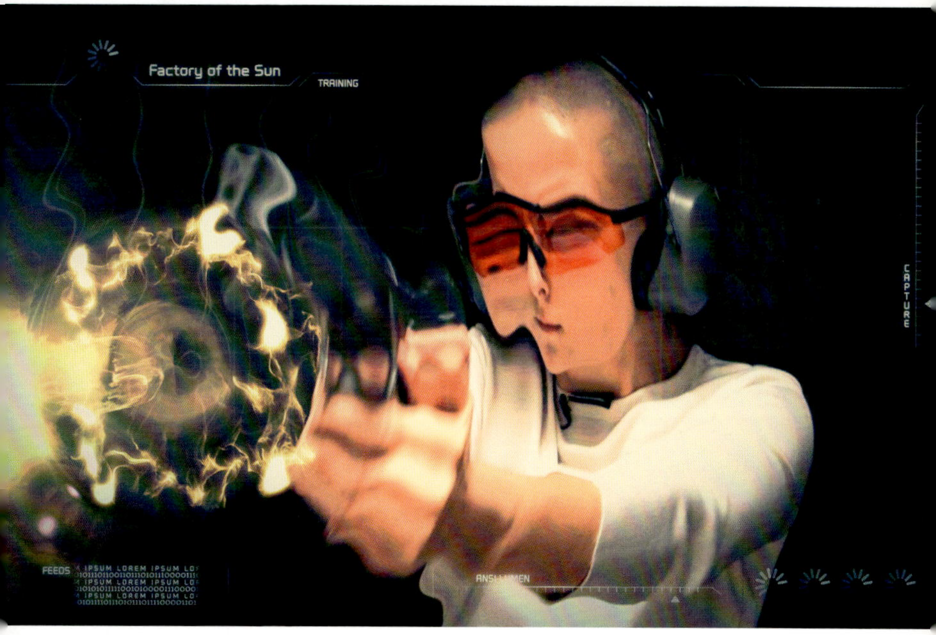
Factory of the Sun
TRAINING
CAPTURE
FEEDS

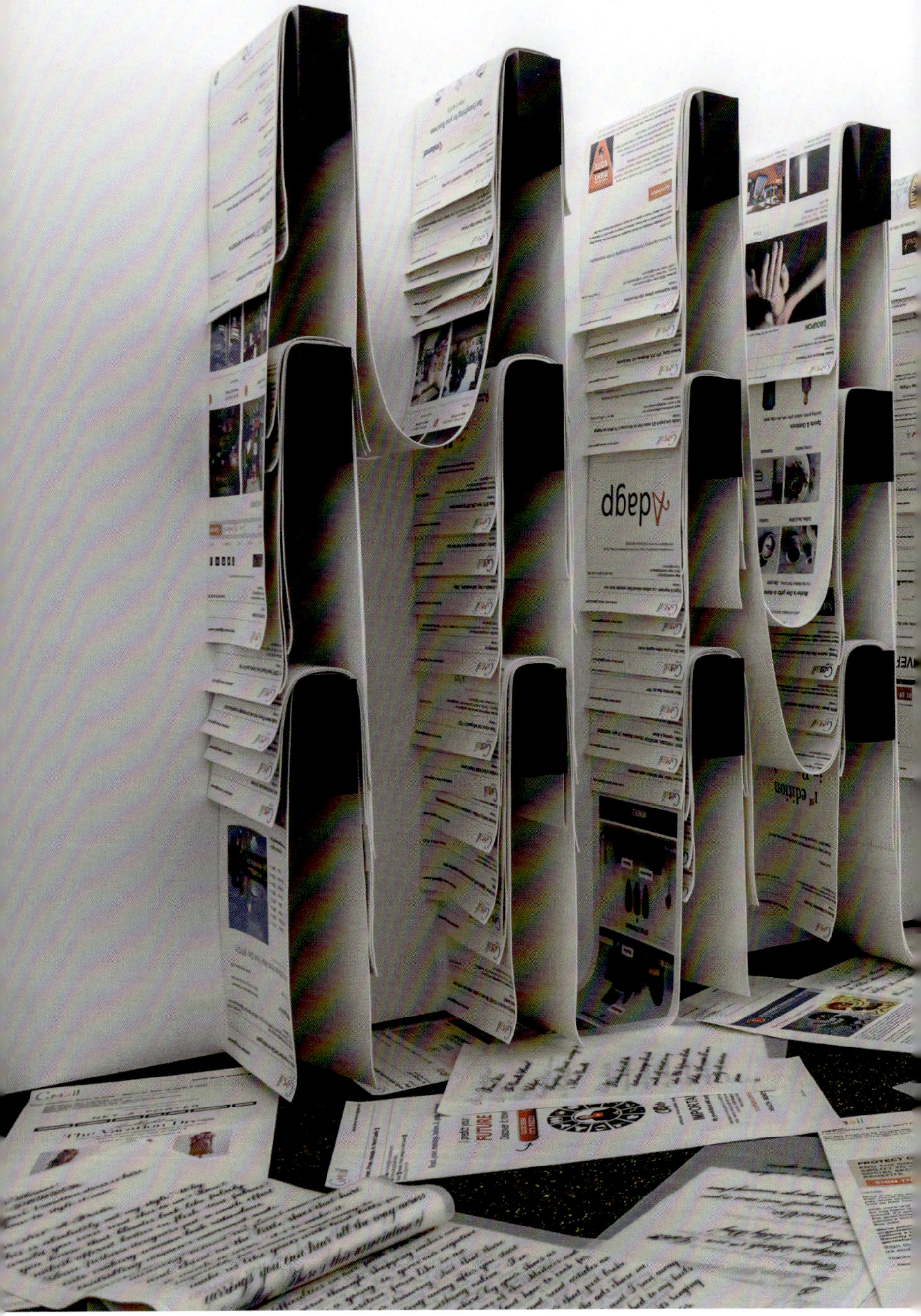

E Camille Henrot

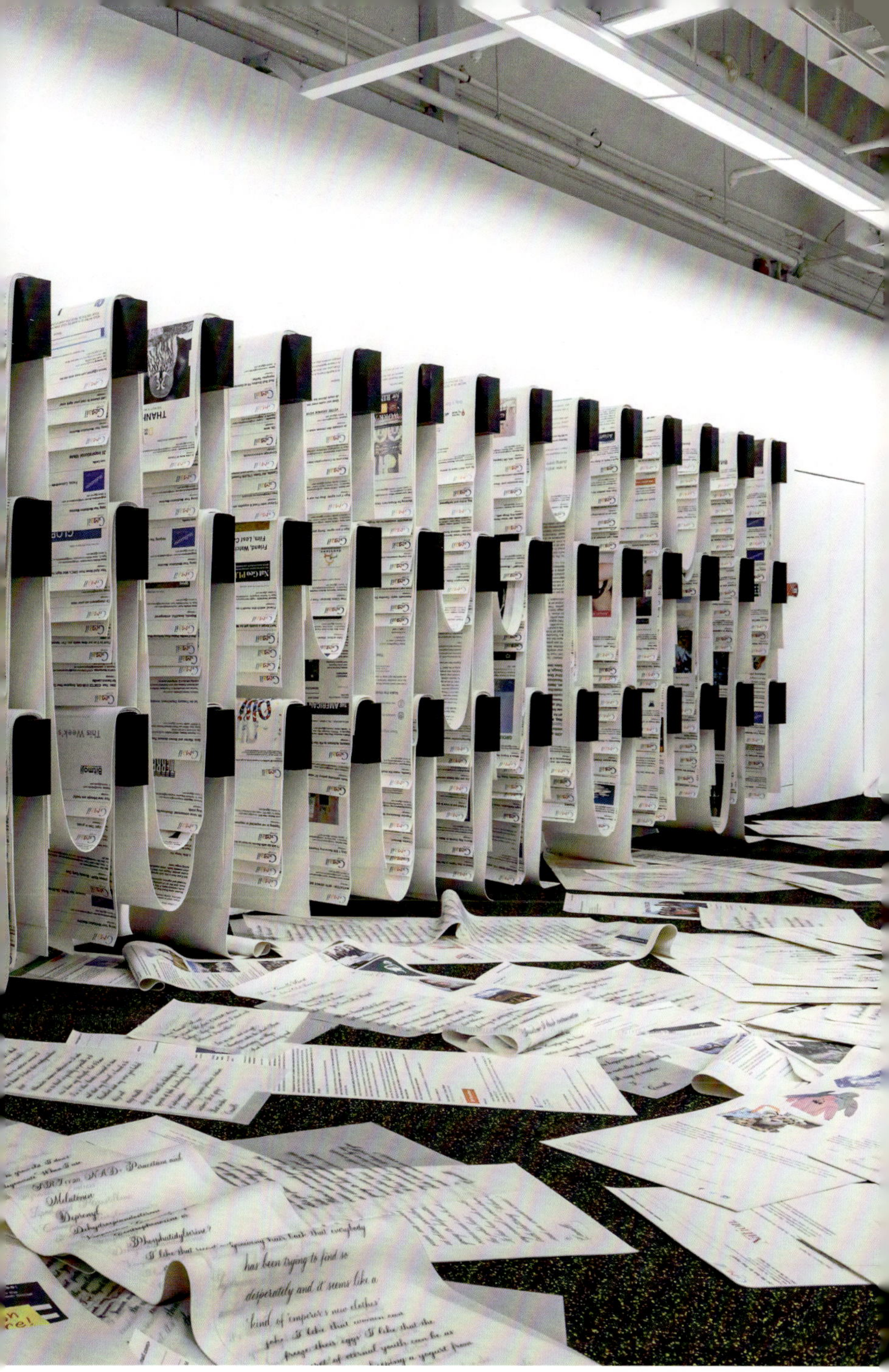
This Week's
has been trying to find so
desperately and it seems like a
kind of emperor's new clothes

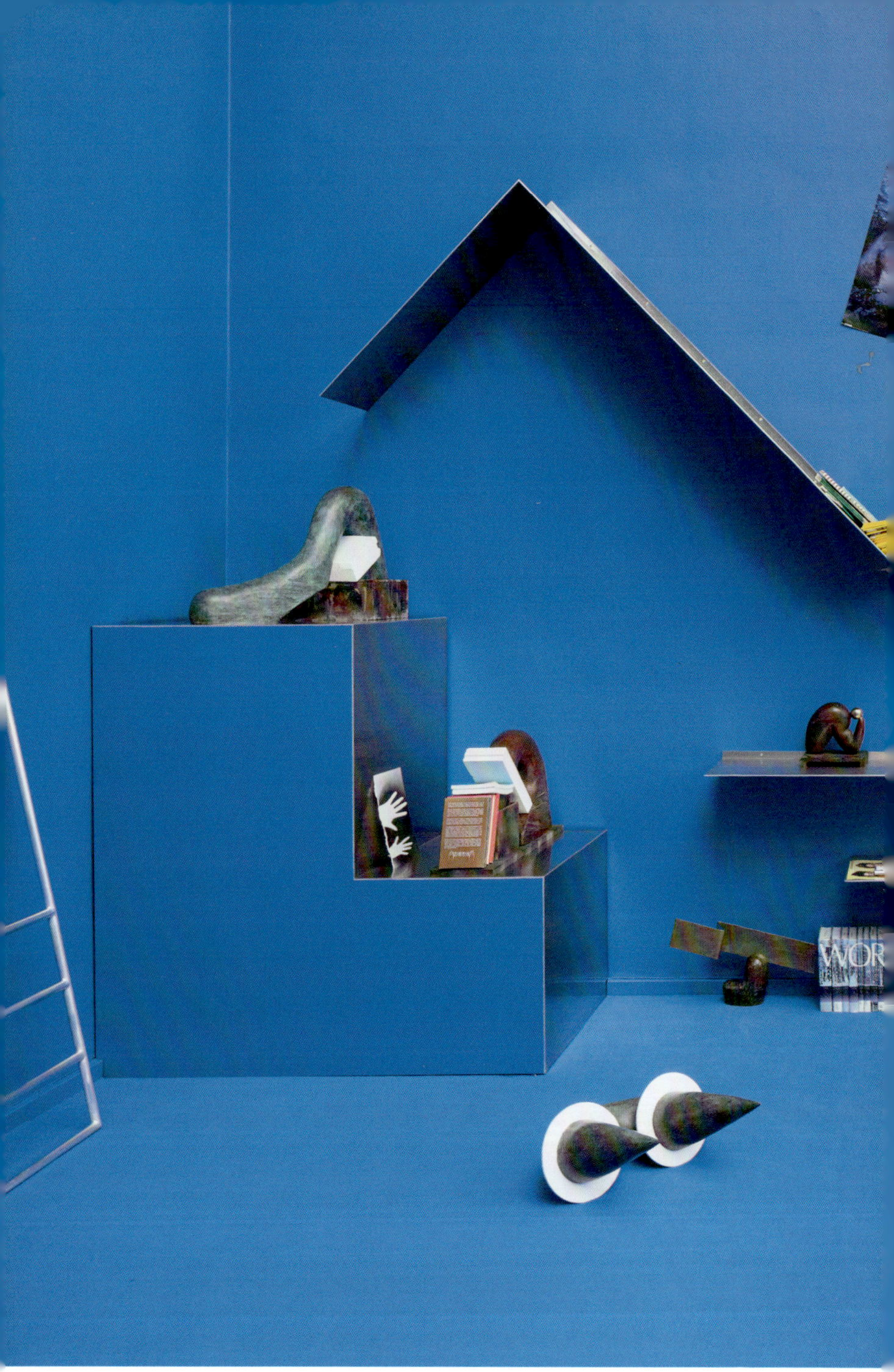

F Camille Henrot

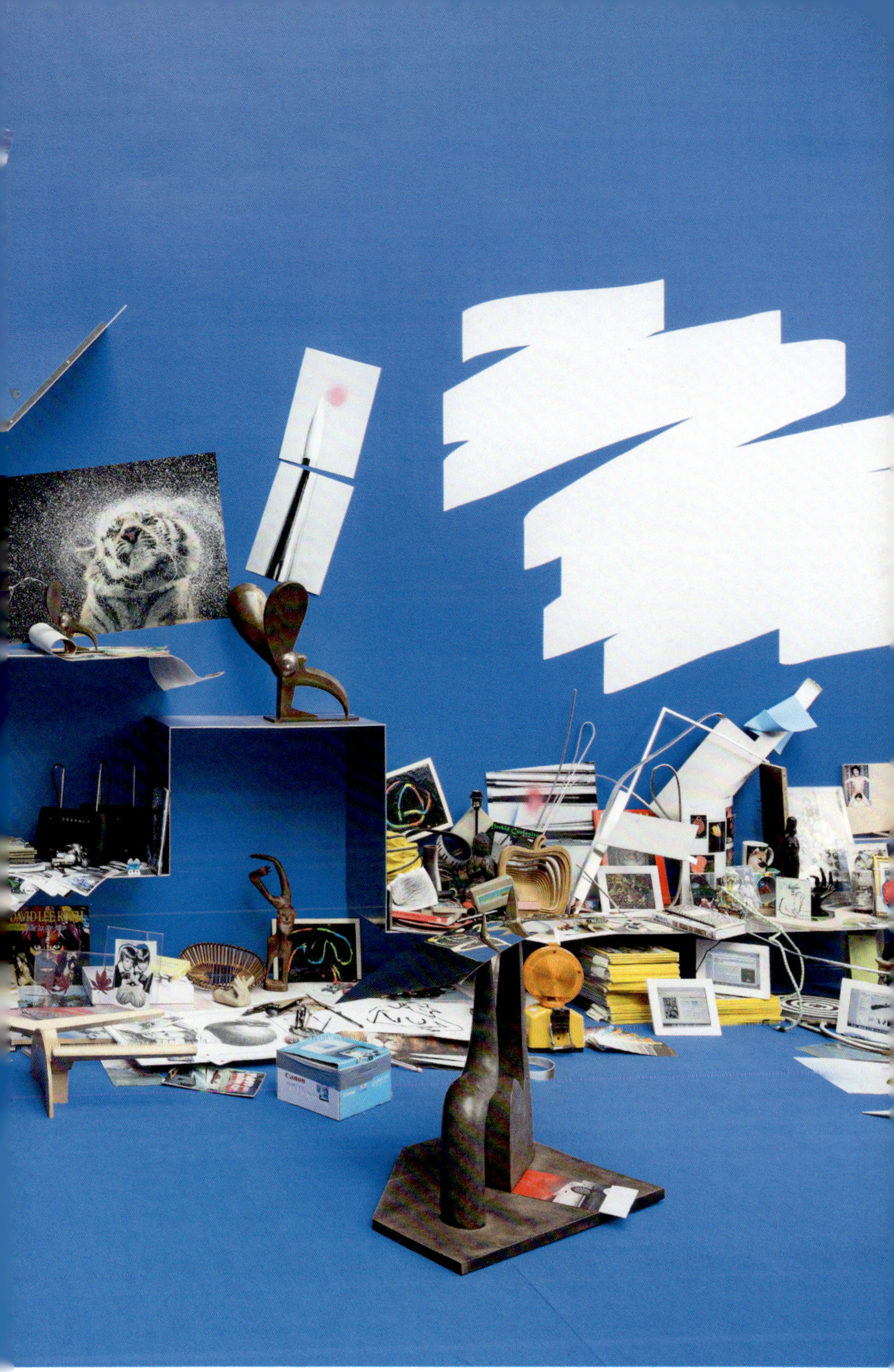

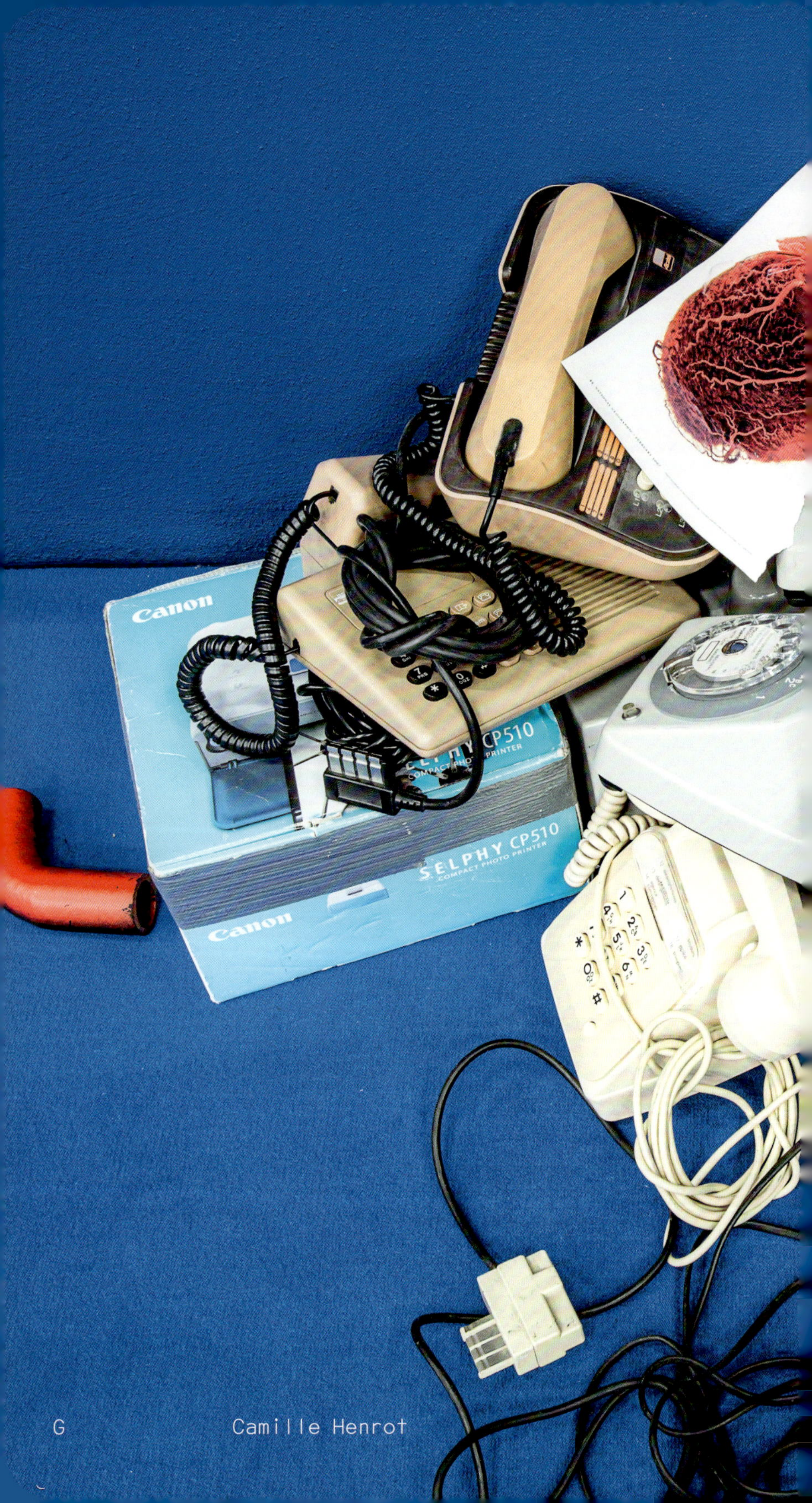
Canon
SELPHY CP510
COMPACT PHOTO PRINTER
Canon

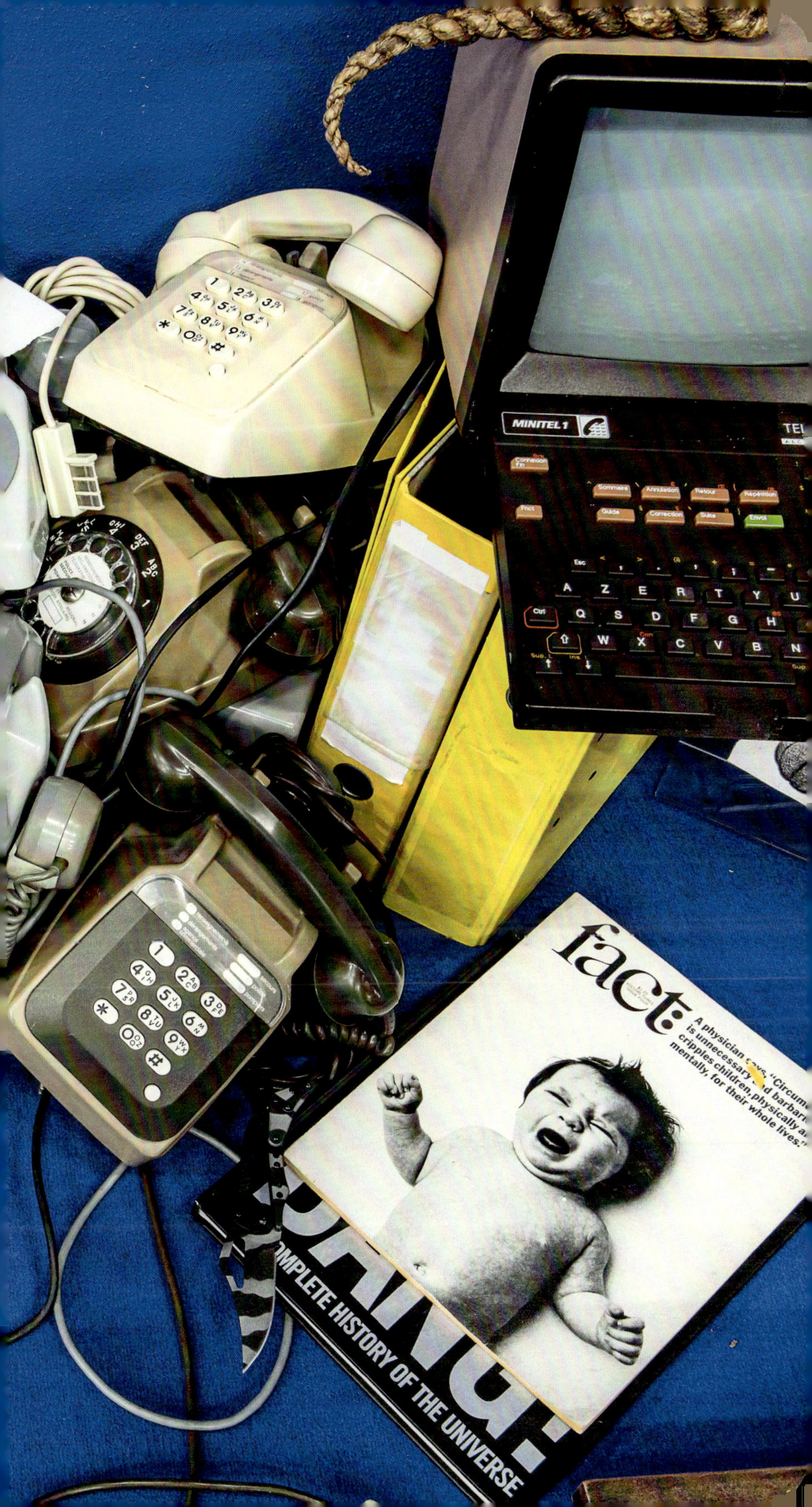
MINITEL 1
Sommaire
Annulation
Retour
Répétition
Guide
Correction
Suite
Envoi
fact:
HISTORY OF THE UNIVERSE

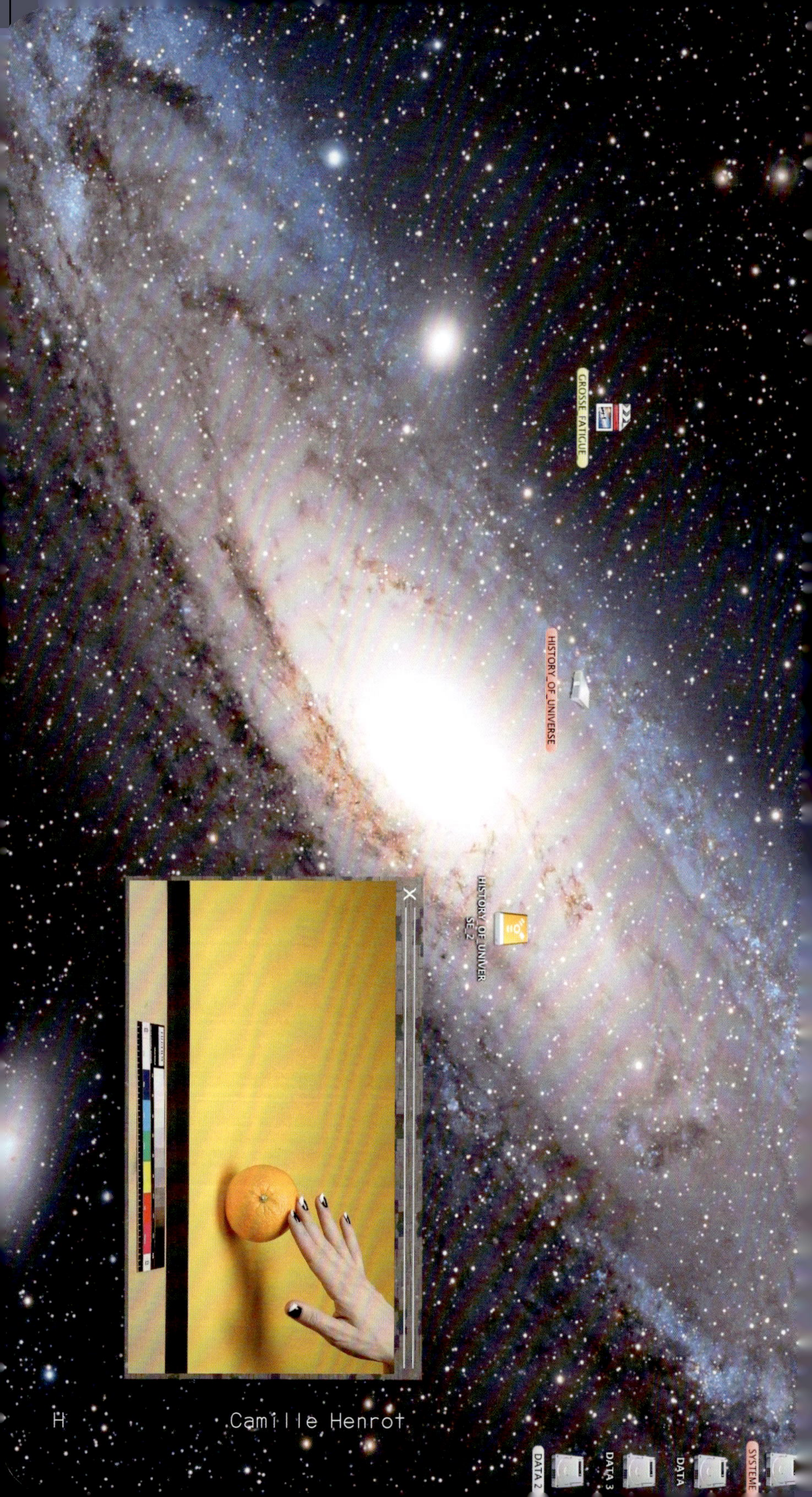
GROSSE_FATIGUE
HISTORY_OF_UNIVERSE
HISTORY_OF_UNIVERSE_2
SYSTEME
DATA
DATA 3
DATA 2

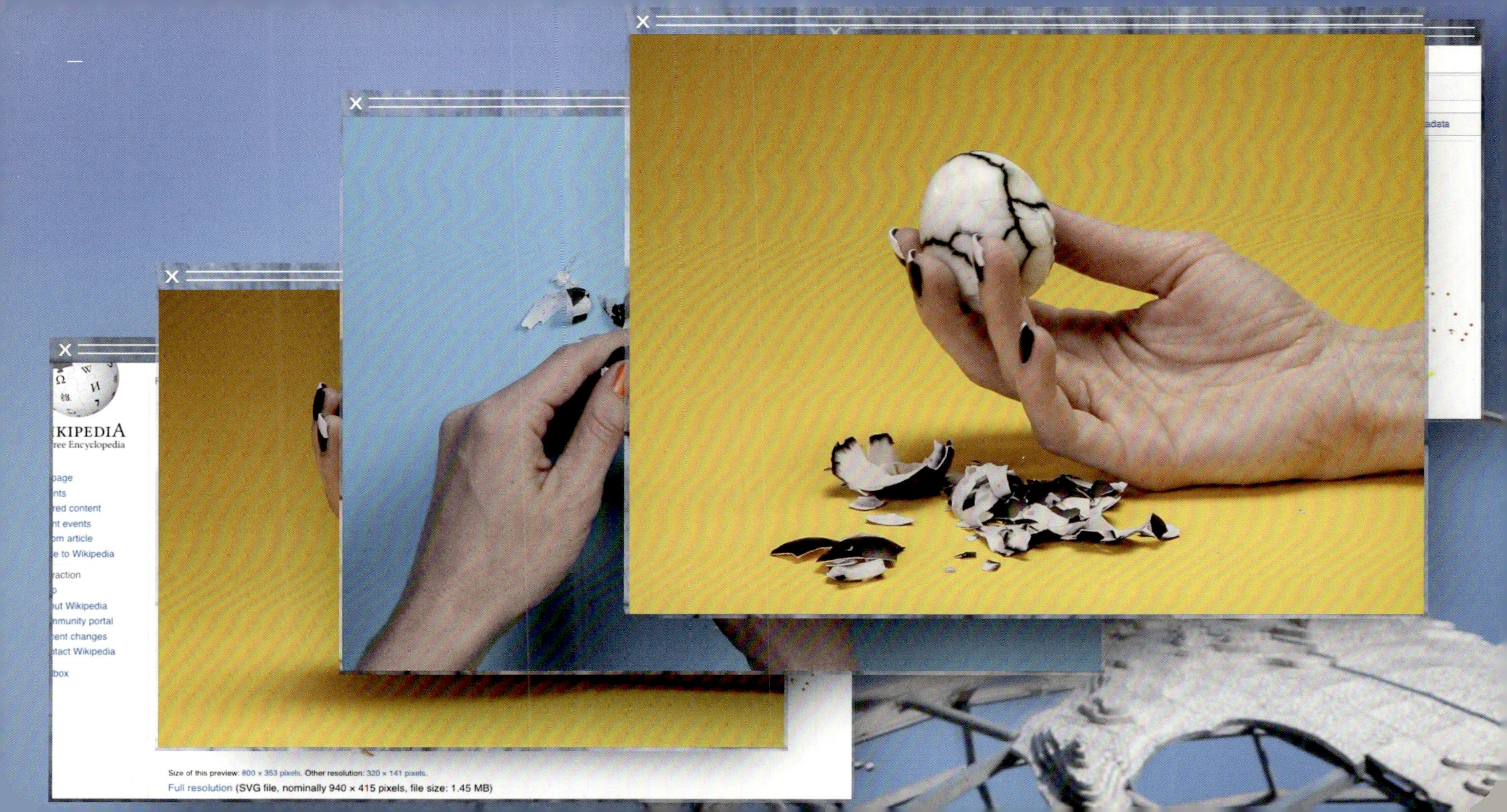

IKIPEDIA
ree Encyclopedia
page
nts
red content
nt events
om article
e to Wikipedia
raction
ut Wikipedia
nmunity portal
ent changes
tact Wikipedia
box
Size of this preview: 800 × 353 pixels. Other resolution: 320 × 141 pixels.
Full resolution (SVG file, nominally 940 × 415 pixels, file size: 1.45 MB)
adata

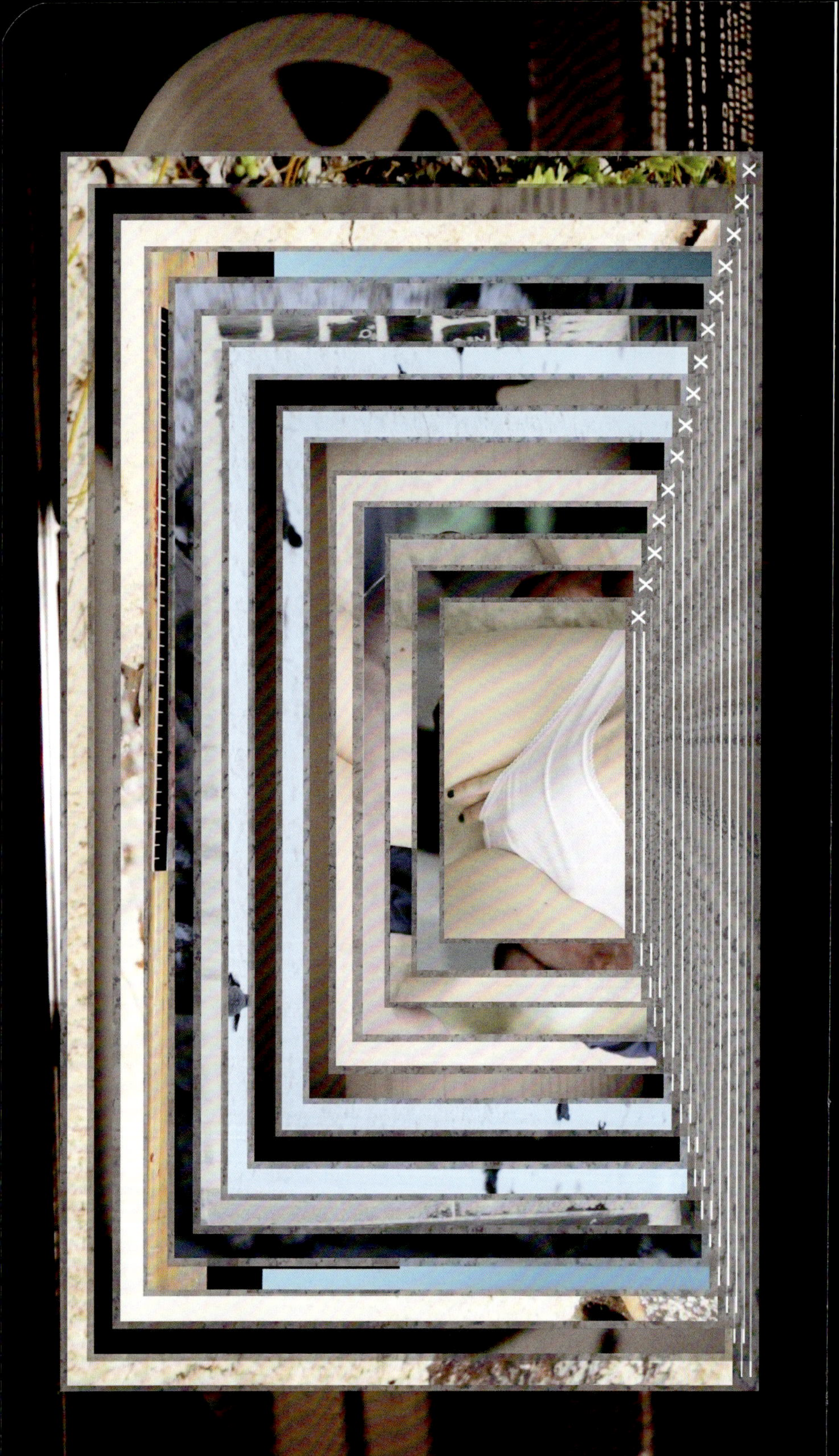

J Camille Henrot

Anachrony, Contemporaneity, and Historical Imagination

Chapter 6

An anachronistic manner of encountering actuality need not necessarily miss out on what is most present today.
— Jacques Derrida[1]

If we bear in mind Giorgio Agamben's observation that "every culture is first and foremost a particular experience of time"[2] — which I understand as a particular experience of what is operative in the present, in the very constitution of the present, thus also a particular experience of which parts of the past that are shared — then the interconnection of different times, temporalities and histories, i.e. the condition of contemporaneity itself, fundamentally challenges ways that time and history have been experienced throughout (post) modernity.

With reference to what might be called an "anachronic" exhibition curated by Georges Didi-Huberman, I would like to elaborate on the notion of contemporaneity discussed throughout this book, and how this relates to the end of a certain history of art, as theorized by art historians and theorists such as Yves Michaud, Arthur C. Danto, Hans Belting, Nicolas Bourriaud, and Didi-Huberman himself. At the same time, I also criticize the ahistorical notion of the contemporary as an "untimely" *person* or *subject* who is capable of entering into a disjunctive or anachronistic relationship with their own time, as Agamben suggests. The overall aim is to make an argument for what I call "the contemporary contemporary" as the point of departure for any anachronic relationship with time today; and as the inescapable point of departure for any possible historical imagination.

When discussing the art historical move from modern to contemporary art, philosopher and art critic Arthur C. Danto explains that his famous declaration, of the end of art, should be understood as the death of *a certain history* of art, namely the linear and teleological one, where each era builds upon and develops from the previous era:

> It was not my view that there would be no more art, which "death" certainly implies, but that whatever art there was to be would be made without benefit of a reassuring sort of narrative in which it was seen as the appropriate next stage in the story. What had come to an end was that narrative but not the subject of the narrative.[3]

He then quotes art historian Hans Belting: "Contemporary art manifests an awareness of a history of art but no longer carries it forward."[4] Thus, Danto employs the notion of the contemporary to describe an art historical period in which there no longer are periods or unifying traits, or, rather, contemporary art does not designate a period, but a post-historical era in which there are no more periods, no more progress to the grand art historical teleology, where each era develops from the preceding one: Renaissance, Baroque, Neoclassicism, Romanticism, Realism, Impressionism, etc.

Danto claims contemporary art to be post-historical art. But this idea about art now being post-historical may not only pertain to contemporary art. A significant artwork or artistic practice — we need not confine ourselves to delimited individual objects — not only changes the way we see the work produced subsequently but also influences how we conceive of the work that came before it. Art after the end of the teleological history of art therefore also changes our relation to the art that is imagined to belong to that history. It is not only contemporary art that is post-historical, it is also the artworks that the historical narrative of chronological progression was based upon. Contemporary art questions the art historical narrative that has been established as the interpretive framework of the practice in which it takes part, rendering this narrative obsolete, or at least deficient, not only with regard to itself, but with regard to works of art in general and at all times. The art historical narrative is dismantled by its own subject. It seems, therefore, that we may not yet have learned the full lesson of Danto's art historical observation: What are its consequences for our experience of time? What are the consequences for the way we do art history? And for our historical interpretation of the world in general?

In 2016–2017, Didi-Huberman curated the exhibition "Soulèvements" (Uprisings) at Jeu de Paume in Paris, and in the leaflet accompanying the exhibition he muses over what makes us rise up, stating:

> It is also *forms*: *forms* through which all of this will be able to appear and become visible in the public space. Images, therefore; images to which this exhibition is devoted. Images of all times, from Goya to today, and of all kinds: paintings, drawings, sculptures, films, photographs, videos, installations, documents, etc. They interact in dialogue beyond all differences of their times.[5]

Rather than showing and communicating the results of a research project, "Soulèvements" was a phase in an ongoing research project. After the show at Jeu de Paume, it travelled to Museu Nacional d'Art de Catalunya in Barcelona, Museo de la Universidad nacional de tres de febrero in Buenos Aires, Sesc in São Paulo, MUAC Museo Universitario Arte Contemporáneo in Mexico City, and Galerie de l'UQÀM in Montreal, undergoing "site-specific" transformations along the way. It arranged uprisings in five sections, whereby it re-articulated the very diversified image material in new constellations or narratives, which, in a sense, disregarded the temporal and spatial distance of the origin of the images in question. Across geographical places and historical situations — from the French Revolution to the Arab Spring — it thus explores uprisings: I. with elements (unleashed); II. with gestures (intense); III. with words (exclaimed); IV. with conflicts (flared up); and V. with desires (indestructible).[6] What interests me is this "dialogue beyond all differences of their times," or what I see as an activation of a number of different images — articulating or giving form to uprisings that took place at different times and in different places — to take part in the same present, constituted by the exhibition. The following is an endeavor to address some of the theoretical issues relating to time and history occasioned by Didi-Huberman's exhibition rather than an analysis of the exhibition itself, which I see as a way to make art history after "art history" in the traditional sense, and as a way to practice historical imagination. It should be kept in mind, however, that it is a particular understanding of history that Danto's prefix, "post," refers to; it is still possible — and, as should hopefully be clear, urgently necessary — to act and to think historically. Before I return to some of the temporal implications of Didi-Huberman's exhibition and his concept of anachronism, I would like to touch upon a couple of other theoretical challenges to the ideas of unity and progression in traditional art historical thinking that have to do with the absence of generally shared aesthetic criteria and with formal and medial discontinuity.

Around the same time as Danto and Belting, that is, in the late 1990s, philosopher and former director of École nationale supérieure des Beaux-Arts in Paris, Yves Michaud, in his book *La crise de l'art contemporain* (The crisis of contemporary art) also questions the validity of a certain interpretive framework for art.[7] Thus, the crisis that Michaud detects in contemporary art is of the concept and representation of art, rather than in contemporary art practices themselves. In parallel to Danto's Hegelian declaration of the end of a particular art historical narrative, he declares "the end of the utopia of art," which refers to a universal human community of taste, largely based on the Kantian concept of *sensus communis*.[8] Today, there are no universal aesthetic criteria — if there ever were — and art, in reality, only gives rise to relatively small and limited communities of taste. Any group and any individual are endowed with a right to pass a legitimate judgment of taste, and this legitimization of any aesthetic judgment occasions a "multicultural" fragmentation of taste. In other words, the idea of the communicative function of art and a universal community of taste has been challenged by a democratic generalized pluralism or "multiculturalism" that does not profess the ideal of a universal community, which was a cornerstone of modern art and of Kantian inspired aesthetic theory. This democratization and pluralism also challenges the universalizing art historical narrative. Once the idea of a universal community of taste is dismantled, the history of *the objects* of taste is pluralized too. It is no longer one, unified history of art, namely the Western one — which in reality itself became internally pluralized in different modernisms long before "contemporary art" took over as designator of the art of our times — but multiple histories of art.

Nicholas Bourriaud formulated another important critique of traditional art historical thinking, addressing its inability to account for the formal and medial discontinuities of contemporary art. In *Relational Aesthetics*, published in 1998, Bourriaud understands art as a semantic remainder of a narrative called "art history" which is now obsolete:

> A certain aspect of the programme of modernity has been fairly and squarely wound up (and not, let us hasten to emphasise in these bourgeois times, the spirit informing it). This completion has drained the criteria of aesthetic judgement we are heir to of their substance, but we go on applying them to present-day artistic practices.[9]

Bourriaud therefore defines "art" as a:

> 1. General term describing a set of objects presented as part of a narrative known as *art history*. This narrative draws up the critical genealogy and discusses the issues raised by these objects, by way of three sub-sets: *painting, sculpture, architecture*. 2. Nowadays, the word "art" seems to be no more than a semantic leftover of this narrative, whose more accurate definition would read as follows: Art is an activity consisting in producing relationships with the world with the help of signs, forms, actions and objects.[10]

In other words, art historical progress has now been suspended, as coexisting contemporary art practices do not necessarily take part in the development of the same or a shared narrative. In the present context, this art historical analysis is far more significant than the relational artistic micro-utopias or "arty parties" Bourriaud's book has been thought to legitimize theoretically.

The art historical problematic outlined above, and the move from modern to contemporary art, is, of course, not independent of "history at large" and should be seen in relation to the modern concepts of time and history and how they have changed in the last decades of the twentieth century (a conceptual change which, of course, is dependent upon the massive material transformations of the world during the last century).

The dominant modern conception of time is based on continuity and progress. History — unified, since the late eighteenth century, in the collective singular, as shown by historian Reinhart Koselleck — was seen as a continuous process toward a qualitatively different future; a process that could be planned, created, and accelerated by humans.[11] Thus, modernity is characterized by a "progress-oriented articulation of past, present and future, in which the future is constituted through the devaluing of the past and the erasure of the present."[12] The qualitatively different future toward which the temporal logic of modernity is orientated implies a certain idea of linear historical progression. Modernity as a discourse of progress, acceleration and teleology therefore also constitutes a practice of totalization, excluding those who do not comply with its parameters. It attributes lateness to colonized nations and subaltern subjects, and progress is thus defined in terms of the projection of certain — that is, Western — people's presents as other people's futures.

The grand narratives and the all-encompassing history authorized by modernity claims to have unified a vast plurality — in particular in the "imagined communities" of nation states — but, as historian Harry Harootunian has pointed out, this history "is actually undermined by the special histories and coexisting mixed temporalities that have steadily resisted its assimilating ambition."[13] Philosopher and cultural critic Ernst Bloch remarked on this failed assimilation or synchronization as early as the 1930s, writing of the temporality of "non-contemporaneous contemporaneities" (*die Gleichzeitigkeit des Ungleichzeitigen*):

> Not all people exist in the same Now. They do so only externally, through the fact that they can be seen today. But they are thereby not yet living at the same time with the others. They rather carry an earlier element with them; this interferes.[14]

In other words, there were experiences of time — in this case, in the developing national-socialist Germany of the mid-1930s — that could not or resisted inclusion in the modern project and its temporality; that *interfered* with the temporality of modernity.

In our current times we seem to have lost the modern belief in progress and all societies moving toward a better future. This lack of futurity has generated a feeling that a contemporary extension of the present is substituting for the temporal logic of modernity, as, among others, Boris Groys observes:

> The present has ceased to be a point of transition from the past to the future, becoming instead a site of the permanent rewriting of both past and future — of constant proliferations of historical narratives beyond any individual grasp or control.[15]

Thus, the self-reproducing presentness of the contemporary seems to have replaced the structurally momentary category of modernity, defined by a permanent transitoriness, by an inherent self-surpassing character.[16]

The category of the present has developed into "presentism," and has, according to François Hartog, become omnipresent.[17] In the modern regime of historicity, actions were guided by the future and they ceased to be understood in *direct* continuity with the past — the "horizon of expectation" was increasingly severed from the "space of experience" in the anthropological terminology of Reinhart Koselleck. In the contemporary regime of historicity, on the other hand, the present has become the privileged temporal category according to which the past and the future is conceived, but also a category that absorbs the past and the future, whereby historical time and any ideas about a qualitatively different future seem to be suspended.[18] The present reproduces itself without leading to any future, creating a feeling that the historical present in which we live is no longer defined by any directional vector of historical development.[19] This was of course, it may be remarked parenthetically, already Fredric Jameson's understanding of the postmodern, which, for him, referred to the overwhelming of the imaginary, rendering it easier to imagine the deterioration of planet Earth and its ecosystems than the breakdown of the very capitalist system that had caused climatic and ecological catastrophe.[20]

The present ways of articulating past, present, and future therefore not only makes our present, here and now, different from previous presents, but it also testifies to a change in our experience of time itself; an experience of an ever expanding, perpetual present, which, in a certain sense, can be seen as a time-relation with no temporal horizon other than itself. The virtual effacement of the categories of the past and the future means that the present is indeed omnipresent, but, if presence is all there is, if there is no outside the present, no temporal differentiation, then nothing is really present any longer. Presentism names the dissolution of presence and the present. It is a crisis of time — a present marked more by presentist circulationism and accumulation of the same than by social change or historical transformation.

It should be noted, however, that Hartog deals almost exclusively with experiences of time within a European framework. What I find crucial about our present, the present present, is that it is conditioned by *con*-temporaneity, understood as a *global* interconnection of *different* presents, with different pre-histories, and of different time-experiences or *Eigenzeiten* in the *same* present.[21] It is an idea of contemporaneity as a shared present across divisive cultural and historical differences; of a temporal unity of the present across the planet. This means that it is necessary to try to establish a global, or even planetary, perspective on the present. As Okwui Enwezor remarks with reference to Hans Belting, we should also be aware, when analyzing the global art world, that

> contemporary Western artists see themselves as being in a post-historical situation, whereas non-Western artists wish to be in a post-ethnic one. To be no longer identified by race, ethnicity, or tribe [...] [T]he main struggle of contemporary Western artists is to come to terms with the logic of tradition, with the way in which history is both a resource and a negation of the now. In the rest of the world — India, China, Africa, wherever — the self-consciousness that follows from established historical identity has not been achieved.[22]

We have, in other words, arrived at contemporaneity via different paths, but the post-historical situation and the struggle to become post-ethnic are now inevitably interconnected.

Against this background, I would like to argue that Didi-Huberman's concept of anachronism and "the dialogue beyond all differences of their [the images'] times" in "Soulèvements" appears to pave the way for at least *imagining* a qualitatively different world, for projecting a futural moment that transcends the all-encompassing temporal horizon of presentism without falling back into the synchronizing and universalizing discourse of progress which characterizes Western modernity. An anachronic approach is, moreover, a way to wrest the image, or the work of art, and its expressive value free from the straitjacket of a particular historical narrative and the restrained possibilities of generating signification that it provides. Thus, Didi-Huberman's anachronistic, or, what I would prefer to call, *anachronic* approach — to stress that I am using it in a positive, not a pejorative sense — not only questions a linear teleological history of art, but it is also a way to break the impasse of presentism, understood as the regeneration of the past and the future only to valorize the immediate moment.

Didi-Huberman's notion of anachrony resonates with Agamben's theory of the contemporary. As mentioned in chapter 4, Agamben makes an explicit connection between anachronism and contemporariness, which is based on a particular *experience* of and relationship with time, in "What Is the Contemporary?":

> Those who are truly contemporary, who truly belong to their time, are those who neither perfectly coincide with it nor adjust themselves to its demands. They are thus in this sense irrelevant. But precisely because of this condition, precisely through this disconnection and this anachronism, they are more capable than others of perceiving and grasping their own time. [...] Contemporariness is, then, a singular relationship with one's own time, which adheres to it and, at the same time, keeps a distance from it. More precisely, it is *that relationship with time that adheres to it through a disjunction and an anachronism*. Those who coincide too well with the epoch, those who are perfectly tied to it in every respect, are not contemporaries, precisely because they do not manage to see it; they are not able to firmly hold their gaze on it.[23]

Agamben, however, like Hartog and Danto, deals almost exclusively with Western tradition and history, that is, with history in the singular. His, in other respects compelling, understanding of the contemporary as non-coincidence with one's own time, as a sort of refusal of contemporaneity, is therefore not adequate to account for contemporaneity as the coexistence of a multiplicity of traditions and histories in the same here and now. Furthermore, his notion of the contemporary seems to be relatively ahistorical; a category that is applicable in any historical context. His conception of the contemporary is therefore in need of historicization. With Danto, Michaud, and Bourriaud in mind one could argue that the contemporary art historical present makes it very difficult to be untimely or anachronistic, as it becomes increasingly difficult to identify a hegemonic time and history from which to differ; how can one be avant-garde without any tradition or hegemony from which to break away and distinguish oneself?

The task, in spite of this difficulty, is to establish a disjunctive relationship not only with the presentist present, but with a homogeneous linear history of art too. Anachrony, according to Didi-Huberman, is the interconnection of heterogeneous times. Partly inspired by the psychoanalytical vocabulary of Sigmund Freud and Jacques Lacan, he thinks that images haunt time — somewhat similar to how Freud's *Nachträglichkeit* and Lacan's *après-coup* has to do with a symptom as an eruption of the past into the present, an anachronism experienced on the body. What Erwin Panofsky wanted to exorcise from his iconology and art history was, according to Didi-Huberman, the "life" of images that haunt time, their overdetermination and dynamic aspects.[24] Panofsky wanted to exorcise "the alteration effected by images themselves on historical knowledge built on images."[25] He did not want images to interfere with the established historical narrative. The idea of anachrony is, on the contrary, related to the contemporary interest in heterochronicity, and should be distinguished from achrony and anachronism in its ordinary art historical sense of assigning a work a temporal frame foreign to it.[26] Terry Smith thus speaks of "the idea of anachrony, of an artwork being, in some or all respects, in an open, adventitious relationship to time," and finds this "a much more interesting idea than achrony, and richer than anachronism, which implies being out of a determined temporal sequence."[27] The idea of anachrony implies that an artwork might do more than simply embody its moment of origin, and that it articulates an intricate temporal complexity.

In an article with the telling title "Before the Image, Before Time: The Sovereignty of Anachronism," Didi-Huberman argues in favour of an anachronic interpretive approach to a fresco by Fra Angelico at the convent of San Marco in Florence, probably painted in the 1440s.[28] According to Didi-Huberman, anachronism is something positive, internal to images, the history of which the art historian tries to reconstruct. "Anachronism," he states, "would be the temporal way of expressing the exuberance, complexity, and overdetermination of images."[29] Before Fra Angelico's fresco, or any other image for that matter, we are thus before an object of complex, impure temporality:

> an *extraordinary montage of heterogeneous times forming anachronisms*. In the dynamic and complexity of this montage, historical notions as fundamental as those of "style" or "epoch" suddenly take on a dangerous plasticity (dangerous only for those who would like everything to be in its place once and for all in the same epoch: the fairly common figure of what I shall call the "historian with time phobia"). So to raise the question of anachronism is to question this fundamental plasticity, and with it the combination — so difficult to analyze — of the temporal differentiation at work in each image.[30]

Images are temporally impure and overdetermined with a potential to activate and connect to a number of different temporalities and times.[31]

Jacques Rancière likewise relates anachronic thinking to making history. Understanding the meaning of the central terms differently,

Rancière sees a critical potential in anachrony, which, in his vocabulary, is close to being synonymous with the positive version of what I — in extension of Osborne and Smith — am calling contemporaneity, which, on the other hand, in Rancière's terminology, however, is a term that refers to something like temporal self-coincidence:

> There is no anachronism. But there are modes of connection that in a positive sense we can call anachronies: events, ideas, significations that are contrary to time, that make meaning circulate in a way that escapes any contemporaneity, any identity of time with "itself." An anachrony is a word, an event, or a signifying sequence that has left "its" time, and in this way is given the capacity to define completely original points of orientation (*les aiguillages*), to carry out leaps from one temporal line to another. And it is because of these points of orientation, these jumps and these connections that there exists a power to "make" history. *The multiplicity of temporal lines, even of senses of time, included in the "same" time is the condition of historical activity.*[32]

Rancière understands contemporaneity as a kind of undivided present, as time's becoming present to and contemporaneous with itself. Such an achievement of Hegelian modernity, he argues, is, however, refuted by modernist avant-garde art forms, which are not ahead of their times, but located in the difference of modern times with themselves.[33] I am interested in how such temporal differentiation can be seen to be at work in contemporary art practices which try to register, and sometimes even produce, different temporalities in the constitution of our — at a certain "higher," more abstract level — globally shared present.[34] It is this globally and even planetary shared present which makes the contemporary contemporary different from earlier spatially and culturally more restricted versions of the contemporary — including that of modernist avant-gardes, whose untimeliness was established in relation to a relatively easily identifiable progressive and unified modern time.

Undeniably biased toward the Western history of art and image-making, Didi-Huberman's exhibition seems to try to transcend this singular history of art by including images and material from historical and recent uprisings in South and Latin America, North Africa and Asia as well as Europe, along with online material of a transnational, more global character. The latter was presented in a section called "Résistances Numériques" (Forms of Digital Resistance) curated by journalist Marie Lechner, made up of a selection of projects exploring the theme of uprisings on the Internet and on social networks, including, for example, the online project titled "Anonymous: Shared identity in the era of a global networked society" by Robert Sakrowski (2011). *Soulèvements* could be — and has been — criticized for aestheticizing the gestures of uprising and for neglecting historical specificity, but this kind of Warburg-inspired political anthropology of images, however, explores the *forms* that the desire for emancipation and uprising take. It is, thus, about forms and images, and not an attempt to impute some transhistorical "style" to past and present uprisings. It is rather a dialectical *montage* of images, in which they are brought into "dialogue beyond all differences of their times," forming different constellations that make us see and imagine new histories. According to Didi-Huberman, in a wall text in the last section of the exhibition: "Whenever a wall is erected, there will always be 'people arisen' to 'jump the wall.' If only by *imagining*. As though inventing images contributed — a little here, powerfully there — to reinventing our political hopes." When thinking about the exhibition as a whole, critic and cultural theorist Mark Fisher's observation — when it had become apparent that the Global Financial Crisis of 2007–2008 would not have any consequences for the capitalist system — springs to mind that: "When the present has given up on the future, we must listen for the relics of the future in the unactivated potential of the past."[35]

In the first volume of his magnum opus, *L'œil de l'histoire* (*The Eye of History*) — which is a pun on George Bataille's *Histoire de l'œil* (*The Story of the Eye*) — called *Quand les images prennent position* (*When Images take Positions*) Didi-Huberman claims — based on a reading of Bertolt Brecht and Walter Benjamin — that the political (*la politique*) can only be shown through the conflicts, paradoxes and the reciprocal shocks of which all history is woven, and that montage is the procedure *par excellence* to expose the political.[36] In montage, things only appear by taking positions; they only appear by first having been taken out (*se démonter*) of the usual order, of their place in the usual order. Montage is to forms what the political is to actions, he argues. Montage is about positions and transgression; about making things exit their habitual or usual places and affirming their existence beyond or outside of what he calls "the bed of time" (*hors du lit du temps*). Montage proceeds by reconfiguring or reassembling history (*remonter l'histoire*); in a dialectical deconstruction of historicism in which historical moments are taken out of their usual places and reassembled outside or beyond established facts (*faites constatés*).

Didi-Huberman thus also draws on Benjamin's critique of the historicist conception of time as only the abstract form of an "empty, homogeneous continuum" that the historian need only fill with a succession of facts, thereby producing a "history of events." As laid out in chapters 3 and 4 above, such abstract notion of time and the historicist notion of history as a linear development is problematic because once time is divided into a chronological series of instants, any moment in the past becomes unreachable, irrevocably severed from the present by an infinite number of instants.[37] It is no longer a dynamic object of knowledge and becomes something that can be accumulated without end, but which will never form what Benjamin calls the "true picture of the past."[38] One can only construct historical knowledge philosophically by exposing — alongside the chronologically ordered stories, currents and factual events — the heterochronies or anachronies of the elements composing every historical moment; by exposing also those elements which resist or work against the chronological narrative, suggesting, perhaps, other possible stories. In Didi-Huberman's vocabulary, the term "heterochrony" stresses effects of heterogeneity or disparity, whereas the term "anachrony" emphasizes anamnesis or recollection. This implies that there is no teleology to history, only heterochronies and anachronies of processes with multiple directions and speeds. Didi-Huberman thus understands Bloch's notion of "non-contemporaneity" as synonymous with "anachronism" (or rather "anachrony"), and montage is a means to render such "non-contemporaneity" dialectical, that is, politically fecund. In this way, montage is an *exposition of anachronies*, while, at the same time, working as an *explosion of chronology*. It separates things that are habitually united and connects things that are habitually separated.

Any work of art embodies a complex temporality, not only as we stand "before the image" in "the present of our own experience," as art historian and critic Hal Foster phrases it, but also as different times are inscribed in the work through its history of reception and through its travel through history (Picasso's *Guernica* is an obvious case in point), "whereby it comes to double as the record of its own material alterations or programmatic transformations."[39] My point, however, is that we need to add to this complexity. Today, "the present of our own experience" is a present constituted by a number of different, interconnected temporalities, including the omnipresent co-presence of others via digital technologies. And perhaps the sense of a shared present is most clearly articulated on the Internet, where all the times of the world are present at the same time in a state of global interactivity. Or, as Sarai-CSDS and Raqs Media Collective formulates it in relation to the conference "What Time Is It? — Technologies of life in the contemporary" that took place in New Delhi in December 2017:

> Growing computational grids inaugurate storage and surveillance technologies that are affecting fields like the environment, finance and law. Machine time disturbs historical continuity and sequence. Genetic engineering and life storage technologies disrupt the idea of the biological life span; media memory and recording technologies have already transformed the lives of mobile phone users in the world. Media-enabled populations in Asia, Africa and Latin America are now part of a new infrastructure of the senses.[40]

"Soulèvements'" formal interconnection of previously unrelated images of different origins opens up possibilities for other histories in which hitherto unseen and invisible elements become visible and, perhaps, active in a shared present. The exhibition re-writes or re-imagines the prehistories of the contemporary present, and through these image constellations it articulates a desire for uprising and generates a sense of history and historical change as possible.

The anachronic intertwinement of heterogeneous temporalities should therefore not only be thought vertically, as connections between past, present, and future within one singular unified history (most often the Western one), but also horizontally as the interconnection of different vertical histor*ies* in the *same* present. The anachronic approach itself is practiced under specific historical conditions and, today, these conditions are characterized by a global contemporaneity, constituted by the coming together of *different* times in the *same* historical present. An historical understanding of anachrony and how it challenges a linear, chronological, and unified understanding of history has therefore to take contemporaneity as a new historical condition and idea into consideration.

A
<u>Soulèvements</u>, Jeu de Paume, Paris 2016-2017
Installation of exhibition

B
<u>Soulèvements</u>, Jeu de Paume, Paris 2016-2017
Installation of exhibition (Sigmar Polke)

C
<u>Soulèvements</u>, Jeu de Paume, Paris 2016-2017
Installation of exhibition (Charles-François Thibault)

D
<u>Soulèvements</u>, Jeu de Paume, Paris 2016-2017
Installation of exhibition (Joseph Beuys)

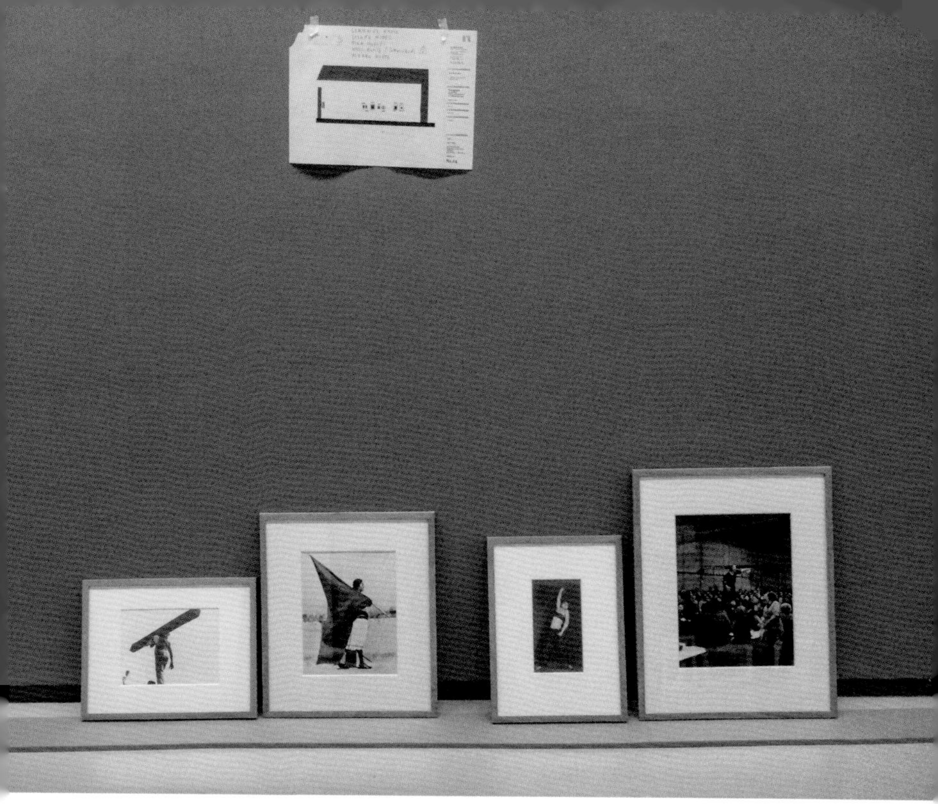

A Soulèvements

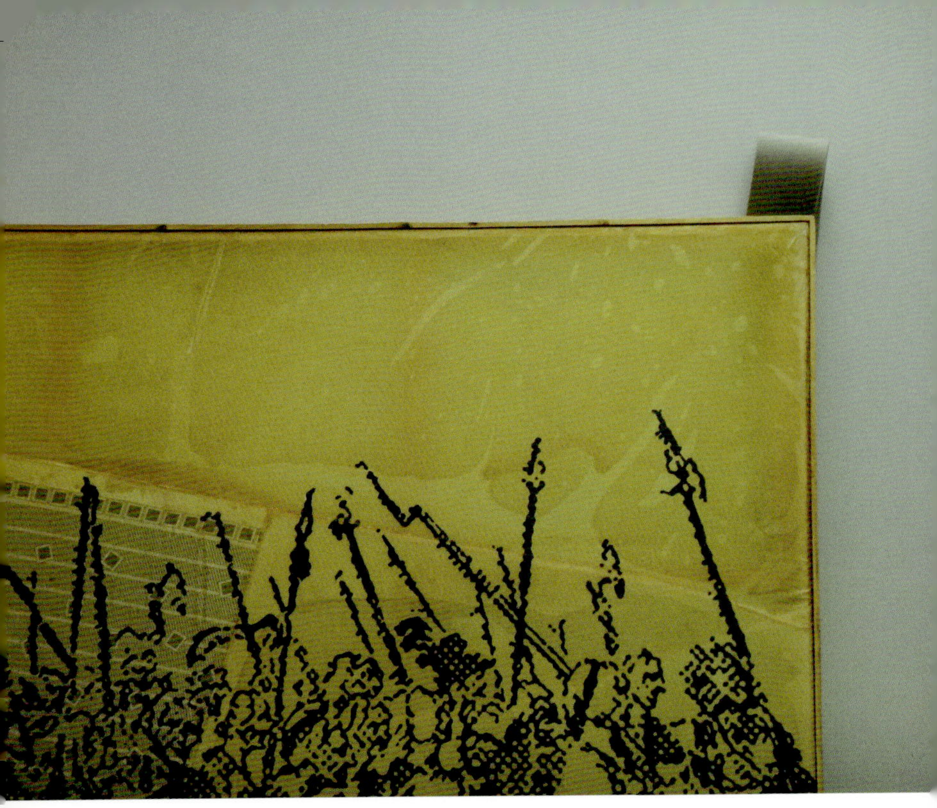

B Soulèvements

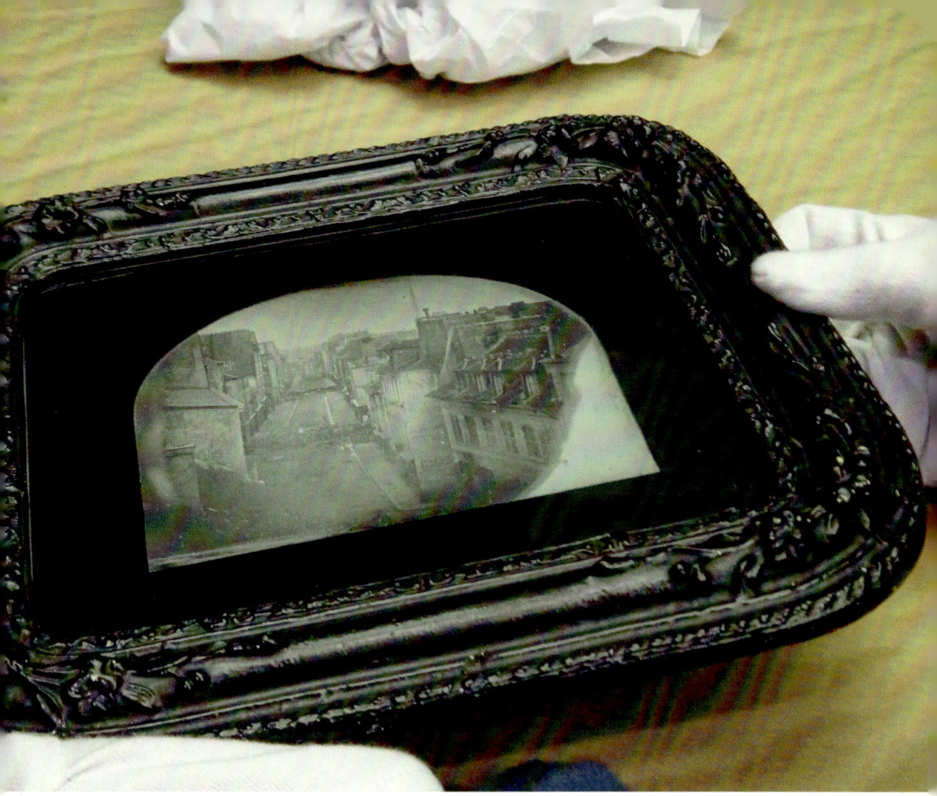

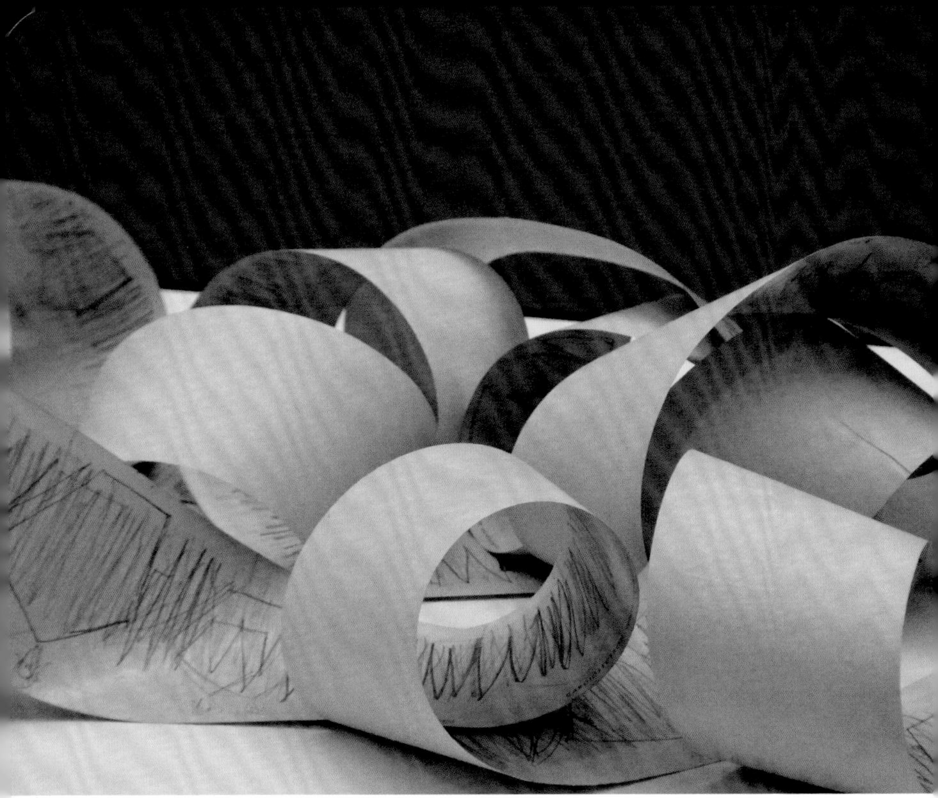

D Soulèvements

Notes

1 "The Deconstruction of Actuality: An Interview with Jacques Derrida," *Radical Philosophy*, no. 68 (1994): 31.

2 Giorgio Agamben, *Infancy and History: On the Destruction of Experience*, trans. Liz Heron (London: Verso, 1993 [1978]), 99.

3 Arthur C. Danto, *After the End of Art* (Princeton, NJ: Princeton University Press, 1998), 4–5.

4 Danto quotes Belting from *The End of the History of Art*, trans. Christopher S. Wood (Chicago: University of Chicago Press, 1987).

5 The exhibition was on show from October 18, 2016 through January 15, 2017.

6 See Georges Didi-Huberman, *Soulèvements*, exh. cat. (Paris: Gallimard & Jeu de Paume, 2016).

7 Yves Michaud, *La crise de l'art contemporain. Utopie, démocratie et comédie* (Paris: Presse Universitaires de France, 1997).

8 Yves Michaud, "The End of the Utopia of Art," in *Think Art: Theory and Practice in the Art of Today*, ed. Bartomeu Mari and Jean-Marie Schaeffer (Rotterdam: Witte de With, 1999), 131–156. See also Jacob Lund, "*Sensus Communis* and the Public," in *Nyhedsavisen: Peer-reviewed Newspaper About Public Interfaces* (2011): 10–11, and Thierry de Duve and Jacob Lund, "'The Glimpse of Hope That Religion or Politics Can No Longer Promise...' An Interview with Thierry de Duve," *Nordic Journal of Aesthetics*, no. 36–37 (2008–2009): 6–10.

9 Nicolas Bourriaud, *Relational Aesthetics*, trans. Simon Pleasance et al. (Dijon: Les presses du réel, 2002), 11.

10 Ibid., 107.

11 Reinhart Koselleck, "'Neuzeit': Remarks on the Semantics of the Modern Concepts of Movement," in *Futures Past: On the Semantics of Historical Time*, trans. Keith Tribe (Cambridge, MA: MIT Press, 1985), 246: "[T]he collective singular form of *Geschichte*, which since around 1780 can be conceived of as history in and for itself in the absence of an associated subject or object."

12 Christine Ross, *The Past Is the Present; It's the Future Too: The Temporal Turn in Contemporary Art* (New York: Continuum, 2012), 7.

13 Harry Harootunian, "Remembering the Historical Present," *Critical Inquiry*, vol. 33, no. 3 (Spring 2007): 481. See Benedict Anderson, *Imagined Communities: Reflections on the Origin and Spread of Nationalism* (London: Verso, 1983) regarding the notion of "imagined communities."

14 Cf. Ernst Bloch, *The Heritage of Our Times*, trans. Neville and Stephen Plaice (Cambridge: Polity Press, 1991 [1935]), 90 and 97.

15 Boris Groys, "Comrades of Time," in *Going Public* (Berlin: Sternberg Press, 2010), 90.

16 Cf. Peter Osborne, *Anywhere or Not at All: Philosophy of Contemporary Art* (London: Verso, 2013), 24.

17 François Hartog, *Regimes of Historicity: Presentism and Experiences of Time*, trans. Saskia Brown (New York: Columbia University Press, 2015).

18 Cf. Christine Ross, *The Past Is the Present,* 13f.

19 See Juliane Rebentisch, "The Contemporaneity of Contemporary Art," *New German Critique*, no. 124, 42:1 (2015): 225. For an analysis of a suspension of historical agency see also Mikkel Bolt Rasmussen, *Hegel after Occupy* (Berlin: Sternberg Press, 2018).

20 Fredric Jameson, *The Seeds of Time* (New York: Columbia University Press, 1994), xi–xii.

21 On the notion of *Eigenzeit* see Helga Nowotny, *Time: The Modern and Postmodern Experience* [*Eigenzeit: Entstehung und Strukturierung eines Zeitgefühls*, 1989], trans. Neville Plaice (Cambridge: Polity, 1994).

22 Okwui Enwezor, "World Platforms, Exhibiting Adjacency, and the Surplus Value of Art," in Terry Smith, *Talking Contemporary Curating* (New York: Independent Curators International, 2015), 91–92.

23 Giorgio Agamben, "What Is the Contemporary?," in *What Is an Apparatus? and Other Essays*, trans. David Kishik and Stefan Pedatella (Stanford, CA: Stanford University Press, 2009), 41.
24 Georges Didi-Huberman, "Preface to the English Edition: The Exorcist," in *Confronting Images: Questioning the Ends of a Certain History of Art*, trans. John Goodman (University Park: Pennsylvania State University Press, 2005 [1990]), xxiii.
25 Georges Didi-Huberman, *Confronting Images*, xxi.
26 Cf. Hal Foster, "Preposterous Timing," *London Review of Books*, vol. 34:21 (2012): 12. See also Keith Moxey, *Visual Time: The Image in History* (Durham, NC: Duke University Press, 2013); Mieke Bal, *Quoting Caravaggio: Contemporary Art, Preposterous History* (Chicago: University of Chicago Press, 1999); and Mieke Bal and Jacob Lund, "An Ethically Nonindifferent Aesthetics: An Interview with Mieke Bal," *Nordic Journal of Aesthetics*, no. 42 (2011): 69–86.
27 Terry Smith, "Seeing Art Historically Today: Where We Are, And Ways To Go," Power Lecture, Domain Theatre, Art Gallery of New South Wales, July 20, 2016. Full text version of unpublished manuscript dated 7.19.2016.
28 Georges Didi-Huberman, "Before the Image, Before Time: The Sovereignty of Anachronism," in *Compelling Visuality: The Work of Art in and out of History*, ed. Claire Farago and Robert Zwijnenberg (Minneapolis: University of Minnesota Press, 2003), 31–44.
29 Didi-Huberman, "Before the Image, Before Time," 37.
30 Ibid., 38. On Fra Angelico see also Georges Didi-Huberman, *Fra Angelico: Dissemblance and Figuration*, trans. Jane Marie Todd (Chicago: University of Chicago Press, 1995).
31 In connection with the temporal overdetermination of the image, Knut Ebeling brought my attention to a passage Walter Benjamin wrote in a letter to F. C. Rang in 1923, where he muses over the question of how the artwork relates to historical life. The artwork is without history (*geschichtslos*), he claims: "Der Versuch das Kunstwerk in das geschichtliche Leben hineinzustellen, eröffnet nicht Perspektiven, die in sein Innerstes führen [...] eine Geschichte der Kunstwerke selbst kommt dabei garnicht in Frage." [Attempts to insert the work of art into historical life opens no perspective leading to its core, its innermost part (...) a history of the work of art itself, therefore, does not come into question.] Walter Benjamin, *Gesammelte Briefe*, vol. II, *1919–1924* (Frankfurt am Main: Suhrkamp, 1996), 392f.
32 Jacques Rancière, "The Concept of Anachronism and the Historian's Truth," *In/Print*, vol. 3:1 (2015 [1996]): 47f., accessed January 27, 2022, http://arrow.dit.ie/cgi/viewcontent.cgi?article=1020&context=inp. Emphasis added.
33 Cf. Jacques Rancière, "Rethinking Modernity," *Diacritics*, 42:3 (2014): 10–11.
34 For more on this, see chapter 4.
35 Mark Fisher, "The Metaphysics of Crackle: Afrofuturism and Hauntology," *Dancecult: Journal of Electronic Dance Music Culture*, 5:2 (2009): 53. Didi-Huberman's strategy is, of course, debatable, and it could be objected that "Soulèvements" actually returns the revolutionary energy — that I claim it actualizes — to history, thus making this revolutionary energy a thing of the past rather than the present (I owe this point to philosopher John Rajchman).
36 Georges Didi-Huberman, *Quand les images prennent position. L'Œil de l'histoire*, 1 (Paris: Les Éditions de Minuit, 2009), 29ff.
37 Cf. Monica Dall'asta, "The (Im)possible History," in *For Ever Godard*, eds. Michael Temple et al. (London: Black Dog Publishing, 2004), 350–363.
38 Walter Benjamin, "Theses on the Philosophy of History," in *Illuminations*, trans. Harry Zohn (New York: Schocken Books, 1969), 255.
39 Foster, "Preposterous Timing," 12.
40 See http://sarai.net/what-time-is-it-14-16-december-2017/, accessed January 27, 2022.

Imagination in the Contemporary Society of the Spectacle

Chapter 7

We are currently witnessing fundamental changes in the conditions and the status of images: more and more images are networked; cameras and screens (portable or fixed) are everywhere; image data is geotagged; databases can be navigated in real time; the prevalence of operative images and "machine vision" detached from human control and sense perception is increasing rapidly, etc. These transformations are, of course, closely connected to the digitalization and the digital production of images, which has raised a number of interesting questions about their material support and the infrastructure of their dissemination, about connectivity, circulation, distribution, formats, etc. At first glance, these changes are happening primarily at a technical and infrastructural level — the digital transformation of the image from geometry to algorithm, from projection to processing, from a passive, fixed representational form to being active and multiplatform.[1] This chapter, however, focuses on how such changes also problematize the cultural and social significance of images and the role of the human subject; the ways in which they shift how we see — or *do not* see — the world, ourselves, and each other.

In his 1988 *Comments on the Society of the Spectacle*, Guy Debord remarks that "images chosen and constructed by *someone else* have everywhere become the individual's principal connection to the world he formerly observed for himself," and, with regard to the didactics of spectacle, that "the computer's binary language is an irresistible inducement to the continual and unreserved acceptance of what has been programmed according to the wishes of someone else and passes for the timeless source of a superior, impartial and total logic."[2] Even if Debord writes of the *global* spectacle he does not — and perhaps, in 1988, when global contemporaneity had not yet become a condition to the extent it is today, could not — reflect the wider implications of this globality and how contemporaneity affects our experience of time and history.[3] (And, with the climate emergency, the era of the so-called Anthropocene, etc., we should, following historian Dipesh Chakrabarty, perhaps speak of planetarity rather than globality.)[4] Debord, of course, gave the fifth chapter of *The Society of the Spectacle* the title "Time and History," and describes both a society that has become detached from its capacity to consciously shape and determine its future, and a condition in which individuals become alienated from their ability to shape and direct their own time, but the historical crisis or presentism he describes is — like most notions of postmodernity — still located within a very Western context with a very Western prehistory.[5]

What I would propose calling *the contemporary* society of the spectacle calls for critical attention to the workings of *the networked* image and the image economy, or *iconomy,* of which it takes part, as the global circulation of images and the workings of new media realities, digital cultures and network relations seem increasingly to mediate social relations and the social imaginary rather than those of *place*. The society of the spectacle not only concerns an accumulation of images: "The spectacle is not a collection of images," Debord explains in paragraph 4 of *The Society of the Spectacle*, "rather, it is a social relationship between people that is mediated by images."[6] Yet, as art historian Claire Bishop remarks, social relations today are not mediated by monodirectional media imagery (as theorized by Debord in 1967) but through the interactive screen, "activating" and training us as "prosumers" who coproduce content, rather than passively consuming what has been devised for them — but who, most of the time, only act as nodes of circulation.[7] "[W]e respond to a selfie with other selfies, one image follows another, with algorithms recording these exchanges within a vast economy of attention," as philosopher and curator Emmanuel Alloa writes in a catalogue text for the exhibition "The Supermarket of Images" on show at the Jeu de Paume in Paris in 2020.[8]

What film scholar Pasi Väliaho calls "biopolitical screens" constitute the imagery that currently composes our affective and conceptual reality, producing and articulating our lived experience, as well as foreclosing alternative ways of inhabiting the world. Images are powerful as they modulate feelings, gestures and thinking, which has a bearing on how we structure existence and define and perceive social space.[9] Images, in other words, seem to become more and more decisive in the distribution of the sensible, in determining what can be seen and sensed, and what makes sense (what constitutes our *common* sense). Images inform our imaginative capacity as the imagination operates as a hinge between the collective and the individual, between the material and the mental; and we use imagination to represent possibilities rather than the actual, to represent other times than the present — including a qualitatively different future.

My point is that the question of the image and of our relation to images has gained ever more importance since Debord's classic analysis of the society of the spectacle over fifty years ago. In relation to Debord's *Society of the Spectacle*, Giorgio Agamben writes:

> The "becoming-image" of capital is nothing more than the commodity's last metamorphosis, in which exchange value has

> completely eclipsed use value and can now achieve the status of absolute and irresponsible sovereignty over life in its entirety, after having falsified the entire social production.[10]

It seems, however, that our relation to images is even more complex than it appeared in 1967. The spectacle is not merely external to us, it is part of who we are, part of our consciousness, and — as mentioned above — strongly influences the ways in which we experience the world, our social reality, and ourselves. “We are not,” Jacques Rancière remarks, “in front of the images; we are in the middle of them, just as they are in the middle of us. The question is to know how to circulate among them, and how to get them to circulate as well.”[11]

Our relation to images and language is of vital importance as they are the media through which we are subjectified and desubjectified, individuated and disindividuated, as well as the media through which we communicate and form communities. As psychoanalyst Jacques Lacan teaches us, we receive the image of ourselves from an external image (a mirror), or — as Émile Benveniste and Giorgio Agamben argue — we become subjects through appropriation of the linguistic shifter “I,” that is, from symbolic media that are external to us, so to speak. Reflecting upon how to think with, or in continuation of, Debord today, in the age of the complete triumph of the spectacle, Agamben writes in his “Marginal Notes on *Commentaries on the Society of the Spectacle*” from 1990:

> It is evident, after all, that the spectacle is language, the very communicativity and linguistic being of humans. This means that an integrated Marxian analysis should take into consideration the fact that capitalism (or whatever other name we might want to give to the process dominating world history today) not only aimed at the expropriation of productive activity, but also, and above all, at the alienation of language itself, of the linguistic and communicative nature of human beings, of that *logos* in which Heraclitus identifies the Common. The extreme form of the expropriation of the Common is the spectacle, in other words, the politics in which we live.[12]

The spectacle is an expropriation of our common language and images, of our very communicativity. This expropriation calls for a re-appropriation, a re-familiarization; it calls for a creative or imaginative destruction and a puncture of the alienating spectacle in order to save our very communicativity, our community etc. A few pages later, Agamben continues:

> in the society of the spectacle it is this very communicativity, this generic essence itself [...], that is being separated in an autonomous sphere. What prevents communication is communicability itself; human beings are kept separate by what unites them. Journalists and the media establishment (as well as psychoanalysts in the private sphere) constitute the new clergy of such an alienation of the linguistic nature of human beings.[13]

What we share, what ties us together and which we individuate ourselves through, what, indeed, makes human community possible, namely language — comprising images as well as verbal language — has been alienated and expropriated by the media establishment; has been separated in an autonomous sphere, dissociated from the speaking and communicating human subjects. This expropriation is related to what Bernard Stiegler calls a short-circuiting of transindividuation, leading to a disindividuation of the individuals that take part — or that were meant to take part — in the social and symbolic exchange.[14] As mentioned above, Stiegler's concept of "transindividuation" does not refer exclusively to the individuated *I* or the inter-individuated *we*, but designates the process of co-individuation within a pre-individuated milieu or medium in which the *I* and the *we* are interdependent and in which they are transformed through one another.[15] Transindividuation takes place through an "associated symbolic milieu" where all members belonging to this milieu participate in and are functions of it.[16] Transindividuation, then, conditions all social transformation; and images — media and technologies of communication — are *pharmacological*, both poison and remedy, and can be part of processes of both trans and disindividuation.

As our culture becomes more and more digitalized, images — like every cultural object — are more open to a potentially global *social* distribution via the Internet. The digitally produced and distributed images seem to transform our social relations. The continuous moving on of the image — post-producing, launching, and accelerating it, what Hito Steyerl has called circulationism[17] — changes, as Peter Osborne has argued, not only the status or ontology of the image, but changes also the social field in which it appears and across which it is shared as that social field is now largely constituted by the production and distribution of images.[18] More and more images seem to gain meaning and social significance through their relationships with other images, and from being networked, as much as through their reference to our lifeworld, even if at some point they came into being as registrations or recordings of the "reality" of that lifeworld.

The tendentially globalized image space and the contemporary society of the spectacle that dominates it seem, in other words, to lead a separate life in a semi-autonomous sphere which nevertheless mediates our social relations, gives us a sense of taking part and living in a kind of globally or planetarily shared present — the networked and distributed image is not only here and now, it is (in principle) everywhere. (The increasing image mediation of our social relations became very palpable during the COVID-19 pandemic, where large parts of our social interaction were relegated to the screens of real-time communication technologies.)

As hinted at, this, of course, points to the need for critical *artistic* thematizations and articulations of this tendentially globalized, networked image space — to a need, if you will, for the creation of dynamic, "transindividuating" relationships with the images that surround us. Circulationism makes it harder to engage with images, but not impossible.

W.J.T. Mitchell's distinction between a picture and an image might be useful in this context. According to Mitchell, a picture is a material object, which can be burnt, broken or torn, whereas an image is what appears in a picture, and what survives its destruction; in memory, in narrative, in copies and traces in other media. The picture is the image as it appears on a concrete material support or in a specific place, it is the embodiment of an image. An image can be thought of as an immaterial entity, a phantasmatic appearance that comes to life via a specific material support.[19] To this I would add that an image *is dependent on recognition* — in line with Walter Benjamin's notion of "the image in the now of its recognizability" — an image is dependent on the involvement of a human agent; it is something that develops out of the spectator's *relation* with the image.[20] Or, as Jean-Luc Godard puts it with reference to his artistic practice of montage: "But an image doesn't exist. This is not an image, it's a picture. The image is the relation with me looking at it dreaming up a relation at [*sic*] someone else. An image is an association."[21] The spectator, so to speak, animates the image.

It is therefore a decisive aspect of the work of art — as noun *and* as verb — that it, at least implicitly, *addresses a viewer*, *someone*, who is invited to take part in its process of signification and production of meaning, not least in light of the proliferation of machine imagery that operates independently of human perception and cognition. These "operative images" are, in filmmaker and author Harun Farocki's definition in the first part of his three-part installation *Eye/Machine* from 2001–2003, "images without a social goal, not for edification, not for reflection" — they "do not represent an object, but rather are part of an operation."[22] Today, in the words of artist Trevor Paglen:

> [M]ost of the images in the world are descendants of the "operational" images in *Eye/Machine*: namely images made by machines for other machines. From quality control systems in manufacturing to Automated License Plate Readers (ALPR) throughout cities, and from retail motion tracking systems in supermarkets and malls to automated pattern-recognition systems in military drones, images are operating upon the world on a scale orders of magnitude greater than at the moment of *Eye/Machine*. [23]

Furthermore, nowadays operational images are overwhelmingly invisible (uninterpretable to the human eye, the *meat-eye*), even as they are ubiquitous, actively regulating and intervening in everyday life and sculpting physical reality in ever more dramatic ways.[24] (According to Paglen, digital images are revolutionary because they are fundamentally machine-readable and can only be seen by humans in special circumstances and for short periods of time. This machine-readability of digital images allows for the automation of vision on an enormous scale.)[25]

Machine vision, however, does not see an image in Godard's sense; it merely registers and processes pictures (visible and invisible). Simply put, what Paglen does in his artistic practice is to try to let us view the world as the machines see it; through this *address* and communicative act he, in a certain sense, creates an *image* out of the *pictures* that to a large extent make up our social field.[26] Paglen's *From 'Apple' to 'Anomaly'* was, for instance, described in the following way when it was on show in 2019–2020 at the Barbican in London:

> Explore the underbelly of our digital world in this exhibition revealing the powerful, and often hidden, forces at play in artificial intelligence. Artist Trevor Paglen's new Curve commission takes as its starting point the way in which AI networks are taught how to "see" and "perceive" the world by taking a closer look at image datasets. Paglen has incorporated approximately 30,000 individually printed photographs, largely drawn from ImageNet, the most widely shared, publicly available dataset. This dataset is archived and preselected in categories by humans, and widely used for training AI networks. In some cases, the connotations of categories are uncontroversial, others, for example "bad person" or "debtors," are not. These categories, when used in AI, suggest a world in which machines will be able to elicit forms of judgement against humankind. Discover

how the advent of autonomous computer vision and AI has developed, rife with hidden politics, biases and stereotypes.[27]

Paglen's work demonstrates that deciding what images mean is the root of power. Computer vision and AI operate according to image taxonomies — relationships between images and concepts/meanings — that are often highly political rather than merely objective descriptions and classifications, for instance with regard to gender and race. The norms that guide the meanings given to the images of the AI training sets support spectacle in several ways (are part of its complex of visuality, to draw on the terminology of visual culture scholar Nicholas Mirzoeff), and the constant endeavor to extract value from us.[28]

In fact, one of the characteristics of what I propose calling the *contemporary* society of the spectacle is its increasing integration of operational images and machine vision. One could think here of Benjamin Bratton's oft-quoted concept of "the Stack." According to Bratton, smart grids, cloud computing, mobile software and smart cities, universal addressing systems, ubiquitous computing and robotics are not unrelated genres of computation but constitute a larger aligned and coherent whole, an accidental megastructure in the form of a planetary-scale computing system.[29] Bratton's notion of the Stack marks the interconnection of all these multiple layers, the interpenetration of digital and analogue times, of technological, material and human times — bringing into being a kind of planetary instantaneity, a present in which every*one* and every*thing* takes part. In this way, the Stack may be seen as a way of visualizing the technological infrastructure that enables contemporaneity and the coming together of times on a planetary scale. Across the Stack, however, technical, social, human and nonhuman layers of temporality are folded together in what theorist and activist Tiziana Terranova — in the article "Red Stack Attack! Algorithms, Capital and the Automation of the Common" — understands as an "infrastructure of autonomization," which, in fact, does not seem to enhance, but rather to limit our operational and imaginative potential.[30]

My point is that machine vision and operational images seep into and penetrate our contemporary image space and co-constitute it. In Benjamin's terms, operational images and machine vision are technical apparatuses (*Apparate*) that act on the human "sensorium," and take part in configuring and organizing "the *Medium* of perception" (*Medium der Wahrnehmnung*).[31] According to Benjamin, sensory experience — the forms and rhythms of perception, the extension and coordinates of the visible, the audible, the tactile, etc. — has a history that is determined by the different ways in which a historically evolving set of such technical *Apparate* acted on the human sensorium. The term "Medium" here indicates the spatially extended environment, the *milieu*, the atmosphere, the *Umwelt* in which perception take place.[32] So, in Benjaminian terms, the operational images take part in a reorganization of our "*Medium* of perception," of the environment or *milieu* in which perception occurs — and which co-determines our imaginative potential.

Of interest here is the agency of the contemporary *networked* image and its ability to shape and affect people, politics and social systems. I am particularly interested in ways in which different aesthetic and artistic practices intervene in and reconfigure our surrounding image space and may be said to bring what Jacques Rancière has called "pensive images" into being. Pensive images invite us to pay attention to the image, to how it becomes an image, and how it functions, to what it does — what it affirms and makes seen, and what it blinds us from seeing and renders invisible. The notion of the pensive image refers to a zone of indeterminacy between the passive and the active, between the image as duplicate of a thing — as a representation or reproduction of the world — and the image as artistic operation — as creative agent — and also to a zone of indeterminacy between non-art and art; between the image as part of society's image circulation, parading as a representation, on the one hand, and the image as resistance, a space for imagination, on the other. The connected and distributed images constituting our contemporary image space allow, to give an example instead of a conclusion, for aesthetic practices such as those carried out by the interdisciplinary research agency Forensic Architecture, which seeks to invert the institutionalized forensic gaze — of actors like the police, the military, the secret service and border agencies, which usually seek to monopolize information — and, in its "counter-forensic" image generation, uses images, footage, and other material, gathered mainly from social networks and online sources, as testimonies to political violence and human rights violations, operating simultaneously in the art world (as Turner Prize nominees and exhibiting at the Whitney, ICA, documenta, etc.) and in juridical and social activist contexts (including as expert witnesses in courts of law). It is — to paraphrase Harun Farocki — a matter of making images testify against themselves.

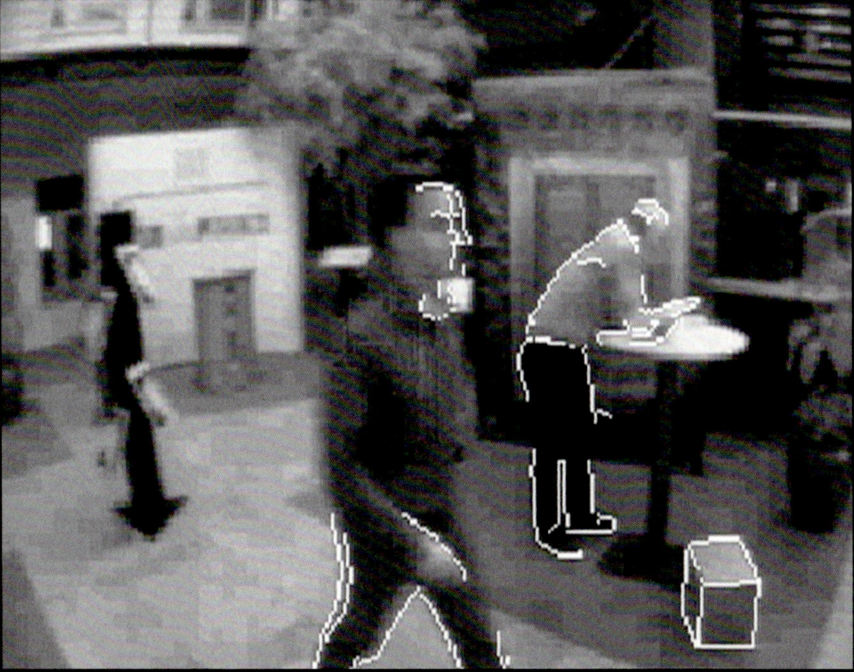

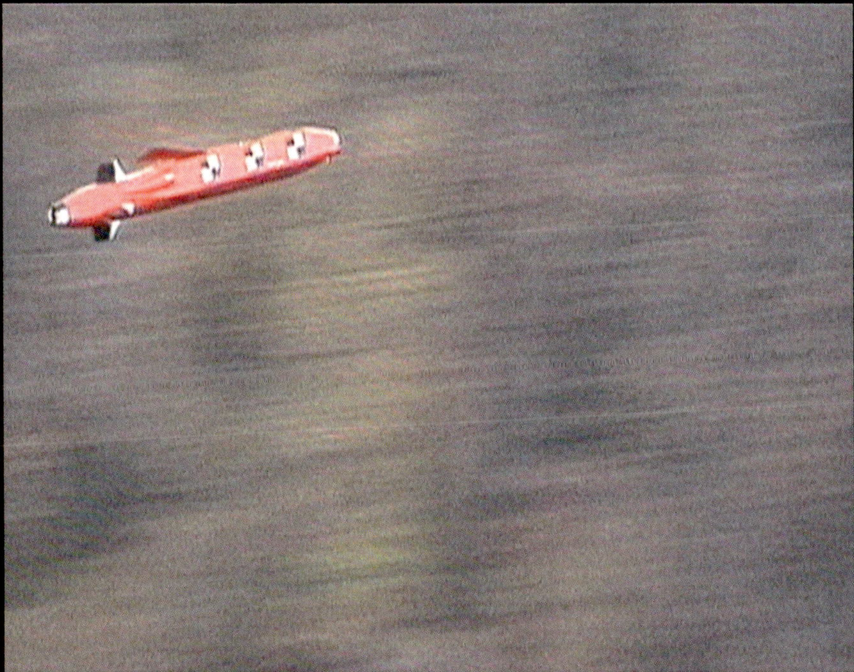

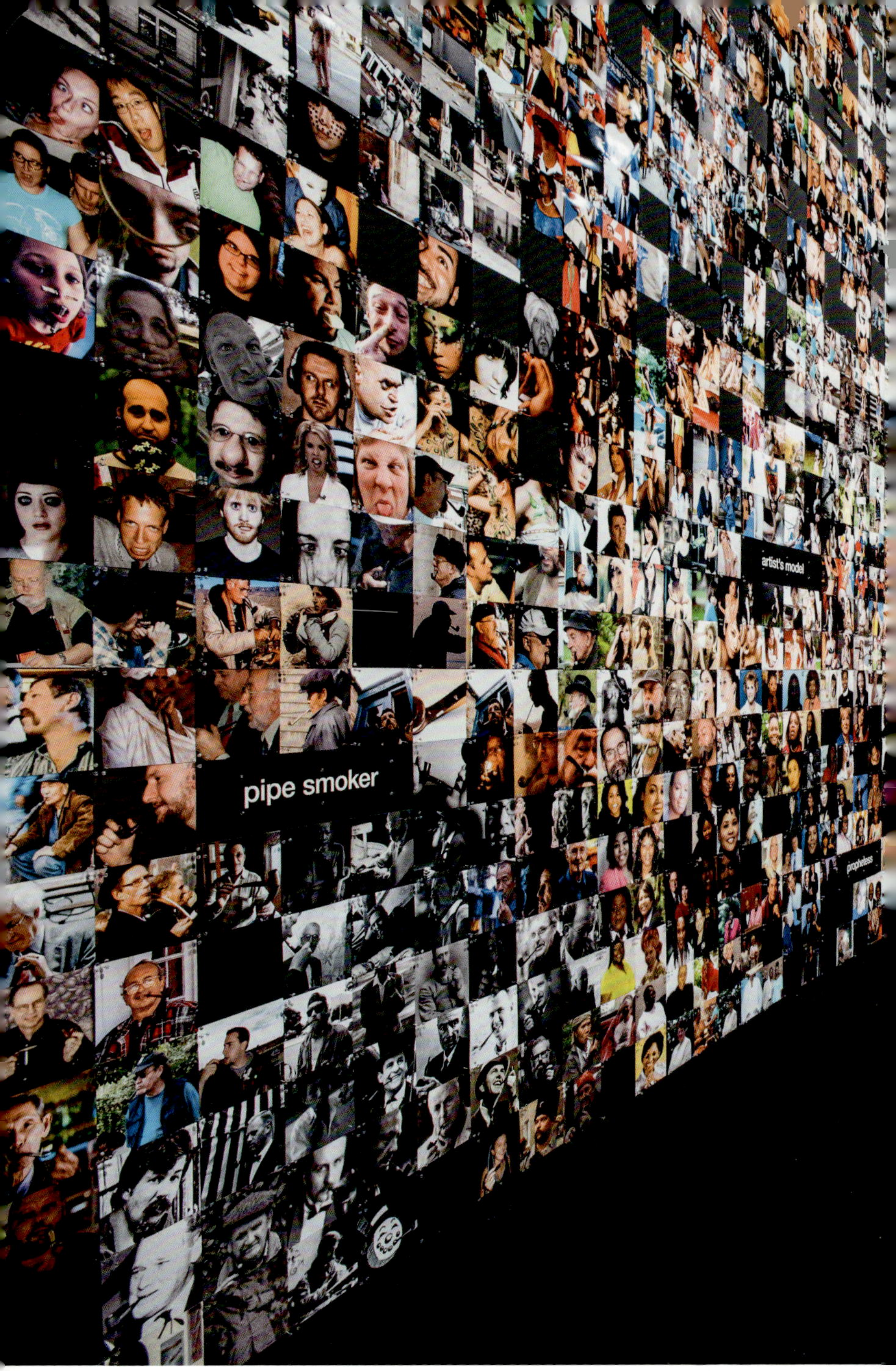

C Trevor Paglen

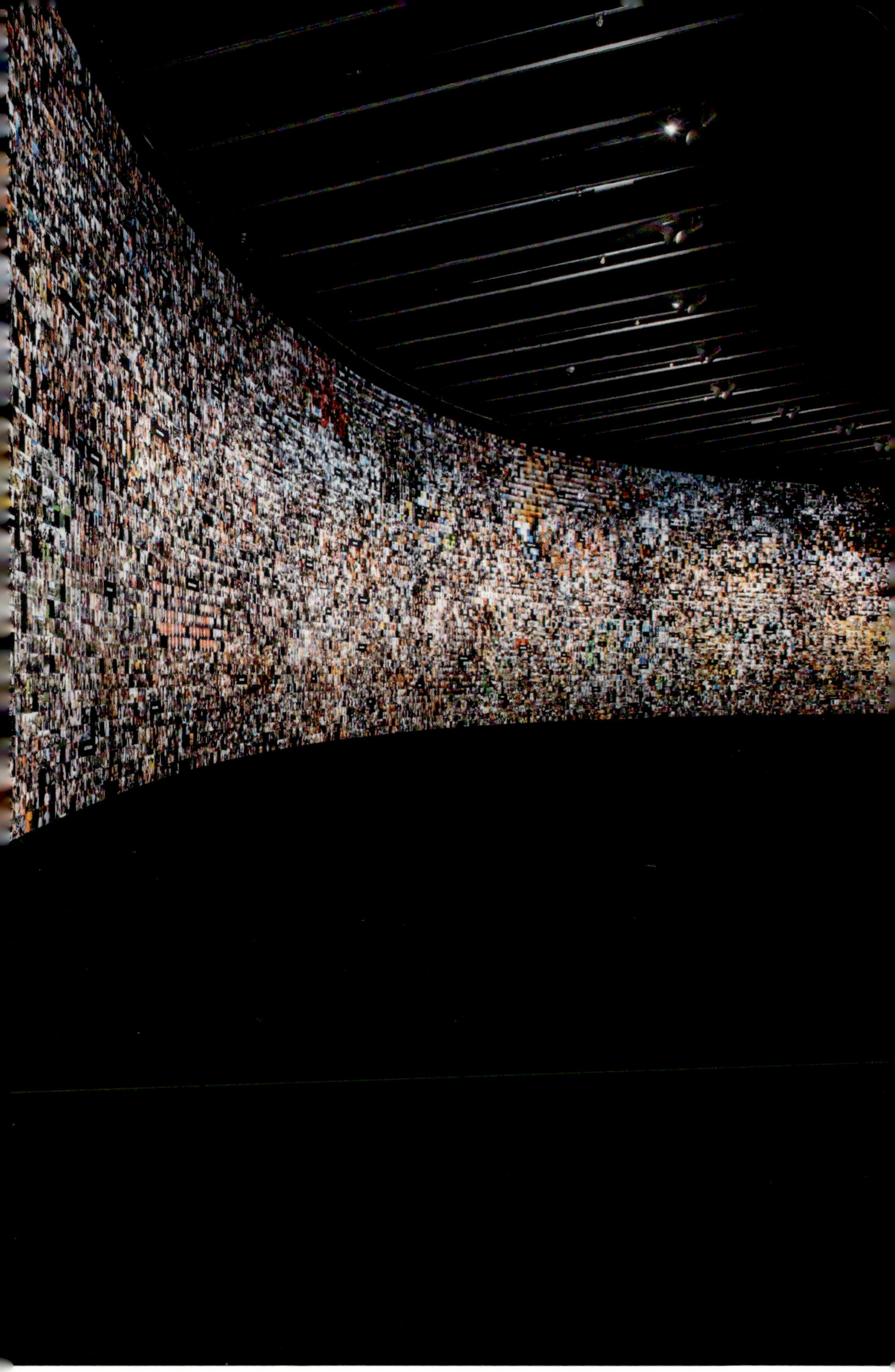

A–B
Harun Farocki
Eye/Machine, 2000

C
Trevor Paglen
From 'Apple' to 'Anomaly', 2019

1 Cf. Aud Sissel Hoel, "Operative Images: Inroads to a New Paradigm of Media Theory," in *Image — Action — Space: Situating the Screen in Visual Practice*, ed. Luisa Feiersinger et al. (Berlin: De Gruyter, 2018), 11–18, accessed January 28, 2022, https://doi.org/10.1515/9783110464979-002. Hoel draws upon Ingrid Hoelzl and Rémi Marie, *Softimage: Towards a New Theory of the Digital Image* (Bristol, UK: Intellect, 2015), 3–4.

2 Guy Debord, *Comments on the Society of the Spectacle*, trans. Malcolm Imrie (London: Verso, 1998), 27 and 28–29.

3 Ibid., 33, where Debord writes of "the global spectacle's present vulgarity."

4 Dipesh Chakrabarty, *The Climate of History in a Planetary Age* (Chicago: University of Chicago Press, 2021).

5 Cf. Tom Bunyard, *Debord, Time and Spectacle* (Leiden: Brill, 2018).

6 Guy Debord, *The Society of the Spectacle*, trans. Donald Nicholson-Smith (New York: Zone Books, 1994), §4.

7 Claire Bishop, "Digital Divide: Contemporary Art and New Media," *Artforum* (September 2012), accessed January 27, 2022, https://www.artforum.com/print/201207/digital-divide-contemporary-art-and-new-media-31944.

8 Emmanual Alloa, "Abstracting," in *The Supermarket of Images*, ed. Peter Szendy et al. (Paris: Gallimard, 2020), 73–94: 75.

9 Pasi Väliaho, *Biopolitical Screens: Image, Power, and the Neoliberal Brain* (Cambridge, MA: MIT Press, 2014), ix.

10 Giorgio Agamben, "Marginal Notes on *Commentaries on the Society of the Spectacle*," in *Means without End: Notes on Politics*, trans. Vincenzo Binetti and Cesare Casarino (Minneapolis: University of Minnesota Press, 2000), 73–90: 76.

11 Jacques Rancière, "Die Arbeit des Bildes/The Work of the Image," in Esther Shalev-Gerz, *MenchenDinge/The Human Aspect of Objects* (Weimar: Stiftung Gedenkstätten Buchenwald und Mittelbau-Dora, 2006), 8–25: 10.

12 Agamben, "Marginal Notes," 82.

13 Ibid., 84.

14 See chapter 1.

15 Cf. Bernard Stiegler and Irit Rogoff, "Transindividuation," in *e-flux journal*, #14 (March 2010), 01/06, accessed January 27, 2022, http://www.e-flux.com/journal/transindividuation/.

16 Cf. Bernard Stiegler, "Technics, Media, Teleology. Interview with Bernard Stiegler," *Theory, Culture & Society*, vol. 24 (7–8) (2007): 334–341, 335.

17 Hito Steyerl, "Too Much World: Is the Internet Dead?" *e-flux journal*, #49 (November 2013), accessed January 27, 2022, https://www.e-flux.com/journal/49/60004/too-much-world-is-the-internet-dead/.

18 Peter Osborne, "The Distributed Image," in *The Postconceptual Condition* (London: Verso, 2018), 143–144.

19 W. J. T. Mitchell, *Image Science: Iconology, Visual Culture, and Media Aesthetics* (Chicago: University of Chicago Press, 2015), 16–17.

20 Walter Benjamin, *The Arcades Project*, trans. Howard Eiland and Kevin McLaughlin (Cambridge, MA: Belknap Press of Harvard University Press, 1999), 463. In what Benjamin calls "dialectical images," ibid., 262f., "what has been comes together in a flash with the now to form a constellation. [...] [I]mage is dialectics at a standstill. For while the relation of the present to the past is purely temporal, the relation of what-has-been to the now is dialectical: not temporal in nature but figural [*bildlich*]." To the one recognizing it it therefore effects a counter rhythm in the ordinary course of events. Cf. Georges Didi-Huberman, *Devant le temps: Histoire de l'art et anachronisme des images* (Paris: Éditions de Minuit, 2000), 117, and chapter 3.

21 Gavin Smith, "Interview: Jean-Luc Godard," *Film Comment* (March/April 1996), accessed January 27, 2022, https://www.filmcomment.com/article/jean-luc-godard-interview-nouvelle-vague-histoires-du-cinema-helas-pour-moi/.
22 Harun Farocki, "Phantom Images," *Public*, no. 29 (2004): 17.
23 Trevor Paglen, "Operational Images," *e-flux journal*, #59 (November 2014), accessed January 27, 2022, https://www.e-flux.com/journal/59/61130/operational-images/.
24 Ibid.
25 Trevor Paglen, "Invisible Images (Your Pictures are Looking at You)," *The New Inquiry* (December 2016), accessed January 27, 2022, https://thenewinquiry.com/invisible-images-your-pictures-are-looking-at-you/.
26 Even Joanna Zylinska's *Nonhuman Photography* (Cambridge, MA: MIT Press, 2017), for instance, is, ultimately, addressed to perceiving human beings.
27 https://www.barbican.org.uk/whats-on/2019/event/trevor-paglen-from-apple-to-anomaly, accessed January 27, 2022.
28 Cf. Nicholas Mirzoeff, *The Right to Look: A Counterhistory of Visuality* (Durham, NC: Duke University Press, 2011).
29 Benjamin H. Bratton, "The Black Stack," in *e-flux journal*, #53 (March 2014), accessed January 27, 2022, http://www.e-flux.com/journal/53/59883/the-black-stack/.
30 http://www.euronomade.info/?p=2268, accessed January 27, 2022. See also Stamatia Portanova, *Whose Time Is It? Asocial Robots, Syncolonialism, and Artificial Chronological Intelligence*, The Contemporary Condition vol. 17 (Berlin: Sternberg Press, 2021).
31 Cf. Antonio Somaini, "Walter Benjamin's Media Theory: The *Medium* and the *Apparat*," *Grey Room*, no. 62 (Winter 2016): 6–41, 7, who refers to Benjamin's "The Work of Art in the Age of Its Technological Reproducibility."
32 Ibid., 7–8.

Exhibition as Reflexive Transformation

Chapter 8

I

In response to an invitation to participate in the 2019 Whitney Biennial at the Whitney Museum of American Art in New York, Forensic Architecture carried out a research project called *Triple-Chaser*, the story of which they presented, in partnership with Laura Poitras's Praxis Films, as a video investigation that premiered at the biennial.[1] In November 2018, US border police fired tear gas grenades at civilians. Photo documentation shows that many of those grenades were manufactured by the Safariland Group, which is owned by Warren B. Kanders, then also vice chair of the board of trustees of the Whitney Museum of American Art. Triple-Chaser is a Safariland manufactured grenade, and a major part of Forensic Architecture's investigation consisted in training computer vision classifiers to detect the canisters of this tear gas grenade among the millions of images shared on the internet, using digital models and photorealistic synthetic environments. They exposed Kanders's connection to the violence committed by the Israeli military against Palestinians in Gaza through the US bullet manufacturer Sierra Bullets as well as — at the request of Decolonize This Place, who led weeks of protest against Kanders's connection to the Whitney — the use of Safariland products by police during civil unrest in Puerto Rico in 2018. Due to the lack of action by the Whitney in response to the allegations against Kanders, Forensic Architecture withdrew from the biennial along with several other artists. Five days later, Kanders resigned from the museum's board of trustees and Forensic Architecture withdrew their request to have their work withdrawn from the exhibition. A couple of weeks later, when the Triple-Chaser tear gas grenade was used by police against Black Lives Matter activists across the US, Kanders announced that he would divest Safariland of its crowd control products divisions, including those that sell tear gas.

The *Triple-Chaser* case raises a number of questions about the relationship between art, aesthetics, society and reality in contemporary practices, and the function of exhibition in this relationship. Forensic Architecture is an agency composed not "merely" of artists, but of an interdisciplinary team of architects, filmmakers, artists, scientists, coders, journalists, and lawyers. "Our work is indicative of the advent of a new kind of political art: one that is less interested in commenting on than intervening in political realities," they state in an opinion piece in *The Guardian* in 2021.[2] Their practice consists in the production of architectural evidence in the form of building surveys, physical or digital models, animations, video, and maps of various forms, and, in the presentation of this evidence, in juridical, political, and — as in the case of *Triple-Chaser* — artistic forums.[3] With reference to the etymology of the term "forensics," the origins of which can be traced back to the Latin *forensis*, which means "pertaining to the forum," they regard their practice as a mode of public address.[4] It is also, founder and head Eyal Weizman stresses, an *aesthetic* practice "because it depends on both the modes and the means by which reality is sensed and presented publicly."[5] Following Bruno Latour, he understands aesthetics as "the ability to perceive and to be concerned," so that, in their practice, aesthetics concerns an augmentation of the capacity to sense as well as a process of sense-making and composition, a rhetoric of presentation.[6] Even though Weizman calls each forum, including that of art, for instance at the Whitney, a distorting lens of its own kind, politically and socially engaged artistic practices, as well as the kind of aesthetic practice undertaken by Forensic Architecture, necessarily involve some degree of exhibition as part of their public address.[7] What Forensic Architecture tries to avoid, however, is to remain in the grip of any single of any of these forums.[8] The Whitney exhibition, therefore, was not restricted to the museum's dedicated exhibition rooms. Not complying with the structures set up by the Whitney as a platform for presentation, the exhibition — the socialization of their evidence — also took place in the lobby, online, and with friends from Decolonize This Place demonstrating in front of Warren Kanders's townhouse in Greenwich Village.

II

If the Western museum of modern art was founded on the separation of its exhibits from their ritualistic and everyday functions, granting them autonomy by disconnecting them from the sociopolitical reality surrounding the museum, how are we to think of contemporary artistic and aesthetic practices like Forensic Architecture's that constantly move beyond the forum of art and perforate its borders? A case such as *Triple-Chaser* seems particularly suited to lend itself to art theorist Lucy Steeds's suggestion — with reference to Walter Benjamin's notions of *Ausstellbarkeit* (fitness, or capacity, for exhibition, or its exhibitionability) and *Ausstellungswert* (exhibition value) in "The Work of Art in the Age of Its Technological Reproducibility" — to analyze art based on its exposability, understood as "its *capacity to produce sociopolitical entanglement*."[9] In contrast to most modern artworks, a contemporary artwork is often distributed across different instantiations, elements and appearances. In socially engaged art practices, for example, the events by which the work of art becomes public may be distributed across time and space: social interactions in physical spaces with and without an audience; online and offline texts, films, photos, interviews, and different kinds of documentation that function as an integral part of the work rather than "extra-diegetic" representations of it.[10]

As I will try to argue in the following, the moment of appearing, of becoming visible, is a fundamental part of the creation and the production of the artwork. The ostensive, which entails the act of showing, displaying, exhibiting and demonstrating something, is an indispensable part of the manifestation of any artwork — contemporary as well as modern — and hence a condition for its being perceived and experienced. This is not yet, however, what makes the thing being shown art or an aesthetic object, be it physical or not. What makes it artistic, or at least aesthetic, is a certain openness with regard to the meaning or signification of the thing that appears, which ignites a process of reflexivity that, ultimately, is a negotiation of the world and how we live in it. In other words, there is a decisive difference between exhibition as presentation of an object or phenomenon "as it is" (non-artistic), and exhibition as presentation of an object or phenomenon as an object of reflection that sparks a process of sense-making or a renegotiation of the meaning the object is generally attributed. The latter is a socializing image practice which creates what Weizman calls an "open verification" where "[v]erification relates to truth not as a noun or as an essence, but as a practice, one that is contingent, collective, and poly-perspectival."[11]

We live in a time when artistic and aesthetic practices resist the categories of modern art theory, when traditional genres of art have been dissolved in all kinds of hybrid forms, and when art increasingly destabilizes the border between art and non-art in endeavors to address urgent questions about climate change, migration, violence, human rights, decolonization, racism, sexism, etc.[12] The destabilization of the border between art and non-art, between art and political reality, of course, also involves the ways in which these practices are exhibited and our art theoretical notions of "exhibition." According to art historian and critic Kim West's reading of sociologist and museologist Jean Davallon, "an exhibition creates a separate symbolic space, but one featuring 'real' objects rather than representations [...] the exhibited objects always retain a connection to their 'external' reality, transcending their adherence to the exhibition's symbolic dimension."[13] My point is that the double articulation of the objects as real *and* symbolic through an act of exhibition is a decisive element in making a negotiation of reality possible. The act of exhibition makes something/ the work present but, at the same time, it creates a distance, precisely because the appearance of the work has been arranged and addressed to someone/us; what is exhibited is given as having been organized and deliberately made available to appear to us.[14] This distance to the object presented installs a difference and an indeterminacy with regard to its status and meaning. In the language of Jacques Rancière, the object becomes a pensive image in a zone of indeterminacy between passive representation and active operation, between non-art and art.[15] The creation of such difference and indeterminacy is what allows for a reflexive transformation and questioning of the status quo, of hegemonic, authoritative narratives about the world and what is.

For a while now we have been thinking about exhibitions as that through which (most) art becomes known.[16] According to curator Bruce W. Ferguson:

> [E]xhibitions of art are, by virtue of their visible prominence, structurally intrinsic and perhaps psychologically necessary to any full understanding of most art. Exhibitions can be understood then as the *medium* of contemporary art in the sense of being its main agency of communication — the body and voice from which an authoritative character emerges.[17]

In addition, West stresses that exhibitions are the media of art's public realization: "as media, art exhibitions should be conceived of as *affirmative in their mediating functions*. They are the spatial and technical arrangements through which artworks are publicly realized."[18]

The question, then, is, what constitutes an exhibition? Does it have to take on a more or less institutionalized form, in a space or at a site dedicated to art, like the ones Ferguson writes about? What is the relationship between the work of art and its exhibition? Are they still distinguishable? When does the exhibition of a work of art begin? When does a work of art become "an object of appreciation" (in the terminology of philosopher George Dickie's institutional theory of art)?[19] I am in many ways sympathetic to Ferguson's analogy between an exhibition of art and an utterance or a set of utterances and to his proposal to see the art exhibition as the speech act of an institution, but what I am after here is not "how art serves exhibitions as their very element of speech."[20] I am interested in "the public realization" of art both within and beyond the authoritative art museum institution, as I see the work of art as being inescapably bound to an act of exhibition, a making-public. In other words, an element of exhibition is an integral part of the very concept of the work of art. It is not something that is added later. It is produced through the work of art's mode and structure of address.

As curator and art historian James Voorhies remarks in relation to Carsten Höller's exhibition "Experience" at the New Museum in New York in 2011–2012:

> Höller's exhibition demonstrates the fugitive position a critical attitude faces in the midst of globalised contemporary art, an industry that reduces the potency of critique through absorption and the need to produce experiences for generating capital. It also demonstrates that critique cannot ascribe such an obvious cause-and-effect relationship to its intentions. It should arrest the spectator's attention by modeling situations of strangeness and confusion that disrupt expectations without literally instructing how participation transpires.[21]

While I largely agree with Voorhies in this analysis, I would perhaps be more careful about differentiating too clearly between art and its exhibition or being made public. For instance, when he describes an approach that prioritizes the spectator, and that "utilises the exhibition as a productive way to explore and expand what, where, and how art reaches its public."[22] I argue that the exhibition form is constitutive of the work of art — which is why "exposition" might be a more appropriate term than "exhibition," as the latter may perhaps be taken to refer to something pre-existing, i.e. a re-presentation or display. Any work of art has a structure of address — an *Appellstruktur* in the terminology of Wolfgang Iser — that informs the ways in which it can be received.[23] It is thus, in a fundamental way, addressing and exposing itself to a public of indefinite strangers.[24] Subsequently, the curator can make it address a public at another level and in any given context, but the first moment of exhibition already occurs in and through the address of the work "itself" — a work of art always already involves an act of exhibition in its initial address to someone, a you, an audience, readers, listeners, spectators, participants, collaborators. It is open to be "received" by anybody who is able to enter into its structure of enunciation, and who will actualize or concretize it.

III

What, then, has happened to art, and what is it that still qualifies the politically and socially engaged practices — of which Forensic Architecture is an example — as artistic?

The past twenty-thirty years have seen thoroughgoing changes within art that have made it difficult to recognize its works as works of art in modern terms. Art can no longer be placed in specific genres and categories belonging to particular art forms, often it is no longer expressed in a delimited work, and it is hard to distinguish from its surroundings and what is not art. Modernist ideas about delimited works, a shared project and a shared progressive history are no longer valid, or at least they no longer hold a monopoly on the conceptual framework for the work of art.[25] The concepts and categories that were developed to describe and analyze modern art seem to have lost their explanatory force in relation to the art that concerns and speaks to our contemporary times, which is why we, to a large extent, have replaced the term "modern art" with "contemporary art." The emergence of contemporary art thus necessitates a paradigm shift within the study of art in which the very notion of art is at stake, including the ways in which it is exhibited and the ways in which it involves a public.

During the transition from modern to contemporary art, the relationship between artistic practice, sense-making, and the sociopolitical reality in which art takes place and by which it is nourished, has undergone substantial changes. In order to catch up with contemporary art, the disciplines of art history and aesthetics therefore have to revise a number of their traditional notions concerning, among others, the historicity of art, the category of work, artistic autonomy, and how these are interrelated. Such revision will help understand how contemporary artistic practices create meaning in relation to the non-artistic societal reality in which they operate, and how the otherwise very diverse practices and works we designate as contemporary art function *as art*.

From the perspective of the theory, history and critique of art, the social relevance of contemporary art is not only based on the urgent issues it raises: climate change, racism, human rights, etc., but also on *how* these issues are raised and made public through an *artistic* generation of meaning. In contrast to a certain classical understanding of the avant-garde, I do not see the aesthetic as becoming political through an art that lets itself dissolve into everyday life. The aesthetic is political precisely because of its ability to differentiate itself from the normally inconspicuous organization of our everyday lifeworld, and, through such differentiation, provoke critical reflection on this organization — which is what makes a certain degree of exhibition of decisive importance.[26]

Contemporary works of art are difficult to recognize as art from the perspective of modern aesthetic theory because, at a formal, objective level, they can neither be included under the tradition of a particular art form, nor do they limit themselves to the traditional artistic media, but assimilate new technologies and industrial modes of production, among other things, in artistic practice — for instance when Forensic Architecture trains an algorithm to detect Triple-Chaser tear gas canisters while simultaneously shedding critical light on that very technology.[27] When they not only evade comparison with the art of the past, but also seem boundless in relation to their non-artistic outside and the non-aesthetic lifeworld, it often becomes unclear what forms part of the work and what does not. These boundless works, which began, in particular, to appear in the 1960s in performance, Fluxus, Minimalism, Conceptual art, etc., do not enroll in the developmental history of traditional art forms and they are no longer given as something defined *objectively*.[28]

Given that the open, boundless works have made it impossible to connect artistic autonomy to the category of work, we need to revise our notion of artistic autonomy if such an idea is to maintain any usefulness in a critical understanding of contemporary art.[29] I subscribe to Juliane Rebentisch's analysis that the art theoretical answer to the question of the continuation of artistic autonomy in contemporary art lies in the coupling of the boundless form with the effects of art. This means that we have to move our focus from the work as an organic, distinct unity to the ways in which it interacts with its surroundings and the subjectivities that experience it, and that we have to consider the specificity of the aesthetic as characterized by a particular relation between sense-making subjects and objects open to sense-making that mutually affect each other. The contemporary work of art depends on the subjects who take part in it, and it is, so to speak, not until in and through this participation that it is realized as work. The spectators thereby entangle their contemporary social realities in the structure of the work. In the process of sense-making they make their own associations and dissociations, based on their particular spaces of experience.[30] Artist Tania Bruguera's *political-timing-specific art* could be an example of how the work of art is linked to the specificity of the political moment of its realization. According to Bruguera:

> Political-timing-specific art doesn't simply address the news cycle. It's also about understanding how, under certain circumstances, politics can define the aesthetic. This kind of art practice embraces the fact that the work will not have a stable meaning, because this is how politics operates — tackling perceptions as they unfold in real time and mobilizing the emotional landscape these perceptions generate.[31]

The autonomy of art, therefore, has to be understood as something experiential, not to abandon the category of work but to redefine it as a dynamic process in which the aesthetic is no longer separated from the non-aesthetic as something objectifiably different, but where the aesthetic consists in a reflexive transformation of the non-aesthetic.[32] The work of art consists not only of its physical presence, but also of its senses and the values in which it is inscribed and which are inscribed in it. As politically time specific, it takes part in the unfolding of the present.[33]

Contemporary aesthetic practices thus also challenge the ways in which the sphere of art is traditionally granted autonomy. Discussing Rancière's philosophy of emancipation and the celebration of openness, indeterminacy and inefficacy in his account of the aesthetic experience, art historian and critic Sven Lütticken convincingly suggests that "the aesthetic is precisely the domain where a 'politics of the sensible' can unfold that is not to be judged exclusively or primarily by its degree of immediate social efficacy."[34] This, according to Lütticken, means that, "[a]esthetic art" is aesthetic practice to the extent that it questions and challenges the relative autonomy of art. The aesthetic is the constant questioning of art and, more precisely, of claims for art's autonomy, counteracting its reduction from persistent problem to ideological given."[35] Art's structural autonomy is not a given, is not an assumption we can leave unquestioned once and for all, and, in this sense, the aesthetic is exactly what persistently questions and irritates limited notions of autonomous art: "If the aesthetic problematizes the relationship of autonomy and heteronomy, then this means that an act or, beyond that, a praxis can be termed aesthetic insofar as it *lets autonomy appear sensibly as a problem* in a world where subjectivities and objectifications are profoundly entangled, where different agencies coexist and collide."[36]

In the analytical approach to contemporary artistic practices, there is therefore also a need to revise what we understand by the formal aspects of the work of art. The formal does not merely relate to a compositional manipulation of a number of abstract visual or physical properties within a closed and purely self-referential system. Many contemporary aesthetic and artistic practices — including that of Forensic Architecture and different kinds of socially engaged art — operate through and within a highly complex formal system, which, in the words of Grant Kester, "is structured through somatic, social, physical and verbal interaction that is intersubjective and also directed at specific institutional and discursive structures."[37] Contemporary artistic creations not only integrate or include thematic areas of the non-artistic social lifeworld, but also formally open themselves up to these areas — artist Jakob Jakobsen's *Hospital for Self Medication*, for instance, as an alternative to the official hospital in its openness to experimentation in care and treatment — which means that the question of the relationship between art and non-art arises in a new way. The contemporary artistic practices in question here generate a special experience that relates reflexively to the experiences and perceptions of the different areas of our lifeworld, in which they intervene or to which they relate.[38]

In pursuing machine learning technology, which is often put to repressive use in policing or by the military, Forensic Architecture not only use it as part of the composition of their case, but, also, to interrogate and shed critical light on how the technology works;[39] they are simultaneously investigating "the sites of violence and repression, where physical and photographic evidence is contested, and the computational field of the algorithm, striving to unpack and make accountable the very tools of analysis."[40] The video shown at the Whitney — and now on their website — engages the relation between human and machine vision: similarly to Trevor Paglen's work, "the film is addressed to a human public, but," as they explained to *Artforum*, "it is built around the images that we use to train an algorithm to see."[41] Furthermore, the aesthetic practice of Forensic Architecture is a *relational* practice that not only — to paraphrase Jean-Luc Godard — investigates politics, but aims at carrying out these investigations politically.[42] So, the practice of Forensic Architecture not only concerns what goes into a given image, but also the composition of a socially productive practice relation that makes it possible to bring that image into being to begin with.[43] Thus, the Triple-Chaser project at the Whitney was realized on the basis of relations with activists in Tijuana on the Mexican-US border and Palestine, including artist Emily Jacir, who collected material for the investigation, as well as with people from all over the world sending images of the teargas canisters.

IV

Challenges to conventional forms of presenting art and its ideas to the public, guided by ideologies of modernity, have become more and more fundamental since Robert Smithson's non-sites in the 1960s. We therefore need to revise some of the basic notions and categories through which we understand art, in order to bring our theories up to speed with contemporary artistic and curatorial practice. On the other hand, we should not lose sight of the exhibitionary aspect of art as that aspect is still, I claim, one of the defining characteristics of art: when dissolved in the lifeworld, art, at best, becomes activism (caring for how we live together); at worst, it becomes entertainment (addressing consumers rather than what Jacques Rancière would call emancipated spectators). The Latin root of the noun "exhibition," *exhibere*, means "to hold out." I hope to have demonstrated that the exhibition and making perceptible of the work is crucial to its ability to create a reflexive transformation of the non-aesthetic and non-artistic spheres of the lifeworld in which it embeds itself or at which it is directed. The act of exhibition simultaneously presents and creates distance. This distance installs a difference, which makes reflexive transformation of our shared reality possible. When Forensic Architecture, to return to our point of departure, make use of reenactments in their investigations of human rights violations — and address these reenactments to a public — real space is turned into a model of itself, and a negotiation of how this reality should be perceived, what sense to make of it, can begin.

A–E
Forensic Architecture
Triple-Chaser, 2019

F
Decolonize This Place
Action at the Whitney Museum of American Art in New York, 2019

G
Forensic Architecture
The Murder of Halit Yozgat. 77sqm_9:26min, 2017

H
Forensic Architecture
Killing in Umm al-Hiran, 2018

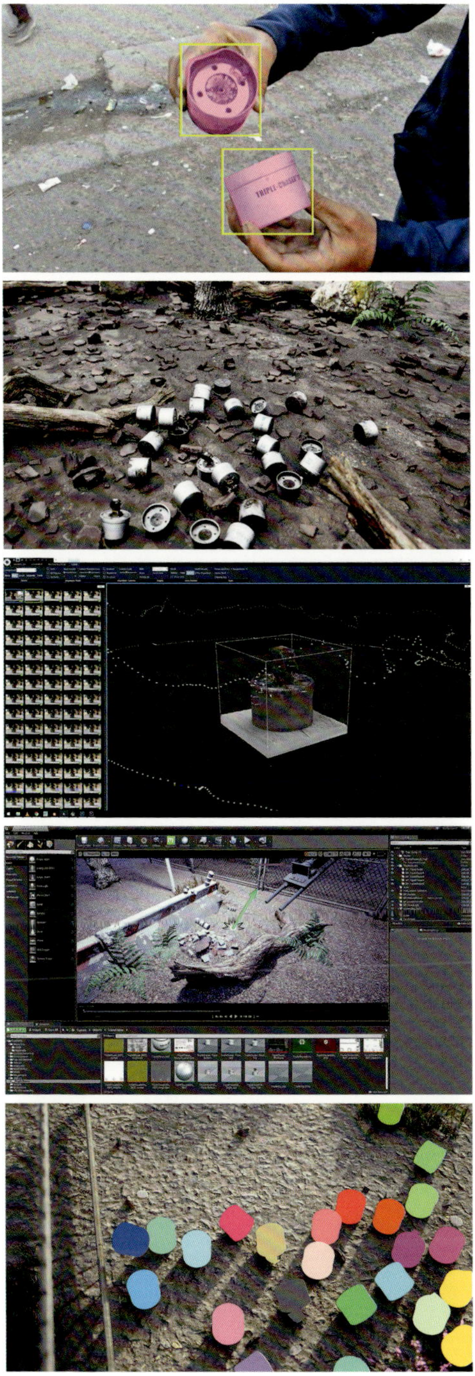

A-E Forensic Architecture

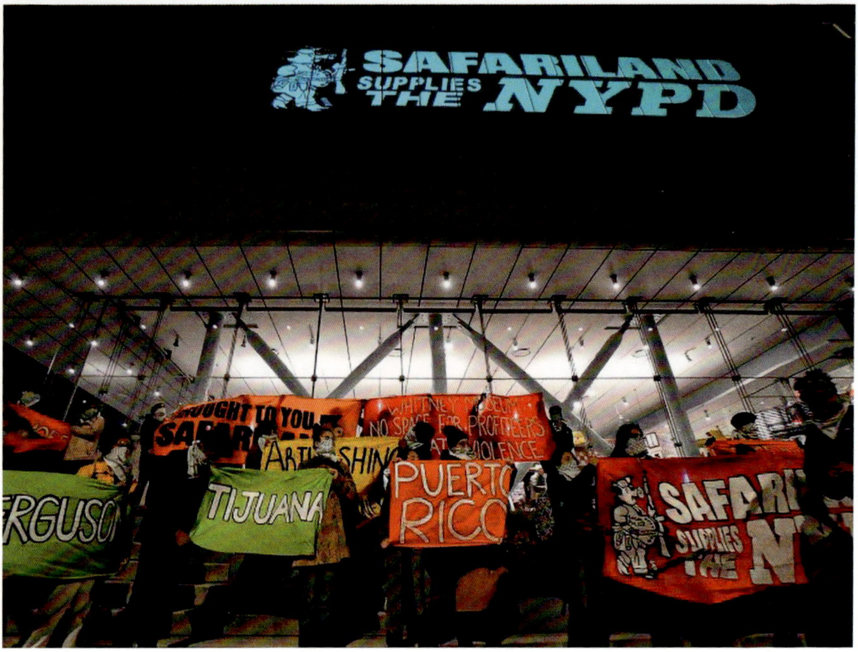

F Decolonize This Place

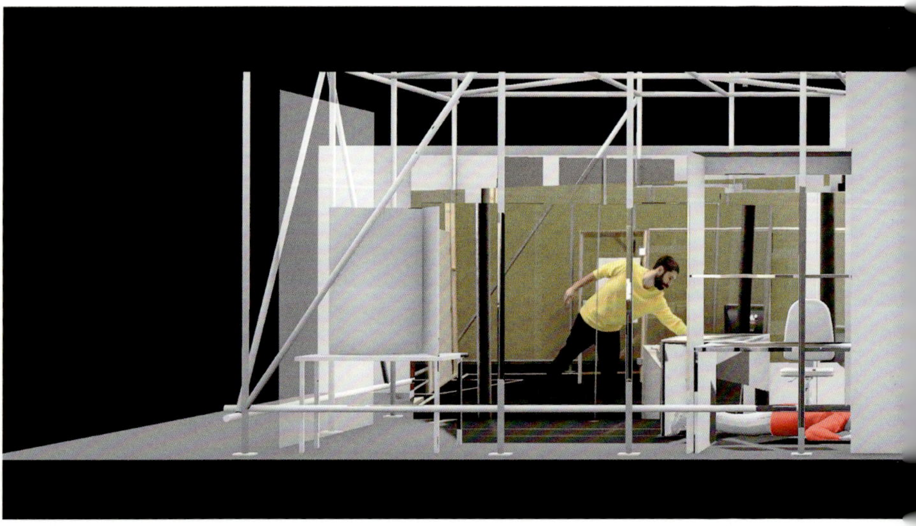

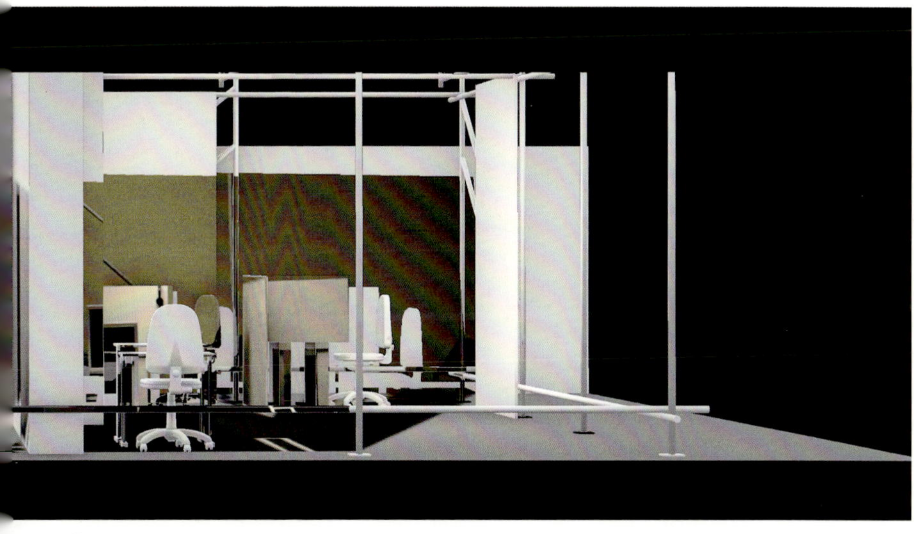

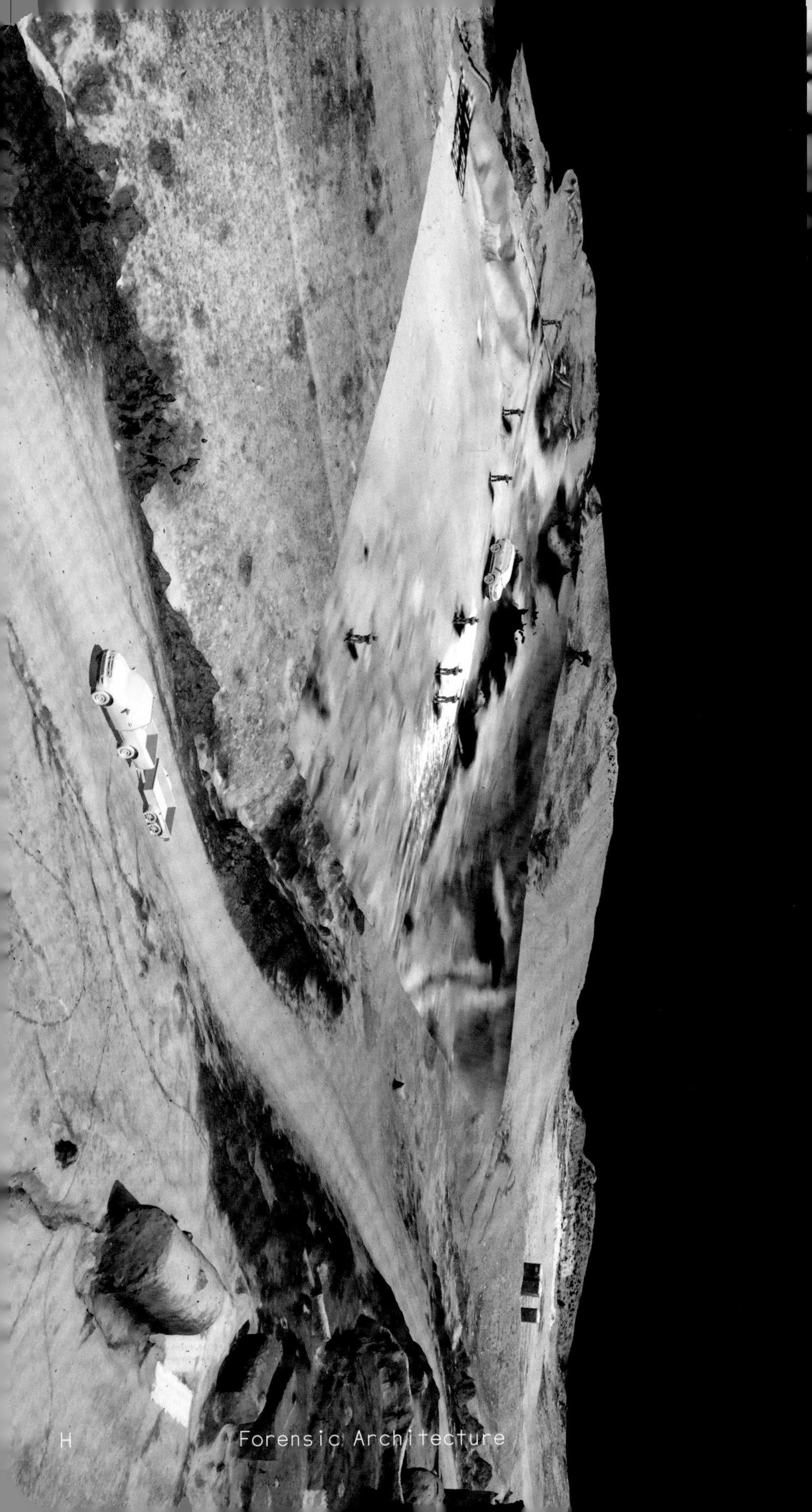

Notes

1 The video is publicly accessible via Forensic Architecture's website, where the project is also described in more detail: https://forensic-architecture.org/investigation/triple-chaser, accessed January 28, 2022. My description is lifted from this website, which also links to the media coverage of the project.

2 Forensic Architecture, "Our art deals with real injustices, some in Palestine: no wonder we faced opposition," *The Guardian*, August 20, 2021, accessed January 28, 2022, https://www.theguardian.com/commentisfree/2021/aug/20/art-real-injustices-palestine-manchester-exhibition-forensic-artchitecture.

3 Cf. Eyal Weizman, *Forensic Architecture: Violence at the Threshold of Detectability* (New York: Zone Books, 2017), 9 and 64.

4 Ibid., 65. Apart from the etymological connection between forensics, forensis and forum, it is worth noticing that we not only use the word "exhibit" for an object that is shown to the public in a museum or gallery, it also designates a thing used as evidence in a juridical context.

5 Ibid., 94. The notion of aesthetics involved in Forensic Architecture's practice is elaborated theoretically in Matthew Fuller and Eyal Weizman, *Investigative Aesthetics: Conflicts and Commons in the Politics of Truth* (London: Verso, 2021).

6 Ibid., 95. Not least Bruno Latour's article "From Realpolitik to Dingpolitik, or How to Make Things Public," seems to have been a major influence on the conception of Forensic Architecture's overall project. For Latour's text, see *Making Things Public: Atmospheres of Democracy*, ZKM exh. cat., eds. Bruno Latour and Peter Weibel (Cambridge, MA: MIT Press, 2005), 4–31.

7 Eyal Weizman, "Forensic Architecture," online lecture as part of the series "Architectures of the New Curatorial" at the Royal College of Art, London, December 10, 2020.

8 Ibid.

9 Lucy Steeds, "Exposability: On the Taking-Place in Future of Art," in *Theater, Garden, Bestiary: A Materialist History of Exhibitions*, eds. Tristan Garcia and Vincent Normand (Berlin: Sternberg Press, 2019), 75–84: 75 (italics in the original).

10 Cf. Kim West, "Concepts for the Critical Study of Art Exhibitions as Media," in *Theater, Garden, Bestiary*, eds. Garcia and Normand, 45–55: 48: "the complex of apparatuses in relation to which exhibitionary apparatuses today achieve their definition is the network of digital media, understood in a wide sense: as the matrix of ubiquitous, interconnected devices and platforms, which forms a global infrastructure of shared information standards and ideals, synchronised with the production models of contemporary capitalism, imposing its rhythms and demands on social, cultural, and political life."

11 Eyal Weizman, "Open Verification," *Becoming Digital*, e-flux Architecture (June 2019), accessed January 28, 2022, https://www.e-flux.com/architecture/becoming-digital/248062/open-verification/. Cf. also Eyal Weizman (in conversation with Jacob Lund), "Inhabiting the Hyper-Aesthetic Image," *Nordic Journal of Aesthetics*, nos. 61–62 (2021): 230-243, 236ff.

12 Cf. for instance Oliver Marchart, "[A]rtistic practices have emerged for which it is more important to be connected to political practices than to art institutions themselves, which in turn, necessarily changes our concept of the public sphere — and of the institution as well." *Conflictual Aesthetics: Artistic Activism and the Public Sphere* (Berlin: Sternberg Press, 2019), 144.

13 West, "Concepts for the Critical Study," 45. West's observations are based on Jean Davallon's *L'exposition à l'œuvre: Stratégies de communication et médiation symbolique* (Paris: L'Harmattan, 1999), 11.

14 Tristan Garcia, "Neither Gesture nor Work of Art: Exhibition as Disposing for Appearance," in *Theater, Garden, Bestiary*, eds. Garcia and Normand, 181–194: 183.

15 Jacques Rancière, “The Pensive Image,” in *The Emancipated Spectator*, trans. Gregory Elliott (London: Verso, 2009), 107–132.
16 Cf. *Thinking about Exhibitions,* eds. Reesa Greenberg et al. (London: Routledge, 1996).
17 Bruce W. Ferguson, “Exhibition Rhetorics: Material speech and utter sense,” in *Thinking about Exhibitions*, eds. Greenberg et al., 175–190: 176.
18 West, “Concepts for the Critical Study,” 45.
19 Cf. George Dickie, *Art and the Aesthetic: An Institutional Analysis* (Ithaca, NY: Cornell University Press, 1974).
20 Ferguson, “Exhibition Rhetorics,” 183–184.
21 James Voorhies, *Beyond Objecthood: The Exhibition as a Critical Form Since 1968* (Cambridge, MA: MIT Press, 2017), 10.
22 Ibid., 12.
23 Cf. Wolfgang Iser, *Die Appellstruktur der Texte. Unbestimmtheit als Wirkungsbedingung literarischer Prosa* (Konstanz: Verlag der Druckerei und Verlagsanstalt Konstanz Universitätsverlag, 1970).
24 Cf. Michael Warner, “Publics and Counterpublics,” *Public Culture*, 14:1 (2002): 59–90.
25 See chapter 6.
26 Cf. Jacques Rancière, *The Politics of Aesthetics: The Distribution of the Sensible*, trans. Gabriel Rockhill (London: Continuum, 2004), and Juliane Rebentisch, *Theorien der Gegenwartskunst — zur Einführung* (Hamburg: Junius, 2013); Juliane Rebentisch, *Aesthetics of Installation Art*, trans. Daniel Hendrickson with Gerrit Jackson (Berlin: Sternberg Press, 2012); and Juliane Rebentisch, *The Art of Freedom: On the Dialectics of Democratic Existence* [2011], trans. Joseph Ganahl (Cambridge: Polity, 2016). These and the following points are heavily influenced by Rebentisch’s work.
27 Cf. Weizman, “Inhabiting the Hyper-Aesthetic Image,” 240.
28 Cf. Rebentisch, *Theorien der Gegenwartskunst*, passim.
29 For an analysis of autonomy and contemporary aesthetic practices, cf. also Sven Lütticken, *Cultural Revolution: Aesthetic Practice after Autonomy* (Berlin: Sternberg Press, 2017).
30 Cf. Rancière, *The Emancipated Spectator*, 1–23.
31 Tania Bruguera, “Notes on Political Timing Specificity,” *Artforum*, 57:9 (2019), accessed January 28, 2022, https://www.artforum.com/print/201905/notes-on-political-timing-specificity-79513. Cf. also Claire Bishop, “Rise to the Occasion,” *Artforum*, 57:9 (2019), accessed January 28, 2022, https://www.artforum.com/print/201905/claire-bishop-on-the-art-of-political-timing-79512.
32 Cf. Rebentisch, *Theorien der Gegenwartskunst*, 40–57, and Rancière, *The Politics of Aesthetics*.
33 Cf. Fuller and Weizman, *Investigative Aesthetics*, 221.
34 Lütticken, *Cultural Revolution*, 13–14.
35 Ibid., 14.
36 Ibid.
37 Grant Kester, “The Limitations of the Exculpatory Critique,” *Nordic Journal of Aesthetics*, no. 53 (2017): 73–98, 97.
38 Cf. Rebentisch, *Theorien der Gegenwartskunst*, 117f.
39 Cf. Weizman, “Inhabiting the Hyper-Aesthetic Image,” 240.
40 Fuller and Weizman, *Investigative Aesthetics*, 188.
41 *Artforum*, May 13, 2019, accessed January 28, 2022, https://www.artforum.com/interviews/forensic-architecture-on-safariland-and-their-whitney-biennial-commission-79785.
42 Fuller and Weizman, *Investigative Aesthetics*, 195.
43 Weizman, “Inhabiting the Hyper-Aesthetic Image,” 237.

Chapter 1

A
Iñigo Manglano-Ovalle
Phantom Truck, 2007
Aluminum and epoxy paint
10 x 2.5 x 4 m
Project for documenta 12, Kassel, 2007
© Iñigo Manglano-Ovalle
Courtesy of Iñigo Manglano-Ovalle and Galerie Thomas Schulte, Berlin

B–E
Thomas Hirschhorn
Touching Reality, 2012
Video, silent, endless loop, 4:45 min.
Courtesy of the artist and Galerie Chantal Crousel, Paris
© Thomas Hirschhorn / ADAGP, Paris (2022)

F–H
Alfredo Jaar
The Sound of Silence, 2006
Wood structure, aluminum, fluorescent tubes, LED lights, flashlights, tripods, video projection (8:00 min. loop)
Software design: Ravi Rajan
Overall dimensions variable
Courtesy of MONA, Hobart, Goodman Gallery, Johannesburg/Cape Town, Galeria Oliva Arauna, Madrid, kamel mennour, Paris, Galerie Thomas Schulte, Berlin, Museum of Contemporary Art, Chicago, Philadelphia Museum of Art, Philadelphia, Galerie Lelong & Co., New York, and the artist

I
Alfredo Jaar
May 1, 2011, 2011
Two LCD monitors and two framed prints
Original White House photograph by Pete Souza
Overall dimensions variable
Photography: Frazer Spowart
Courtesy of Galerie Lelong & Co., New York, kamel mennour, Paris, Galerie Thomas Schulte, Berlin, and the artist

J–K
Alfredo Jaar
Lament of the Images, 2002
Three illuminated texts, light screen, text by David Levi Strauss
Overall dimensions variable
Courtesy of Galerie Lelong & Co., New York, Louisiana Museum of Modern Art, Humlebæk, Museum of Modern Art, New York, and the artist, New York

Chapter 2

A
Esther Shalev-Gerz
Between Listening and Telling: Last Witnesses, Auschwitz 1945–2005, 2005
Installation view
Photograph by P. Simon. © Esther Shalev-Gerz

B
Esther Shalev-Gerz
Between Listening and Telling: Last Witnesses, Auschwitz 1945–2005, 2005
Video projections
Photograph by Arno Gisinger. © Esther Shalev-Gerz

C
Esther Shalev-Gerz
MenschenDinge/The Human Aspect of Objects, 2006
Installation view
Photograph by Arno Gisinger. © Esther Shalev-Gerz

D
Esther Shalev-Gerz
MenschenDinge/The Human Aspect of Objects, 2006
Pewter broach
Photograph by Esther Shalev-Gerz. © Esther Shalev-Gerz

Chapter 3

A
Jean-Luc Godard
Histoire(s) du cinéma, 1998
Film still
Reproduced from Jean-Luc Godard, *Histoires du cinéma*, vol. 1, *Toutes les histoires et Une histoire seule* (Paris: Gallimard – Gaumont, 1998), p. 110
© Éditions Gallimard

B
Jean-Luc Godard
Histoire(s) du cinéma, 1998
Film still
Reproduced from Jean-Luc Godard, *Histoire(s) du cinéma*, vol. 1, *Toutes les histoires et Une histoire seule* (Paris: Gallimard – Gaumont, 1998), p. 133
© Éditions Gallimard

C
Jean-Luc Godard
Histoire(s) du cinéma, 1998
Film still
Reproduced from Jean-Luc Godard, *Histoire(s) du cinéma*, vol. 1, *Toutes les histoires et Une histoire seule* (Paris: Gallimard – Gaumont, 1998), p. 134
© Éditions Gallimard

D
Jean-Luc Godard
Histoire(s) du cinéma, 1998
Film still
Reproduced from Jean-Luc Godard, *Histoire(s) du cinéma*, vol. 4, *Le contrôle de l'univers et Les signes parmi nous* (Paris: Gallimard – Gaumont, 1998), p. 192
© Éditions Gallimard

Chapter 4

A
Kader Attia
Oil and Sugar #2, 2007
Single channel video projection, color, sound, 4:30 min.
Courtesy of the artist, Galerie Nagel Draxler, Collection Tate Modern, London; and ICA Institute for Contemporary Art Boston

B
Kader Attia
Holy Land, 2006
Site-specific installation. Mirrors
Installation view on the Canary Islands, 2007
Courtesy of the artist
Photo by Kader Attia

C
Kader Attia
Untitled (Ghardaïa), 2009
Installation, cooked couscous on plinth, digital prints on paper
Installation view, "But a Storm Is Blowing from Paradise: Contemporary Art of the Middle East and North Africa," Solomon R. Guggenheim Museum, New York, April 29–October 5, 2016
Courtesy of the artist
Photograph by David Heald

D
Kader Attia
Reflecting Memory, 2016
Single-channel HD digital video projection, color, sound, 48:01 min.
Courtesy of the artist, Collection MACVAL, France, Collection MAC Marseille, France, Galleria Continua, Galerie Krinzinger, Lehmann Maupin, and Galerie Nagel Draxler

E–F
Kader Attia
Le grand miroir du monde, 2017
Site-specific installation. Fragments of mirrors
Exhibition view, "Continua Sphères Ensemble," Galleria Continua, Le Centquatre, Paris, 2017
Courtesy of the artist and Galleria Continua
Photo by Oak Taylor-Smith

Chapter 5

A–B
Hito Steyerl
Duty Free Art, 2015
Three channel HD video with sound
38:21 min.
Image CC 4.0 Hito Steyerl
Courtesy of the artist

C–D
Hito Steyerl
Factory of the Sun, 2015
Single channel high-definition video, environment, luminescent LE grid, beach chairs
23:00 min.
Image CC 4.0 Hito Steyerl
Courtesy of the artist, Andrew Kreps Gallery, New York, and Esther Schipper, Berlin

E
Camille Henrot
Office of Unreplied Emails, 2016
Exhibition view, "Dissolving Margins," ICA Singapore, 2018
© ADAGP Camille Henrot
Courtesy of the artist and Hauser & Wirth

F
Camille Henrot
The Pale Fox, 2014
Exhibition view, Westfälischer Kunstverein, Münster, 2015
© ADAGP Camille Henrot
Courtesy of the artist, kamel mennour, Paris / London and Hauser & Wirth
Photo by Thorsten Arendt
Featured in the installation: image of "Tiger Shaking," photography by Tim Flach

G
Camille Henrot
The Pale Fox, 2014
Exhibition view, Kunsthal Charlottenborg, Copenhagen, 2014
© ADAGP Camille Henrot
Courtesy of the artist, kamel mennour, Paris / London, and König Galerie, Berlin / London / Seoul
Photo by Anders Sune Berg

H–J
Camille Henrot
Grosse Fatigue, 2013
© ADAGP Camille Henrot
Courtesy of the artist, Silex Films, and kamel mennour, Paris/London

Chapter 6

A
"Soulèvements," Jeu de Paume, Paris, 2016–2017
Installation of exhibition
© Georges Didi-Huberman
Photo by Georges Didi-Huberman

B
"Soulèvements," Jeu de Paume, Paris, 2016–2017
Installation of exhibition (Sigmar Polke)
© Georges Didi-Huberman
Photo by Georges Didi-Huberman

C
"Soulèvements," Jeu de Paume, Paris, 2016–2017
Installation of exhibition (Charles-François Thibault)
© Georges Didi-Huberman
Photo by Georges Didi-Huberman

D
"Soulèvements," Jeu de Paume, Paris, 2016–2017
Installation of exhibition (Joseph Beuys)
© Georges Didi-Huberman
Photo by Georges Didi-Huberman

Chapter 7

A–B
Harun Farocki
Eye/Machine, 2000
© Harun Farocki GbR

C
Trevor Paglen
From 'Apple' to 'Anomaly', 2019
Selections from the ImageNet dataset for object recognition
C-Prints, pins, labels, approx. 24000 individual images
5.8 × 81 m
Installation view, Barbican Centre – The Curve, London,
September 2019–February 2020
Photo by Max Colson
© Trevor Paglen
Courtesy of the artist and Barbican Centre – The Curve, London

Chapter 8

A
Forensic Architecture
Triple-Chaser, 2019
During the process of training a 'computer vision' classifier, bounding boxes and 'masks' tell the classifier where in the image the Triple-Chaser grenade exists.
© Forensic Architecture/Praxis Films

B
Forensic Architecture
Triple-Chaser, 2019
Using the Unreal engine, Forensic Architecture generated thousands of photorealistic 'synthetic' images, situating the Triple-Chaser in approximations of real-world environments.
© Forensic Architecture/Praxis Films

C
Forensic Architecture
Triple-Chaser, 2019
Forensic Architecture asked activists around the world to find, and film, examples of the Triple Chaser grenade. They used photogrammetry to turn those images into a precise 3D model.
© Forensic Architecture/Praxis Films

D
Forensic Architecture
Triple-Chaser, 2019
The Unreal game engine allows Forensic Architecture to set parameters for variables such as sun position, camera focal length, and dirt on the grenade.
© Forensic Architecture/Praxis Films

E
Forensic Architecture
Triple-Chaser, 2019
Using the Unreal engine, Forensic Architecture generated thousands of photorealistic 'synthetic' images, situating the Triple-Chaser in approximations of real-world environments. Coloured 'masks' tell the classifier where in the image the Triple-Chaser grenade exists.
© Forensic Architecture/Praxis Films

F
Decolonize This Place
Action at the Whitney Museum of American Art in New York, 2019
Image courtesy of Decolonize This Place

G
Forensic Architecture
The Murder of Halit Yozgat. 77sqm_9:26min, 2017
A composite of Forensic Architecture's physical and virtual reconstructions of the internet cafe in which the murder of Halit Yozgat on 6 April 2006 occurred.
© Forensic Architecture

H
Forensic Architecture
Killing in Umm al-Hiran, 2018
Projecting thermal footage from a police helicopter establishes the spatial relationship of figures and vehicles, reflected in a photogrammetry 3D site model.
© Forensic Architecture

Agamben, Giorgio. *Homo Sacer: Sovereign Power and Bare Life* [1995]. Translated by Daniel Heller-Roazen. Stanford, CA:: Stanford University Press, 1998.
—. *Infancy and History: On the Destruction of Experience* [1993]. Translated by Liz Heron. London: Verso, 2007.
—. "Kommerell, or On Gesture" [1991]. In *Potentialities: Collected Essays in Philosophy.* Translated by Daniel Heller-Roazen, 77–85. Stanford, CA: Stanford University Press, 1999.
—. "Marginal Notes on Commentaries on the Society of the Spectacle." In *Means without End: Notes on Politics* [1996]. Translated by Vincenzo Binetti and Cesare Casarino, 73–90. Minneapolis: University of Minnesota Press, 2000.
—. "Notes on Gesture." In *Means without End.* Translated by Vincenzo Binetti and Cesare Casarino, 49–62. Minneapolis: University of Minnesota Press, 2000.
—. *Remnants of Auschwitz: The Witness and the Archive* [1998]. Translated by Daniel Heller-Roazen. New York: Zone Books, 1999.
—. "The Idea of Language." In *Potentialities.* Translated by Daniel Heller-Roazen, 39–47. Stanford, CA: Stanford University Press, 1999.
—. "What Is the Contemporary?" In *What Is an Apparatus? And Other Essays* [2008]. Translated by David Kishik and Stefan Pedatella, 39–54. Stanford, CA: Stanford University Press, 2009.

Aikens, Nick, ed. *Too Much World: The Films of Hito Steyerl.* Einhoven: Van Abbemuseum & Berlin: Sternberg Press, 2014.

Alloa, Emmanual. "Abstracting." In *The Supermarket of Images.* Edited by Peter Szendy et al., 73–94. Paris: Gallimard, 2020.

Anderson, Benedict. *Imagined Communities: Reflections on the Origin and Spread of Nationalism.* London: Verso, 1983.

Attia, Kader. *Repair*. Edited by Léa Gauthier. Paris: Blackjack éditions, 2014.
—. "Kader Attia Speaks about the Idea of Repair" (interview with Judith Benhamou-Huet). YouTube video, 2:38, posted by "Judith Benhamou-Huet Reports." May 22, 2018. Accessed March 14, 2022. https://www.youtube.com/watch?v=PBYoL6z4V7Q.
—. "The Field of Emotion." Kader Attia homepage, 2018. Accessed December 16, 2021, http://kaderattia.de/the-field-of-emotion/.

Augé, Marc. *An Anthropology for Contemporaneous Worlds* [1994]. Translated by Amy Jacobs. Stanford, CA: Stanford University Press, 1999.

Bal, Mieke. *Quoting Caravaggio: Contemporary Art, Preposterous History.* Chicago: University of Chicago Press, 1999.

Bal, Mieke, and Jacob Lund. "An Ethically Nonindifferent Aesthetics: An Interview with Mieke Bal." *Nordic Journal of Aesthetics*, no. 42 (2011): 69–86.

Belting, Hans. *The End of the History of Art* [1983]. Translated by Christopher S. Wood. Chicago: University of Chicago Press, 1987.

Benjamin, Walter. *Gesammelte Briefe*, vol. II, *1919–1924*. Frankfurt am Main: Suhrkamp, 1996.
—. "On the Concept of History" [1942]. In *Selected Writings*, vol. IV, *1938–1940.* Translated by Edmund Jephcott and others. Edited by Howard Eiland and Michael W. Jennings, 389–400. Cambridge, MA: Belknap Press of Harvard University Press, 1992.
—. *The Arcades Project* [1982]. Translated by Howard Eiland and Kevin McLaughlin. Cambridge, MA: Belknap Press of Harvard University Press, 2002.

—. "Theses on the Philosophy of History" [1942]. In *Illuminations*. Translated by Harry Zohn, 255–266. New York: Schocken Books, 1969.

Benveniste, Émile. "Les relations de temps dans le verbe français" [1959]. In *Problèmes de linguistique générale I*, 237–50. Paris: Gallimard, 1966.

Bishop, Claire. "Antagonism and Relational Aesthetics." *October*, 110 (2004): 51–79.
—. *Artificial Hells: Participatory Art and the Politics of Spectatorship.* New York: Verso, 2012.
—. "Digital Divide: Contemporary Art and New Media." *Artforum* (September 2012). Accessed January 27, 2022, https://www.artforum.com/print/201207/digital-divide-contemporary-art-and-new-media-31944
—. "Rise to the Occasion." *Artforum*, 57:9 (2019).

Bloch, David. *Aristotle on Memory and Recollection, Text, Translation, Interpretation, and Reception in Western Scholasticism*, Leiden: Brill, 2007.

Bloch, Ernst. *The Heritage of Our Times* [1935]. Translated by Neville and Stephen Plaice. Cambridge: Polity Press, 1991.

Bourriaud, Nicolas. *Relational Aesthetics* [1998]. Translated by Simon Pleasance and Fronza Woods Dijon: Les presses du réel, 2002.

Bratton, Benjamin H. "The Black Stack." In *e-flux journal*, #53 (March 2014). Accessed January 27, 2022, http://www.e-flux.com/journal/53/59883/the-black-stack/.

Breazeale, Daniel. "Introduction." In Friedrich Nietzsche. *Untimely Meditations.* Edited by Daniel Breazeale. Cambridge: Cambridge University Press, 1997.

Brown, Bill. "Materiality." In *Critical Terms for Media Studies.* Edited by W.J.T. Mitchell & Mark B.N. Hansen, 49–63. Chicago: University of Chicago Press, 2010.

Buergel, Roger and Ruth Noack, eds. *Documenta Kassel: 16/06–23/09 2007, 12.* Cologne: Taschen, 2007.

Bunyard, Tom. *Debord, Time and Spectacle.* Leiden: Brill, 2018.

Carroll, Noël. *Engaging the Moving Image.* New Haven, CT: Yale University Press, 2003.

Chakrabarty, Dipesh. *Provincializing Europe: Postcolonial Thought and Historical Difference.* Princeton, NJ: Princeton University Press, 2000.
—. *The Climate of History in a Planetary Age*. Chicago: University of Chicago Press, 2021.

Cox, Geoff and Jacob Lund. *The Contemporary Condition: Introductory Thoughts on Contemporaneity and Contemporary Art*. The Contemporary Condition 1. Berlin: Sternberg Press, 2016.
—. "Time.now." In *Uncertain Archives: Critical Keywords for Big Data*. Edited by Nanna Bonde Thylstrup, Daniela Agostinho, Annie Ring, Catherine D'Ignazio, and Kristin Veel, 523–31. Cambridge, MA: Mit Press, 2021.

Crary, Jonathan. *24/7: Late Capitalism and the Ends of Sleep*. London: Verso, 2014.

Dall'asta, Monica. "The (Im)possible History." In *For Ever Godard*.

Edited by Michael Temple, James S. Williams, and Michael Witt, 350–363. London: Black Dog Publishing, 2004.

Danto, Arthur C. *After the End of Art: Contemporary Art and the Pale of History.* Princeton, NJ: Princeton University Press, 1997.

Davallon, Jean. *L'exposition à l'œuvre: Stratégies de communication et médiation symbolique.* Paris: L'Harmattan, 1999.

Debord, Guy. *Comments on the Society of the Spectacle* [1988]. Translated by Malcolm Imrie. London: Verso, 1998.
—. *The Society of the Spectacle* [1967]. Translated by Donald Nicholson-Smith. New York: Zone Books, 1994.

Derrida, Jacques. "Aphorism Countertime" [1986]. In *Acts of Literature.* Translated by Nicholas Royle. Edited by Derek Attridge, 414–33. New York: Routledge, 1992.
—. "The Deconstruction of Actuality: An Interview with Jacques Derrida." *Radical Philosophy*, no. 68 (1994): 28–41.

Dickie, George. *Art and the Aesthetic: An Institutional Analysis.* Ithaca: Cornell University Press, 1974.

Didi-Huberman, Georges. "Before the Image, Before Time: The Sovereignty of Anachronism." Translated by Peter Mason. In *Compelling Visuality: The Work of Art in and out of History.* Edited by Claire Farago and Robert Zwijnenberg, 31–44. Minneapolis: University of Minnesota Press, 2003.
—. *Devant le temps: Histoire de l'art et anachronisme des images.* Paris: Éditions de Minuit, 2000.
—. "Emotion does not say 'I': Ten Fragments on Aesthetic Freedom." In *Alfredo Jaar: La politique des* images. Exhibition catalogue. Edited by Nicole Schweizer, 57–70. Musée Cantonal des Beaux-Arts, Lausanne. Zurich: JRP Ringier, 2007.
—. *Fra Angelico: Dissemblance and Figuration* [1990]. Translated by Jane Marie Todd. Chicago: University of Chicago Press, 1995.
—. "Preface to the English Edition: The Exorcist." In *Confronting Images. Questioning the Ends of a Certain History of Art* [1990]. Translated by John Goodman, xv–xxvi. University Park: Pennsylvania State University Press, 2005.
—. *Quand les images prennent position. L'Œil de l'histoire*, 1. Paris: Les Éditions de Minuit, 2009.
—. *Soulèvements.* Exhibition catalogue. Paris: Gallimard & Jeu de Paume, 2016.
—. "The 'Blancs Soucis' of Our History." In *Esther Shalev-Gerz: Between Telling and Listening – Entre l'écoute et la parole.* Exhibition Catalogue. Edited by Nicole Schweizer, 57–62. Zurich: JRP Ringier, 2012.

Duve, Thierry de, and Jacob Lund. "'The Glimpse of Hope That Religion or Politics Can No Longer Promise...' An Interview with Thierry de Duve." *Nordic Journal of Aesthetics*, no. 36–37 (2008–2009): 6–10.

Les associés d'EIM, eds. *Les dirigeants face au changement: Baromètre 2004.* Paris: Éditions du Huitième jour, 2004.

Enwezor, Okwui, "World Platforms, Exhibiting Adjacency, and the Surplus Value of Art." In Terry Smith, *Talking Contemporary Curating*, 85–113. New York: Independent Curators International, 2015.

Enwezor, Okwui, with Mélanie Bouteloup, Abdellah Karroum, Émilie Renard and Claire Staebler, eds. *Intense Proximity: An Anthology of the Near and the Far. La Triennale 2012.* Paris: Palais de Tokyo, 2012.

Ernst, Wolfgang. “Printed Letters, Acoustic Space, Real Time Internet: The Message of Current Communication Media, Deciphered with (and Beyond) McLuhan.” *SITE* 33 (2013): 197–212.

Fabian, Johannes. *Time and the Other: How Anthropology Makes its Object.* New York: Columbia University Press, 1983.

Farocki, Harun. “Phantom Images.” Translated by Brian Poole. *Public*, no. 29 (2004): 12–22.

Ferguson, Bruce W. “Exhibition Rhetorics: Material speech and utter sense.” In *Thinking about Exhibitions.* Edited by Reesa Greenberg, Bruce W. Ferguson, and Sandy Nairne, 175–190. London: Routledge, 1996.

Fisher, Mark. “The Metaphysics of Crackle: Afrofuturism and Hauntology.” *Dancecult: Journal of Electronic Dance Music Culture*, 5:2 (2009): 42–55.

Forensic Architecture, “Our art deals with real injustices, some in Palestine: no wonder we faced opposition.” *The Guardian*, August 20, 2021. https://www.theguardian.com/commentisfree/2021/aug/20/art-real-injustices-palestine-manchester-exhibition-forensic-artchitecture.
—. Website. Accessed February 6, 2022, https://forensic-architecture.org.

Foster, Hal. “Preposterous Timing.” *London Review of Books*, vol. 34:21 (2012): 12.

Foucault, Michel. “Nietzsche, Genealogy, History” [1971]. In *Language, Counter-Memory, Practice: Selected Essays and Interviews by Michel Foucault.* Translated by Donald F. Bouchard and Sherry Simon. Edited by Donald F. Bouchard, 139–64. Ithaca, NY: Cornell University Press, 1977.

Fraser, J.T. “An Embarrassment of Proper Times: A Foreword.” In Helga Nowotny, *Time. The Modern and Postmodern Experience*, 1–5. Cambridge: Polity, 1994.

Garcia, Tristan. “Neither Gesture nor Work of Art: Exhibition as Disposing for Appearance.” In *Theater, Garden, Bestiary: A Materialist History of Exhibitions*. Edited by Tristan Garcia and Vincent Normand, 181–194. Berlin: Sternberg Press, 2020.

Geismar, Haidy. “On Digital Anthropology.” In *Camille Henrot. “Days Are Dogs.” Palais. Le magazine du Palais de Tokyo*, no. 26 (2017): 127–129.

Gjessing, Steinar. “Christian Boltanski – An Interview, November 1993.” *Terskel/Threshold*, no. 11 (1994): 41–50.

Greenberg, Reesa, Bruce W. Ferguson, and Sandy Nairne, eds. *Thinking about Exhibitions.* London: Routledge, 1996.

Groys, Boris. “Comrades of Time.” In *Going Public*. 84–101. Berlin: Sternberg Press, 2011.
—. “The Topology of Contemporary Art.” In *Antinomies of Art and Culture: Modernity, Postmodernity, Contemporaneity.* Edited by Terry Smith, Okwui Enwezor and Nancy Condee, eds., 71–80. Durham, NC: Duke University Press, 2008.

Harootunian, Harry. *Marx after Marx: History and Time in the Expansion of Capitalism*. New York: Columbia University Press, 2015.
—. “Remembering the Historical Present.” *Critical Inquiry*, vol. 33, no. 3 (Spring 2007): 471–494.

Hartog, François. *Regimes of Historicity: Presentism and Experiences of Time* [2003]. Translated by Saskia Brown. New York: Columbia University Press, 2015.

Hegel, Georg Wilhelm Friedrich. *Aesthetics: Lectures on Fine Art* [1818–29]. Translated by T. M. Knox. 2 vols. Oxford: Clarendon Press, 1975.

Henrot, Camille. "The Grasp of Totalizing Systems." In *Art in America* 110:6 (June/July 2013): 44–45. Accessed January 27, 2022, https://www.camillehenrot.fr/en/work/68/grosse-fatigue.

Hirsch, Marianne. *The Generation of Postmemory: Writing and Visual Culture after the Holocaust.* New York: Columbia University Press, 2012.

Hirschhorn, Thomas. "Why it is important – today – to show and look at images of destroyed human bodies?" In *Le Journal de la Triennale #2.* Edited by Émilie Renard, 62–67. Paris: Centre national des arts plastiques, 2012.

Hoel, Aud Sissel. "Operative Images: Inroads to a New Paradigm of Media Theory." In *Image – Action – Space: Situating the Screen in Visual Practice.* Edited by Luisa Feiersinger, Kathrin Friedrich and Moritz Queisner, 11–18. Berlin: De Gruyter, 2018.

Hoelzl, Ingrid and Rémi Marie. *Softimage. Towards a New Theory of the Digital Image.* Bristol, UK: Intellect, 2015.

Huyssen, Andreas. *Present Pasts: Urban Palimpsests and the Politics of Memory.* Stanford, CA: Stanford University Press, 2003.
—. *Twilight Memories: Marking Time in a Culture of Amnesia.* New York: Routledge, 1995.

Jaar, Alfredo. "Between Baudrillard and the Cave: Alfredo Jaar and Simon Critchley in Conversation." *Mute online* (March to May 2011). Accessed February 6, 2022, http://www.metamute.org/editorial/articles/between-baudrillard-and-cave-alfredo-jaar-and-simon-critchley-conversation.
—. "Exhausted States: Alfredo Jaar and Simon Critchley in Conversation." *Mute online* (March to May 2011). Accessed February 6, 2022, http://www.metamute.org/editorial/articles/exhausted-states.
—. "Interview with Luigi Fassi." *Klat* (Winter 2009–2010): 73–74.
—. *It is difficult*, vol. 2. Exhibition catalogue. Verona: Edizioni Corraini, 2008.
—. *Let One Hundred Flowers Bloom*. Exhibition catalogue. Rome: Museo d'arte contemporanea Roma & Electa, 2005.

Iser, Wolfgang. *Die Appellstruktur der Texte. Unbestimmtheit als Wirkungsbedingung literarischer Prosa.* Konstanz: Verlag der Druckerei und Verlagsanstalt Konstanz Universitätsverlag, 1970.

Jameson, Fredric. *The Seeds of Time*. New York: Columbia University Press, 1994.

Kant, Immanuel. *Critique of Judgement* [1790]. Translated by James Creed Meredith. Revised and edited by Nicholas Walker. Oxford: Oxford University Press, 2007.

—. *Critique of Pure Reason* [1781]. Translated by J. M. D. Meiklejohn. London: H. G. Bohn, 1855.

Karlholm, Dan, and Keith Moxey. *Time in the History of Art: Temporality, Chronology and Anachrony.* New York: Routledge, 2018.

Keenan, Thomas and Eyal Weizman. *Mengele's Skull: The Advent of a Forensic Aesthetics.* Berlin: Sternberg Press, 2012.

Kester, Grant H. *Conversation Pieces: Community and Communication in Modern Art.* Berkeley: University of California Press, 2004.
—. "The Limitations of the Exculpatory Critique." *Nordic Journal of Aesthetics* 53 (2017): 73–98.

Ketz, Jan, ed. *Alfredo Jaar. The way it is: Eine Ästhetik des Widerstands/ An Aesthetics of Resistance*. Exhibition catalogue. Berlin: NGBK, 2012.

Koselleck, Reinhart. "'Neuzeit': Remarks on the Semantics of the Modern Concepts of Movement." In *Futures Past: On the Semantics of Historical Time* [1979]. Translated by Keith Tribe, 231–266. Cambridge, MA and London: MIT, 1985.
— "On the Meaning and Absurdity of History" [1997]. In *Sediments of Time: On Possible Histories*. Translated and edited by Sean Franzel and Stefan-Ludwig Hoffmann, 177–96. Stanford, CA: Stanford University Press, 2018.

Langer, Lawrence L. *Holocaust Testimonies: The Ruins of Memory.* New Haven, CT: Yale University Press, 1991.

Lanzmann, Claude. *Shoah: An Oral History of the Holocaust. The Complete Text of the Film.* New York: Pantheon Books, 1985.

Latour, Bruno. "From Realpolitik to Dingpolitik, or How to Make Things Public." In *Making Things Public: Atmospheres of Democracy*. ZKM exhibition catalogue. Edited by Bruno Latour and Peter Weibel, 4–31. Cambridge, MA: MIT Press, 2005.

Lorey, Isabell. "Presentist Democracy: Exodus and Tiger's Leap." Translated by Aileen Derieg. Transversal Texts, June 2014. Accessed February 2, 2022, http://transversal.at/blog/Presentist-Democracy.

Lund, Jacob. "Making History through Anachronic Imagining: Notes on Art History and Temporal Complexities of the Present." In *Retracing the Past: Historical Continuity in Aesthetics from a Global Perspective.* Edited by Zoltán Somhegyi, 165–76. International Yearbook of Aesthetics 19. Santa Cruz, CA: International Association for Aesthetics, 2017.
—. "Sensus Communis and the Public." In *Nyhedsavisen: Peer-reviewed Newspaper About Public Interfaces* (2011): 10–11.

Lütticken, Sven. *Cultural Revolution: Aesthetic Practice after Autonomy.* Berlin: Sternberg Press, 2017.

Lyotard, Jean-François. *Heidegger and "the jews"* [1988]. Translated by Andreas Michel and Mark Roberts. Minneapolis: University of Minnesota Press, 1990.
—. *The Postmodern Condition: A Report on Knowledge* [1979]. Translated by Geoff Bennington and Brian Massumi. Minneapolis: University of Minnesota Press, 1984.

Makkreel, Rudolf. "Imagination and Temporality in Kant's Theory of the Sublime." *Journal of Aesthetics and Art Criticism,* no. 42 (March 1984): 303–316.

Marchart, Oliver. *Conflictual Aesthetics: Artistic Activism and the Public Sphere.* Berlin: Sternberg Press, 2019.

Mbembe, Achille. *On the Postcolony* [2000]. Translated by A. M. Berrett, Janet Roitman, Murray Last, and Steven Rendall. Berkeley: University of California Press, 2001.
—. "How to Develop a Planetary Consciousness." Interview with Nils Gilman and Jonathan Blake, *NOEMA* (January 11, 2022). Accessed January 15, 2022. https://www.noemamag.com/how-to-develop-a-planetary-consciousness/.

McLuhan, Marshall. *Understanding Media: The Extensions of Man.* New York: McGraw Hill, 1965.
—. *Counterblast.* New York: Harcourt, Brace & World, 1969.

Michaud, Yves. *La crise de l'art contemporain. Utopie, démocratie et comédie.* Paris: Presse Universitaires de France, 1997.
—. "The End of the Utopia of Art." In *Think Art: Theory and Practice in the Art of Today.* Edited by Bartomeu Mari and Jean-Marie Schaeffer, 131–156. Rotterdam: Witte de With, 1999.

Mirzoeff, Nicholas. *The Right to Look: A Counterhistory of Visuality.* Durham, NC: Duke University Press, 2011.

Mitchell, W. J. T. *Image Science: Iconology, Visual Culture, and Media Aesthetics.* Chicago: University of Chicago Press, 2015.
—. *What Do Pictures Want? The Lives and Loves of Images.* Chicago: University of Chicago Press, 2005.

Mouffe, Chantal. "Alfredo Jaar: The Artist as Organic Intellectual." In *Alfredo Jaar. The way it is: Eine Ästhetik des Widerstands/An Aesthetics of Resistance.* Exhibition catalogue. Edited by Jan Ketz, 266–282. Berlin: NGBK, 2012.

Moxey, Keith. *Visual Time: The Image in History.* Durham, NC: Duke University Press, 2013.

Nietzsche, Friedrich. "On the Uses and Disadvantages of History for Life" [1873–76]. In *Untimely Meditations.* Edited by Daniel Breazeale. Translated by R. J. Hollingdale, 60–123. Cambridge: Cambridge University Press, 1997.

Nowotny, Helga. *Time: The Modern and Postmodern Experience* [1989]. Translated by Neville Plaice. Cambridge: Polity, 1994.
—. "Eigenzeit Revisited." Keynote lecture at the conference *100 Years of Now* at Haus der Kulturen der Welt, Berlin, September 30, 2015. Accessed February 6, 2022, https://hkw.de/en/programm/projekte/veranstaltung/p_119626.php.

Osborne, Peter. *Anywhere or Not at All: Philosophy of Contemporary Art.* London: Verso, 2013.
— "Contemporary Art Is Post-Conceptual Art." Lecture at Fondazione Antonio Ratti, Villa Sucota, Como, July 9, 2010. Accessed February 6, 2022, https://api.fondazioneratti.org/assets/PDFs/XVI-CSAV_Lectures/Leggi-il-testo-della-conferenza-di-Peter-Osborne-in-PDF1.pdf.
—. "Existential Urgency: Contemporaneity, Biennials and Social Form." *Nordic Journal of Aesthetics*, no. 49–50 (2015): 175–188.
—. "Non-places and the Spaces of Art." *The Journal of Architecture*, vol. 6 (Summer 2011): 183–194.
—. "The Distributed Image." In *The Postconceptual Condition*, 143–44. London: Verso, 2017.
—. "The Kabakov Effect: 'Moscow Conceptualism' in the History of Contemporary Art." In *The Postconceptual Condition*, 167–183. London: Verso, 2017.

—. *The Politics of Time: Modernity and Avant-Garde*. London: Verso, 1995.
—. *The Postconceptual Condition*. London: Verso, 2017.

Paglen, Trevor. "Invisible Images (Your Pictures Are Looking at You)." *The New Inquiry* (December 2016). Accessed February 6, 2022, https://thenewinquiry.com/invisible-images-your-pictures-are-looking-at-you/.
—. "Operational Images." *e-flux journal*, #59 (November 2014). Accessed February 6, 2022, https://www.e-flux.com/journal/59/61130/operational-images/.

Paul, Christiane. "The Myth of Immateriality: Presenting and Preserving New Media." In *MediaArtHistories.* Edited by Oliver Grau, 251–274. Cambridge, MA: MIT Press, 2007.

Pollock, Griselda. "Not-Forgetting Africa." In *Alfredo Jaar: La politique des images.* Exhibition catalogue. Edited by Nicole Schweizer, 113–135. Lausanne: Musée cantonal des beaux-arts, 2007.

Portanova, Stamatia. *Whose Time Is It? Asocial Robots, Syncolonialism, and Artificial Chronological Intelligence*. The Contemporary Condition 17. Berlin: Sternberg Press, 2021.

Poster, Mark. "Global Media and Culture." *New Literary History*, 39.3 (Summer 2008): 685–703.

Rancière, Jacques. "Die Arbeit des Bildes/The Work of the Image." In Esther Shalev-Gerz, *MenschenDinge/The Human Aspect of Objects*, 8–25. Weimar: Stiftung Gedenkstätten Buchenwald und Mittelbau-Dora, 2006.
—. "From Politics to Aesthetics?" In *Paragraph*, 28:1 (2005): 13–25.
—. *Le partage du sensible: Esthétique et politique.* Paris: La fabrique, 2000.
—. "Rethinking Modernity." *Diacritics*, 42:3 (2014): 10–11.
—. "S'il y a de l'irreprésentable." In *L'art et la mémoire des camps : Représenter exterminer.* Edited by Jean-Luc Nancy, 81–102. Paris: Seuil, 2001.
—. "The Aesthetic Revolution and its Outcomes." *New Left Review*, no. 14 (March–April 2002): 133–51.
—. "Theater of Images." In *Alfredo Jaar: La politique des images.* Edited by Nicole Schweizer, 71–80. Lausanne: Musée cantonal des beaux-arts, 2007.
—. "The Concept of Anachronism and the Historian's Truth" [1996]. *In/Print*, vol. 3:1 (2015): 21–52. Accessed February 6, 2022, http://arrow.dit.ie/cgi/viewcontent.cgi?article=1020&context=inp.
—. *The Emancipated Spectator* [2008]. Translated by Gregory Elliott. London: Verso, 2009.
—. *The Politics of Aesthetics: The Distribution of the Sensible* [2000]. Edited and translated by Gabriel Rockhill. London: Continuum, 2004.
—. "What Medium Can Mean." *Parrhesia*, no. 11 (2011): 35–43.

Rancière, Jacques, and Davide Panagia. "Dissenting Words – A Conversation with Jacques Rancière." In *Diacritics*, 30:2 (2000): 113–126.

Rasmussen, Mikkel Bolt. *Hegel after Occupy*. The Contemporary Condition 9. Berlin: Sternberg Press, 2018.

Ravini, Sinziana. "Dialogisk estetik och den relationella estetikens uppgång och fall." *Paletten: tidskrift för konst*, 264.2 (2006) : 4–9.

Rebentisch, Juliane. *Aesthetics of Installation Art* [2003]. Translated by Daniel Hendrickson with Gerrit Jackson. Berlin: Sternberg Press, 2012.
—. *The Art of Freedom: On the Dialectics of Democratic Existence* [2011]. Translated by Joseph Ganahl. Cambridge: Polity, 2016.
—. "The Contemporaneity of Contemporary Art." *New German Critique*, no. 124, 42:1 (2015): 223–237.
—. *Theorien der Gegenwartskunst – zur Einführung.* Hamburg: Junius, 2013.

Renov, Michael. "The Facial Closeup in Audio-Visual Testimony: The Power of Embodied Memory." (2013): 1–8. Accessed February 6, 2022, http://www.preserving-survivors-memories.org/media/presentations/Michael_Renov_The_Facial_Closeup_in_Audio-Visual_Testimony.pdf?1354623339.

Ross, Christine. *The Past Is the Present; It's the Future Too: The Temporal Turn in Contemporary Art*. New York: Continuum, 2012.

Ross. Daniel. "Politics and Aesthetics, or, Transformations of Aristotle in Bernard Stiegler." *Transformations*, no. 17 (2009). Accessed February 6, 2022, http://www.transformationsjournal.org/wp-content/uploads/2017/01/Ross_Trans17.pdf.

Sarai-CSDS and Raqs Media Collective. *What time Is It? – Technologies of Life in the Contemporary*. Accessed February 6, 2022, http://sarai.net/what-time-is-it-14-16-december-2017/.

Shalev-Gerz, Esther. *Est-ce que ton image me regarde?/Geht dein Bild mich an?/Does your image reflect me?.* Exhibition catalogue. Hannover: Sprengel Museum, 2002.
—. *Esther Shalev-Gerz*. Exhibition catalogue. Paris: Fage éditions & Éditions du Jeu de Paume, 2010.
—. "Esther Shalev-Gerz in conversation with Ulrich Krempel." In Esther Shalev-Gerz, *MenschenDinge/The Human Aspect of Objects,* 100–103. Weimar: Stiftung Gedenkstätten Buchenwald und Mittelbau-Dora, 2006.
—. *MenschenDinge/The Human Aspect of Objects.* Exhibition catalogue. Weimar: Stiftung Gedenkstätten Buchenwald und Mittelbau-Dora, 2006a.

Smith, Gavin. "Interview: Jean-Luc Godard." *Film Comment* (March/April 1996). Accessed February 6, 2022, https://www.filmcomment.com/article/jean-luc-godard-interview-nouvelle-vague-histoires-du-cinema-helas-pour-moi/.

Smith, Terry. *Art to Come. Histories of Contemporary Art.* Durham, NC: Duke University Press, 2019.
—. "Biennials/Art Fairs in the Exhibitionary Complex." In *Double Trouble in Exhibiting the Contemporary: Art Fairs and Shows*. Edited by Cristina Baldacci, Clarissa Ricci and Angela Vettese, 23–45. Milan: Scalpendi Editore, 2020.
—. "Contemporary Art and Contemporaneity." *Critical Inquiry,* 32.4 (Summer 2006): 681–707.
—. "Defining Contemporaneity: Imagining Planetarity." *Nordic Journal of Aesthetics,* no. 49–50 (2015): 156–74.
—. "Seeing Art Historically Today: Where We Are, And Ways To Go." Power Lecture, Domain Theatre, Art Gallery of New South Wales, July 20, 2016. Full text version of unpublished manuscript dated 7.19.2016.
—. *The Contemporary Composition.* The Contemporary Condition 2. Berlin: Sternberg Press, 2016.
—. *What Is Contemporary Art?* Chicago: University of Chicago Press, 2009.

Somaini, Antonio. "Walter Benjamin's Media Theory: The Medium and the Apparat." *Grey Room 62* (Winter 2016): 6–41.

Steeds, Lucy. "Exposability: On the Taking-Place in Future of Art." In *Theater, Garden, Bestiary: A Materialist History of Exhibitions*. Edited by Tristan Garcia and Vincent Normand, 75–84. Berlin: Sternberg Press, 2019.

Steyerl, Hito. "Duty-Free Art." In *e-flux journal*, #63 (March 2015). Accessed February 6, 2022, http://www.e-flux.com/journal/duty-free-art/.
—. *Duty Free Art: Art in the Age of Planetary Civil War*. London: Verso, 2017.
—. "Politics of Art: Contemporary Art and the Transition to Post-Democracy." In *e-flux journal*, #21 (December 2010). Accessed February 6, 2022, http://www.e-flux.com/journal/politics-of-art-contemporary-art-and-the-transition-to-post-democracy/.
—. "The Terror of Total Dasein: Economies of Presence in the Art Field." In *Duty Free Art: Art in the Age of Planetary Civil War.* 21–30. London: Verso, 2017.
—. "Too Much World: Is the Internet Dead?" In *e-flux journal*, #49 (November 2013). Accessed February 6, 2022, http://www.e-flux.com/journal/too-much-world-is-the-internet-dead/.

Stiegler, Bernard. "De la misère symbolique." *Le Monde*, October 10, 2003.
—. *De la misère symbolique, 1 : L'époque hyperindustrielle.* Paris: Galilée, 2004.
—. *De la misère symbolique, 2 : La catastrophè du sensible.* Paris: Galilée, 2005.
—. "How I Became a Philosopher." In *Acting Out*. Translated by David Barison et al. Stanford, CA: Stanford University Press, 2009.
—. *La technique et le temps, 1: La faute d'Epiméthée.* Paris: Galilée, 1994.
—. "Suffocated Desire, or How the Cultural Industry Destroys the Individual: Contribution to a Theory of Mass Consumption." *Parrhesia*, no. 13 (2011): 52–61.
—. *Technics and Time, 1: The Fault of Epimetheus* [1994]. Translated by Richard Beardsworth and George Collins. Stanford, CA: Stanford University Press, 1998.
—. "Technics, Media, Teleology. Interview with Bernard Stiegler." In *Theory, Culture & Society,* vol. 24 (7-8), (2007). 334–341.
—. "The Tongue of the Eye: What 'Art History' Means." *Releasing the Image: From Literature to New Media.* Edited by Jacques Khalip and Robert Mitchell, 222–235. Stanford, CA: Stanford University Press, 2011.

Stiegler, Bernard, and Irit Rogoff. "Transindividuation." In *e-flux, journal,* #14 (March 2010). Accessed February 7, 2022, http://www.e-flux.com/journal/transindividuation/.

Väliaho, Pasi. *Biopolitical Screens: Image, Power, and the Neoliberal Brain.* Cambridge, MA: MIT Press, 2014.

Virno, Paolo. *A Grammar of the Multitude: For an Analysis of Contemporary Forms of Life.* Translated by Isabella Bertoletti, James Cascaito and Andrea Casson. Los Angeles: Semiotext(e), 2004.

Voorhies, James. *Beyond Objecthood: The Exhibition as a Critical Form Since 1968.* Cambridge, MA: MIT Press, 2017.

Warner, Michael. "Publics and Counterpublics." *Public Culture* 14:1 (2002): 59–90.

Wayne, Michael. *Red Kant: Aesthetics, Marxism and the Third Critique*. London: Bloomsbury, 2014.

Weizman, Eyal. "Forensic Architecture." Online lecture as part of the series Architectures of the New Curatorial at the Royal College of Art, London, December 10, 2020.
—. "Forensic Architecture: Notes from Fields and Forums." In *dOCUMENTA (13) – The Book of Books.* Edited by Carolyn Christov-Bakargiev, 389–92. Ostfildern: Hatje Cantz, 2012.
—. *Forensic Architecture: Violence at the Threshold of Detectability.* New York: Zone Books, 2017.

Welsch, Wolfgang. "Aesthetics beyond Aesthetics." In *Rediscovering Aesthetics: Transdisciplinary Voices from Art History, Philosophy, and Art Practice.* Edited by Francis Halsall et al., 178–192. Stanford, CA: Stanford University Press, 2009.

West, Kim. "Concepts for the Critical Study of Art Exhibitions as Media." In *Theater, Garden, Bestiary: A Materialist History of Exhibitions*. Edited by Tristan Garcia and Vincent Normand, 45–55. Berlin: Sternberg Press, 2019.

Wittgenstein, Ludwig. *Philosophical Investigations*. Translated by G.E.M. Anscombe. New York: Macmillan, 1953.

Young, James E. *At Memory's Edge: After-Images of the Holocaust in Contemporary Art and Architecture.* New Haven, CT: Yale University Press, 2000.
— "Spaces for Deep Memory: Esther Shalev-Gerz and the First Counter-Monuments." In *Esther Shalev-Gerz: Between Telling and Listening – Entre l'écoute et la parole.* Exhibition catalogue. Edited by Nicole Schweizer, 79–82. Zurich: JRP Ringier, 2012.

Zylinska, Joanna. *Nonhuman Photography.* Cambridge, MA: MIT Press, 2017.

I am very grateful to all the friends and colleagues who have taken part in discussions of issues related to contemporaneity, contemporary art and aesthetics and/or who have organized events where I have been invited to present my work. Thank you, Emmanuel Alloa, Kader Attia, Armen Avanessian, Mieke Bal, Cristina Baldacci, Laura Beloff, Ina Blom, Mikkel Bolt Rasmussen, Maibritt Borgen, Yves Citton, Geoff Cox, Dexter Sinister, Georges Didi-Huberman, Knut Ebeling, Knut Ove Eliassen, Iben Bach Elmstrøm, Wolfgang Ernst, Jale Erzen, Margaret-Anne Hutton, Sven Anders Johansson, Joasia Krysa, Morten Kyndrup, Jørgen Michaelsen, Monica Narula/Raqs Media Collective, Peter Osborne, Nikos Papastergiadis, Jussi Parikka, Juliane Rebentisch, Johnny Rodger, Lionel Ruffel, Max Ryynänen, Michael Schwab, Ludger Schwarte, Simon Sheikh, Karen-Margrethe Simonsen, Terry Smith, Zoltán Somhegyi, Felix Stalder, Ravi Sundaram, Morten Søndergaard, Sally Tallant, Iris van der Tuin, Frederik Tygstrup, Christina Varvia, Angela Vettese, Jacob Wamberg, Eyal Weizman, and Claudia Welz.

The research project *The Contemporary Condition: The Articulation and Experience of Contemporaneity in and through Contemporary Arts Practice* at Aarhus University — made possible by a grant from the Danish Council for Independent Research and running from 2015 to 2020 — has been an important context for the development of many of the ideas presented in these pages. I am grateful to co-director Geoff Cox, postdoc Verina Gfader, and PhD fellows Anne Kølbæk Iversen, Camma Juel Jepsen, Johanne Løgstrup, and Ryan Nolan. I also thank my colleagues in the research program Contemporary Aesthetics and Technology at Aarhus University.

In addition to the Danish Council for Independent Research I owe the Novo Nordisk Foundation thanks for a grant for the research project *The Work of Art In the Age of a Globally Networked Image-Space,* running from 2020 to 2022, which, together with additional funding from the New Carlsberg Foundation, has made the publication of this book possible.

For generously providing images and permissions, I thank Kader Attia, Larissa Scheidt at his studio and the Solomon R. Guggenheim Museum; Decolonize This Place; Georges Didi-Huberman; Antje Ehmann, Harun Farocki GbR; Forensic Architecture; Éditions Gallimard; Camille Henrot and Francisca Frère at galerie kamel mennour; Alfredo Jaar, Kathy Cho and Masahito Ono at his studio; Thomas Hirschhorn and Pauline Assathiany at Galerie Chantal Crousel; Iñigo Manglano-Ovalle, Mareike Spendel and Annika Karpowski at Galerie Thomas

Schulte; Esther Shalev-Gerz; Hito Steyerl and Connor Creagan at Andrew Kreps Gallery; and Trevor Paglen.

For enabling the publication of earlier versions of these essays, I thank Mikkel Bolt Rasmussen; Wolfram Bergande; Diana Popescu and Tanja Schult; Paolo de Assis and Michael Schwab; Cristina Baldacci, Clarissa Ricci, and Angela Vettese; Zoltán Somhegyi; Geoff Cox and Stuart Bertolotti-Bailey; Johnny Rodger; and Camilla Salvaneschi. I am also grateful to James Day for copy-editing and proofreading, to Max Bach for proofreading, and to Claus Due for typesetting and designing the present volume — and to Tatjana Günthner at Sternberg Press for her confidence.

Thank you above all, Bente, Bastian, Kristine and Marie, with whom I share most intensely the changing present on an everyday basis and who help me keep the wonder of the world alive.

This book is dedicated to the memory of my mother, Hanne Lund.

Jacob Lund
The Changing Constitution of the Present
Essays on the Work of Art in Times of Contemporaneity

Published by Sternberg Press

Editor: Tatjana Günthner
Copy editor and proofreader: James Day
Design: Studio Claus Due
Printing and binding: Narayana Press, Odder

This publication has received generous funding
from the Novo Nordisk Foundation (grant 0061314)
and the New Carlsberg Foundation

ISBN 978-3-95679-640-1

Distributed by The MIT Press, Art Data, Les presses du réel,
and Idea Books

Sternberg Press
71–75 Shelton Street
London WC2H 9JQ
www.sternberg-press.com